PRAXIS
EDUCATION OF EXCEPTIONAL STUDENTS 0353

By: Sharon Wynne, M.S.

XAMonline, INC.
Boston

Library of Congress Cataloging-in-Publication Data

Wynne, Sharon A.
    PRAXIS Education of Exceptional Students 0353 / Sharon A. Wynne. 1st ed
    ISBN 978-1-60787-055-5
    1. Education of Exceptional Students 0353
    2. Study Guides
    3. PRAXIS
    4. Teachers' Certification & Licensure
    5. Careers

Disclaimer:

Printed in the United States of America   œ-1

PRAXIS Education of Exceptional Students 0353
ISBN: 978-1-60787-055-5

Table of Contents

DOMAIN II
LEGAL AND SOCIETAL ISSUES

DOMAIN III
DELIVERY OF SERVICES TO STUDENTS 83

COMPETENCY 8
BACKGROUND KNOWLEDGE 85

COMPETENCY 9
CURRICULUM AND INSTRUCTION AND THEIR IMPLEMENTATION ACROSS THE CONTINUUM OF EDUCATIONAL SETTINGS 101

COMPETENCY 10
ASSESSMENT 142

SECTION 1
ABOUT XAMONLINE

XAMonline—A Specialty Teacher Certification Company

Created in 1996, XAMonline was the first company to publish study guides for state-specific teacher certification examinations. Founder Sharon Wynne found it frustrating that materials were not available for teacher certification preparation and decided to create the first single, state-specific guide. XAMonline has grown into a company of over 1,800 contributors and writers and offers over 300 titles for the entire PRAXIS series and every state examination. No matter what state you plan on teaching in, XAMonline has a unique teacher certification study guide just for you.

XAMonline—Value and Innovation

We are committed to providing value and innovation. Our print-on-demand technology allows us to be the first in the market to reflect changes in test standards and user feedback as they occur. Our guides are written by experienced teachers who are experts in their fields. And our content reflects the highest standards of quality. Comprehensive practice tests with varied levels of rigor means that your study experience will closely match the actual in-test experience.

To date, XAMonline has helped nearly 600,000 teachers pass their certification or licensing exams. Our commitment to preparation exceeds simply providing the proper material for study—it extends to helping teachers **gain mastery** of the subject matter, giving them the **tools** to become the most effective classroom leaders possible, and ushering today's students toward a **successful future**.

SECTION 2
ABOUT THIS STUDY GUIDE

Purpose of This Guide

Is there a little voice inside of you saying, "Am I ready?" Our goal is to replace that little voice and remove all doubt with a new voice that says, "I AM READY. **Bring it on!**" by offering the highest quality of teacher certification study guides.

Organization of Content

You will see that while every test may start with overlapping general topics, each is very unique in the skills they wish to test. Only XAMonline presents custom content that analyzes deeper than a title, a subarea, or an objective. Only XAMonline presents content and sample test assessments along with **focus statements**, the deepest-level rationale and interpretation of the skills that are unique to the exam.

Title and field number of test

→Each exam has its own name and number. XAMonline's guides are written to give you the content you need to know for the specific exam you are taking. You can be confident when you buy our guide that it contains the information you need to study for the specific test you are taking.

Subareas

→These are the major content categories found on the exam. XAMonline's guides are written to cover all of the subareas found in the test frameworks developed for the exam.

Objectives

→These are standards that are unique to the exam and represent the main subcategories of the subareas/content categories. XAMonline's guides are written to address every specific objective required to pass the exam.

Focus statements

→These are examples and interpretations of the objectives. You find them in parenthesis directly following the objective. They provide detailed examples of the range, type, and level of content that appear on the test questions. **Only XAMonline's guides drill down to this level.**

How Do We Compare with Our Competitors?

XAMonline—drills down to the focus statement level.
CliffsNotes and REA—organized at the objective level
Kaplan—provides only links to content
MoMedia—content not specific to the state test

Each subarea is divided into manageable sections that cover the specific skill areas. Explanations are easy to understand and thorough. You'll find that every test answer contains a rejoinder so if you need a refresher or further review after taking the test, you'll know exactly to which section you must return.

How to Use This Book

Our informal polls show that most people begin studying up to eight weeks prior to the test date, so start early. Then ask yourself some questions: How much do you really know? Are you coming to the test straight from your teacher-education program or are you having to review subjects you haven't considered in ten years? Either way, take a **diagnostic or assessment test** first. Also, spend time on sample tests so that you become accustomed to the way the actual test will appear.

This guide comes with an online diagnostic test of 30 questions found online at *www.XAMonline.com*. It is a little boot camp to get you up for the task and reveal things about your compendium of knowledge in general. Although this guide is structured to follow the order of the test, you are not required to study in that order. By finding a time-management and study plan that fits your life you will be more effective. The results of your diagnostic or self-assessment test can be a guide for how to manage your time and point you toward an area that needs more attention.

After taking the diagnostic exam, fill out the **Personalized Study Plan** page at the beginning of each chapter. Review the competencies and skills covered in that chapter and check the boxes that apply to your study needs. If there are sections you already know you can skip, check the "skip it" box. Taking this step will give you a study plan for each chapter.

Week	Activity
8 weeks prior to test	Take a diagnostic test found at www.XAMonline.com
7 weeks prior to test	Build your Personalized Study Plan for each chapter. Check the "skip it" box for sections you feel you are already strong in. ✘ SKIP IT ☐
6-3 weeks prior to test	For each of these four weeks, choose a content area to study. You don't have to go in the order of the book. It may be that you start with the content that needs the most review. Alternately, you may want to ease yourself into plan by starting with the most familiar material.
2 weeks prior to test	Take the sample test, score it, and create a review plan for the final week before the test.
1 week prior to test	Following your plan (which will likely be aligned with the areas that need the most review) go back and study the sections that align with the questions you may have gotten wrong. Then go back and study the sections related to the questions you answered correctly. If need be, create flashcards and drill yourself on any area that you makes you anxious.

SECTION 3
ABOUT THE PRAXIS EXAMS

What Is PRAXIS?

PRAXIS II tests measure the knowledge of specific content areas in K-12 education. The test is a way of insuring that educators are prepared to not only teach in a particular subject area, but also have the necessary teaching skills to be effective. The Educational Testing Service administers the test in most states and has worked with the states to develop the material so that it is appropriate for state standards.

PRAXIS Points

1. The PRAXIS Series comprises more than 140 different tests in over seventy different subject areas.

2. Over 90% of the PRAXIS tests measure subject area knowledge.

3. The purpose of the test is to measure whether the teacher candidate possesses a sufficient level of knowledge and skills to perform job duties effectively and responsibly.

4. Your state sets the acceptable passing score.

5. Any candidate, whether from a traditional teaching-preparation path or an alternative route, can seek to enter the teaching profession by taking a PRAXIS test.

6. PRAXIS tests are updated regularly to ensure current content.

Often **your own state's requirements** determine whether or not you should take any particular test. The most reliable source of information regarding this is either your state's Department of Education or the Educational Testing Service. Either resource should also have a complete list of testing centers and dates. Test dates vary by subject area and not all test dates necessarily include your particular test, so be sure to check carefully.

If you are in a teacher-education program, check with the Education Department or the Certification Officer for specific information for testing and testing time-lines. The Certification Office should have most of the information you need.

If you choose an alternative route to certification you can either rely on our Web site at *www.XAMonline.com* or on the resources provided by an alternative certi-fication program. Many states now have specific agencies devoted to alternative certification and there are some national organizations as well:

National Center for Education Information
http://www.ncei.com/Alt-Teacher-Cert.htm

National Associate for Alternative Certification
http://www.alt-teachercert.org/index.asp

Interpreting Test Results

Contrary to what you may have heard, the results of a PRAXIS test are not based on time. More accurately, you will be scored on the raw number of points you earn in relation to the raw number of points available. Each question is worth one raw point. It is likely to your benefit to complete as many questions in the time allotted, but it will not necessarily work to your advantage if you hurry through the test.

Follow the guidelines provided by ETS for interpreting your score. The web site offers a sample test score sheet and clearly explains how the scores are scaled and what to expect if you have an essay portion on your test.

Scores are usually available by phone within a month of the test date and scores will be sent to your chosen institution(s) within six weeks. Additionally, ETS now makes online, downloadable reports available for 45 days from the reporting date.

It is **critical** that you be aware of your own state's passing score. Your raw score may qualify you to teach in some states, but not all. ETS administers the test and assigns a score, but the states make their own interpretations and, in some cases, consider combined scores if you are testing in more than one area.

What's on the Test?

PRAXIS tests vary from subject to subject and sometimes even within subject area. For PRAXIS Education of Exceptional Students (0353), the test lasts for 1 hour and consists of approximately 60 multiple-choice questions. The breakdown of the questions is as follows:

Category	Approximate Number of Questions	Approximate Percentage of the test
I: Understanding Exceptionalities	15-18	25-30%
II: Legal and Societal Issues	9-12	15-20%
III: Delivery of Services to Students with Disabilities	30-36	50-60%

This chart can be used to build a study plan. Twenty-five to thirty percent may seem like a lot of time to spend on Understanding Exceptionalities, but when you consider that amounts to about 1 out of 4 multiple choice questions, it might change your perspective.

Question Types

You're probably thinking, enough already, I want to study! Indulge us a little longer while we explain that there is actually more than one type of multiple-choice question. You can thank us later after you realize how well prepared you are for your exam.

1. Complete the Statement. The name says it all. In this question type you'll be asked to choose the correct completion of a given statement. For example:

> **The Dolch Basic Sight Words consist of a relatively short list of words that children should be able to:**
>
> A. Sound out
>
> B. Know the meaning of
>
> C. Recognize on sight
>
> D. Use in a sentence

The correct answer is A. In order to check your answer, test out the statement by adding the choices to the end of it.

2. Which of the Following. One way to test your answer choice for this type of question is to replace the phrase "which of the following" with your selection. Use this example:

> **Which of the following words is one of the twelve most frequently used in children's reading texts:**
>
> A. There
>
> B. This
>
> C. The
>
> D. An

Don't look! Test your answer. _____ is one of the twelve most frequently used in children's reading texts. Did you guess C? Then you guessed correctly.

3. **Roman Numeral Choices.** This question type is used when there is more than one possible correct answer. For example:

> **Which of the following two arguments accurately supports the use of cooperative learning as an effective method of instruction?**
> I.   Cooperative learning groups facilitate healthy competition between individuals in the group.
> II. Cooperative learning groups allow academic achievers to carry or cover for academic underachievers.
> III. Cooperative learning groups make each student in the group accountable for the success of the group.
> IV. Cooperative learning groups make it possible for students to reward other group members for achieving.
>
> A. I and II
> B. II and III
> C. I and III
> D. III and IV

Notice that the question states there are **two** possible answers. It's best to read all the possibilities first before looking at the answer choices. In this case, the correct answer is D.

4. **Negative Questions.** This type of question contains words such as "not," "least," and "except." Each correct answer will be the statement that does **not** fit the situation described in the question. Such as:

> **Multicultural education is not**
>
> A. An idea or concept
> B. A "tack-on" to the school curriculum
> C. An educational reform movement
> D. A process

Think to yourself that the statement could be anything but the correct answer. This question form is more open to interpretation than other types, so read carefully and don't forget that you're answering a negative statement.

5. **Questions that Include Graphs, Tables, or Reading Passages.** As always, read the question carefully. It likely asks for a very specific answer and not a broad interpretation of the visual. Here is a simple (though not statistically accurate) example of a graph question:

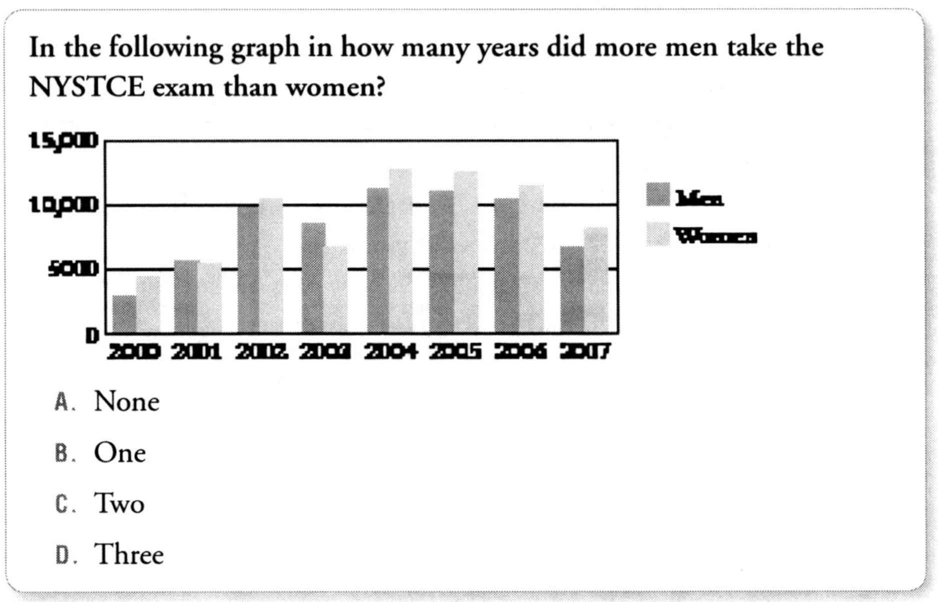

In the following graph in how many years did more men take the NYSTCE exam than women?

A. None

B. One

C. Two

D. Three

It may help you to simply circle the two years that answer the question. Make sure you've read the question thoroughly and once you've made your determination, double check your work. The correct answer is C.

SECTION 4
HELPFUL HINTS

Study Tips

1. **You are what you eat.** Certain foods aid the learning process by releasing natural memory enhancers called CCKs (cholecystokinin) composed of tryptophan, choline, and phenylalanine. All of these chemicals enhance the neurotransmitters associated with memory and certain foods release memory enhancing chemicals. A light meal or snacks of one of the following foods fall into this category:

   - Milk
   - Rice
   - Eggs
   - Fish
   - Nuts and seeds
   - Oats
   - Turkey

   The better the connections, the more you comprehend!

2. **See the forest for the trees.** In other words, get the concept before you look at the details. One way to do this is to take notes as you read, paraphrasing or summarizing in your own words. Putting the concept in terms that are comfortable and familiar may increase retention.

3. **Question authority.** Ask why, why, why? Pull apart written material paragraph by paragraph and don't forget the captions under the illustrations. For example, if a heading reads *Stream Erosion* put it in the form of a question (Why do streams erode? What is stream erosion?) then find the answer within the material. If you train your mind to think in this manner you will learn more and prepare yourself for answering test questions.

4. **Play mind games.** Using your brain for reading or puzzles keeps it flexible. Even with a limited amount of time your brain can take in data (much like a computer) and store it for later use. In ten minutes you can: read two paragraphs (at least), quiz yourself with flash cards, or review notes. Even if you don't fully understand something on the first pass, your mind stores it for recall, which is why frequent reading or review increases chances of retention and comprehension.

5. **The pen is mightier than the sword.** Learn to take great notes. A by-product of our modern culture is that we have grown accustomed to getting our information in short doses. We've subconsciously trained ourselves to assimilate information into neat little packages. Messy notes fragment the flow of information. Your notes can be much clearer with proper formatting. ***The Cornell Method*** is one such format. This method was popularized in *How to Study in College*, Ninth Edition, by Walter Pauk. You can benefit from the method without purchasing an additional book by simply looking up the method online. Below is a sample of how *The Cornell Method* can be adapted for use with this guide.

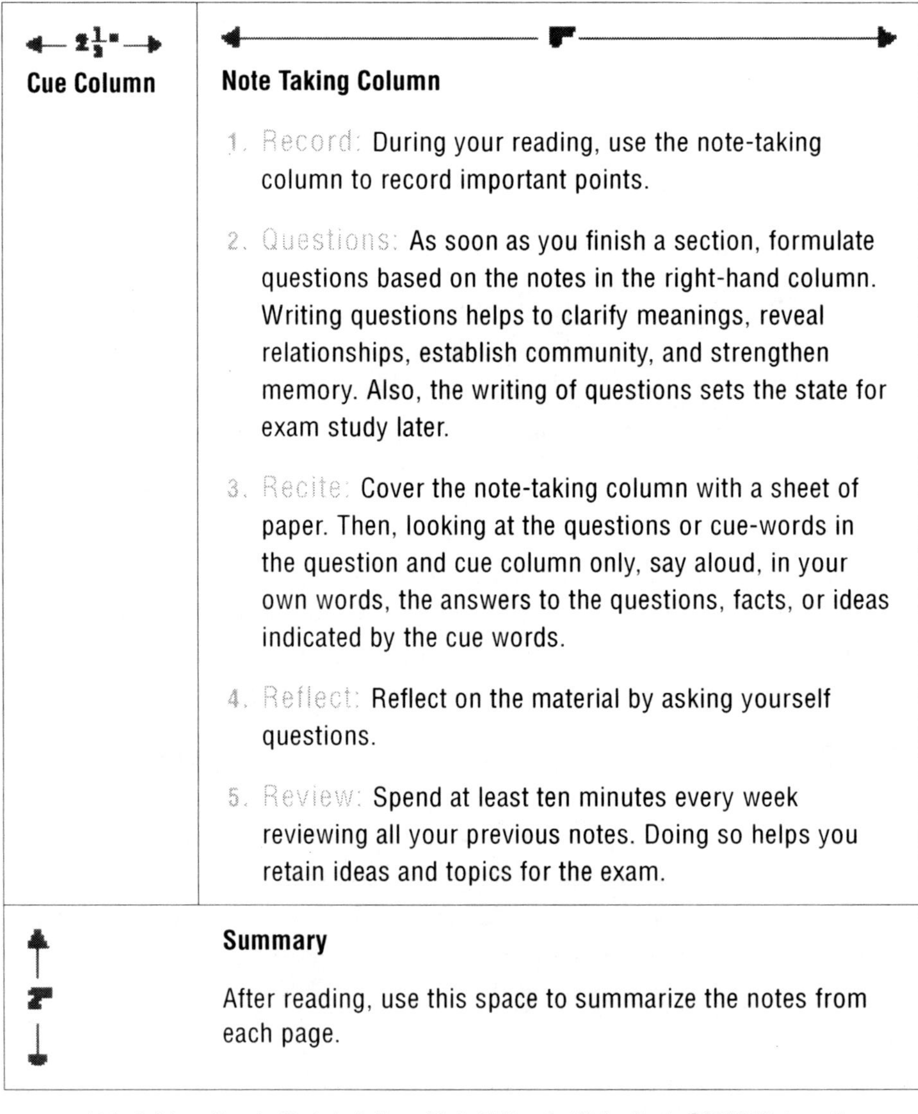

Cue Column	Note Taking Column
	1. Record: During your reading, use the note-taking column to record important points.
	2. Questions: As soon as you finish a section, formulate questions based on the notes in the right-hand column. Writing questions helps to clarify meanings, reveal relationships, establish community, and strengthen memory. Also, the writing of questions sets the state for exam study later.
	3. Recite: Cover the note-taking column with a sheet of paper. Then, looking at the questions or cue-words in the question and cue column only, say aloud, in your own words, the answers to the questions, facts, or ideas indicated by the cue words.
	4. Reflect: Reflect on the material by asking yourself questions.
	5. Review: Spend at least ten minutes every week reviewing all your previous notes. Doing so helps you retain ideas and topics for the exam.
	Summary After reading, use this space to summarize the notes from each page.

*Adapted from How to Study in College, Ninth Edition, by Walter Pauk, ©2008 Wadsworth

6. **Place yourself in exile and set the mood.** Set aside a particular place and time to study that best suits your personal needs and biorhythms. If you're a night person, burn the midnight oil. If you're a morning person set yourself up with some coffee and get to it. Make your study time and place as free from distraction as possible and surround yourself with what you need, be it silence or music. Studies have shown that music can aid in concentration, absorption, and retrieval of information. Not all music, though. Classical music is said to work best

7. **Get pointed in the right direction.** Use arrows to point to important passages or pieces of information. It's easier to read than a page full of yellow highlights. Highlighting can be used sparingly, but add an arrow to the margin to call attention to it.

8. **Check your budget.** You should at least review all the content material before your test, but allocate the most amount of time to the areas that need the most refreshing. It sounds obvious, but it's easy to forget. You can use the study rubric above to balance your study budget.

The proctor will write the start time where it can be seen and then, later, provide the time remaining, typically fifteen minutes before the end of the test.

Testing Tips

1. **Get smart, play dumb.** Sometimes a question is just a question. No one is out to trick you, so don't assume that the test writer is looking for something other than what was asked. Stick to the question as written and don't overanalyze.

2. **Do a double take.** Read test questions and answer choices at least twice because it's easy to miss something, to transpose a word or some letters. If you have no idea what the correct answer is, skip it and come back later if there's time. If you're still clueless, it's okay to guess. Remember, you're scored on the number of questions you answer correctly and you're not penalized for wrong answers. The worst case scenario is that you miss a point from a good guess.

3. **Turn it on its ear.** The syntax of a question can often provide a clue, so make things interesting and turn the question into a statement to see if it changes the meaning or relates better (or worse) to the answer choices.

4. **Get out your magnifying glass.** Look for hidden clues in the questions because it's difficult to write a multiple-choice question without giving away part of the answer in the options presented. In most questions you can readily eliminate one or two potential answers, increasing your chances of answering correctly to 50/50, which will help out if you've skipped a question and gone back to it (see tip #2).

5. **Call it intuition.** Often your first instinct is correct. If you've been studying the content you've likely absorbed something and have subconsciously
retained the knowledge. On questions you're not sure about trust your
instincts because a first impression is usually correct.

6. **Graffiti.** Sometimes it's a good idea to mark your answers directly on the
test booklet and go back to fill in the optical scan sheet later. You don't get
extra points for perfectly blackened ovals. If you choose to manage your test
this way, be sure not to mismark your answers when you transcribe to the
scan sheet.

7. **Become a clock-watcher.** You have a set amount of time to answer the
questions. Don't get bogged down laboring over a question you're not sure
about when there are ten others you could answer more readily. If you choose
to follow the advice of tip #6, be sure you leave time near the end to go back
and fill in the scan sheet.

Do the Drill

No matter how prepared you feel it's sometimes a good idea to apply Murphy's
Law. So the following tips might seem silly, mundane, or obvious, but we're
including them anyway.

1. **Remember, you are what you eat, so bring a snack.** Choose
from the list of energizing foods that appear earlier in the introduction.

2. **You're not too sexy for your test.** Wear comfortable clothes. You'll
be distracted if your belt is too tight or if you're too cold or too hot.

3. **Lie to yourself.** Even if you think you're a prompt person, pretend you're
not and leave plenty of time to get to the testing center. Map it out ahead
of time and do a dry run if you have to. There's no need to add road rage to
your list of anxieties.

4. **Bring sharp number 2 pencils.** It may seem impossible to forget this
need from your school days, but you might. And make sure the erasers are
intact, too.

5. **No ticket, no test.** Bring your admission ticket as well as **two** forms of
identification, including one with a picture and signature. You will not be
admitted to the test without these things.

6. **You can't take it with you.** Leave any study aids, dictionaries, note-
books, computers, and the like at home. Certain tests **do** allow a scientific or
four-function calculator, so check ahead of time to see if your test does.

7. **Prepare for the desert.** Any time spent on a bathroom break **cannot** be made up later, so use your judgment on the amount you eat or drink.

8. **Quiet, Please!** Keeping your own time is a good idea, but not with a timepiece that has a loud ticker. If you use a watch, take it off and place it nearby but not so that it distracts you. And **silence your cell phone**.

To the best of our ability, we have compiled the content you need to know in this book and in the accompanying online resources. The rest is up to you. You can use the study and testing tips or you can follow your own methods. Either way, you can be confident that there aren't any missing pieces of information and there shouldn't be any surprises in the content on the test.

If you have questions about test fees, registration, electronic testing, or other content verification issues please visit *www.ets.org*.

Good luck!

Sharon Wynne
Founder, XAMonline

UNDERSTANDING EXCEPTIONALITIES

PERSONALIZED STUDY PLAN

KNOWN MATERIAL/ SKIP IT

COMPETENCY 1
HUMAN DEVELOPMENT AND BEHAVIOR AS RELATED TO STUDENTS WITH DISABILITIES

SKILL 1.1   Social and emotional development and behavior

Children whose behavior deviates from society's standards for normal behavior for certain ages and stages of development are identified as having disabilities. Behavioral expectations vary from setting to setting; for example, yelling on the football field is acceptable, but yelling when the teacher is explaining a lesson to the class is not. Different cultures have different standards of behavior, further complicating the question of what constitutes a behavioral problem. People also have their personal opinions and standards for what is tolerable and what is not. Some behavioral problems are openly expressed; others are inwardly directed and not very obvious. As a result of these factors, the terms behavioral disorders and emotional disturbance have become almost interchangeable.

While almost all children at times exhibit behaviors that are aggressive, withdrawn, or otherwise inappropriate, the IDEA definition of serious emotional disturbance (SED) focuses on behaviors that persist over time, are intense, and impair a child's ability to function in society. The behaviors must not be caused by temporarily stressful situations or other factors such as depression over the death of a grandparent or anger over the parents' impending divorce. In order for a child to be considered seriously emotionally disturbed, he or she must exhibit one or more of the following characteristics over a *long period of time* and to a *marked degree* that *adversely affects* a child's educational performance.

- Inability to learn that cannot be explained by intellectual, sensory, or health factors

- Inability to maintain satisfactory interpersonal relationships

- Inappropriate types of behaviors

- General pervasive mood of unhappiness or depression

- Physical symptoms or fears associated with personal or school problems

Schizophrenic children are covered under this definition, and social maladjustment by itself does not satisfy this definition unless it is accompanied by one of the other conditions of SED.

> While almost all children at times exhibit behaviors that are aggressive, withdrawn, or otherwise inappropriate, the IDEA definition of serious emotional disturbance (SED) focuses on behaviors that persist over time, are intense, and impair a child's ability to function in society.

The diagnostic categories and definitions used to classify mental disorders come from the American Psychiatric Association's publication *Diagnostic and Statistical Manual of Mental Disorders* (DSM-IV), the handbook used by psychiatrists and psychologists. The DSM-IV is a multiaxial classification system consisting of dimensions (axes) coded along with the psychiatric diagnosis. The axes are listed below.

Axis I	Principal psychiatric diagnosis (e.g., overanxious disorder)
Axis II	Developmental problems (e.g., developmental reading disorder)
Axis III	Physical disorders (e.g., allergies)
Axis IV	Psychosocial stressors (e.g., divorce)
Axis V	Rating of the highest level of adaptive functioning (includes intellectual and social). Rating is called Global Assessment Functioning (GAF) score.

While the DSM-IV diagnosis is one way of diagnosing SED, there are other ways of classifying the various forms in which behavior disorders manifest themselves. The following tables summarize some of these classifications.

Externalizing Behaviors	**Internalizing Behaviors**
Aggressive behaviors expressed outwardly toward others	Withdrawing behaviors that are directed inward to oneself
Manifested as hyperactivity, persistent aggression, irritating behaviors that are impulsive and distractible	Social withdrawal
Examples: hitting, cursing, stealing, arson, cruelty to animals, hyperactivity	Depression, fears, phobias, elective mutism, withdrawal, anorexia, and bulimia

Well-known instruments used to assess children's behavior have their own categories and scales to classify behaviors. The following table illustrates the scales used in some of the widely used instruments.

Walker Problem Identification Checklist	Burks' Behavior Rating Scales (BBRS)	Devereux Behavior Rating Scale (Adolescent)	Revised Behavior Problem Checklist (Quay & Peterson)
Acting out	Excessive self-blame	Unethical behavior	*Major scales*
Withdrawal	Excessive anxiety	Defiant-resistive	Conduct Disorder
Distractibility	Excessive withdrawal	Domineering-sadistic	Socialized aggression
Disturbed peer relations	Excessive dependency	Heterosexual interest	Attention problems—immaturity
Immaturity	Poor ego strength	Hyperactive expansive	Anxiety—withdrawal
	Poor physical strength	Poor emotional control	*Minor scales*
	Poor coordination	Need approval, dependency	Psychotic behavior
	Poor intellectuality	Emotional disturbance	Motor excess
	Poor academics	Physical inferiority—timidity	
	Poor attention	Schizoid withdrawal	
	Poor impulse control	Bizarre speech and cognition	
	Poor reality contact	Bizarre actions	
	Poor sense of identity		
	Excessive suffering		
	Poor anger control		
	Excessive sense of persecution		
	Excessive aggressiveness		
	Excessive resistance		

Disturbance may also be categorized in degrees: mild, moderate, or severe. The degree of disturbance will affect the type and degree of interventions and services required by the student with an emotional disturbance. Degree of disturbance also must be considered when determining the least restrictive environment and the services named for free, appropriate education for these students. An example of a set of criteria for determining the degree of disturbance is the one developed by P. L. Newcomer:

CRITERIA	DEGREE OF DISTURBANCE		
	MILD	**MODERATE**	**SEVERE**
Precipitating Events	Highly stressful	Moderately stressful	Not stressful
Destructiveness	Not destructive	Occasionally destructive	Usually destructive
Maturational Appropriateness	Behavior typical for age	Some behavior untypical for age	Behavior too young or too old
Personal Functioning	Cares for own needs	Usually cares for own needs	Unable to care for own needs
Social Functioning	Usually able to relate to others	Usually unable to relate to others	Unable to relate to others
Reality Index	Usually sees events as they are	Occasionally sees events as they are	Little contact with reality
Insight Index	Aware of behavior	Usually aware of behavior	Usually not aware of behavior
Conscious Control	Usually can control behavior	Occasionally can control behavior	Little control over behavior
Social Responsiveness	Usually acts appropriately	Occasionally acts appropriately	Rarely acts appropriately

Source: Understanding and Teaching Emotionally Disturbed Children and Adolescents, *(2nd ed., p. 139), by P. L. Newcomer, 1993, Austin, TX: Pro-De. Copyright 1993. Reprinted with permission.*

Sample Test Questions and Rationale

(Average)

1. Which behavior would be expected at the mild level of emotional/behavioral disorders?

   A. Attention seeking

   B. Inappropriate affect

   C. Self-injurious

   D. Poor sense of identity

Answer: A. Attention seeking

Children who exhibit mild behavioral disorders are characterized by:

- Average or above average scores on intelligence tests

- Poor academic achievement; learned helplessness

- Unsatisfactory interpersonal relationships

- Immaturity; attention seeking

(Rigorous)

2. Short attention span, daydreaming, clumsiness, and preference for younger playmates are associated with:

   A. Conduct disorder

   B. Personality disorders

   C. Immaturity

   D. Socialized aggression

Answer: C. Immaturity

These disorders show immaturity. The student is not acting age-appropriately.

SKILL 1.2 Language development and behavior

LANGUAGE is the means whereby people communicate their thoughts, make requests, and respond to others. COMMUNICATION COMPETENCE is an interaction of cognitive competence, social knowledge, and language competence. Communication problems can occur in any or all of these areas and have a direct impact on the student's ability to interact with others. Language consists of several components, each of which follows a sequence of development.

Brown and colleagues were the first to describe language as a function of developmental stages rather than age (Reid, 1988 p 44). They developed a formula to group the mean length of utterances (sentences) into stages. Counting the number of morphemes per one hundred utterances, one can calculate a mean length of utterance (MLU). Total number of morphemes / 100 = MLU, e.g., 180/100 = 1.8.

LANGUAGE: the means whereby people communicate their thoughts, make requests, and respond to others

COMMUNICATION COMPETENCE: the interaction of cognitive competence, social knowledge, and language competence

MLU AND LANGUAGE DEVELOPMENT		
Stage	**MLU**	**Developmental Features**
L	1.5–2.0	14 basic morphemes (e.g., in, on, articles, possessives)
LI	2.0–2.5	Beginning of pronoun use, auxiliary verbs
LII	2.5–3.0	Language forms approximate adult forms; beginning of questions and negative statements
IV	3.0–3.5	Use of complex (embedded) sentences
V	3.5–4.0	Use of compound sentences

PHONOLOGY: the system of rules about sounds and sound combinations for a language

MORPHEMES: the smallest units of language that convey meaning or function

FREE MORPHEMES: morphemes that can stand alone as root words, such as walk, or dog

BOUND MORPHEMES: morphological units that do not stand alone and convey or alter meaning when attached to other morphemes

MORPHOLOGY: the rules for making words, including rules for making plurals, possessives, and inflections in verbs

Components of Language

Language learning is composed of five components: phonology, morphology, syntax, semantics, and pragmatics. Developmentally, children progress through each component.

Phonology

PHONOLOGY is the system of rules about sounds and sound combinations for a language. A phoneme is the smallest unit of sound that combines with other sounds to make words. Most phonemes have no meaning in isolation ('a' and 'I' are exceptions). Generally, a phoneme must be combined with other phonemes to compose words or other morphemes. Problems in phonology may be manifested as developmental delays in acquiring consonants, reception problems such as misinterpreting words because a different consonant was substituted, or difficulty learning the sound-symbol code (phonics).

Morphology

MORPHEMES are the smallest units of language that convey meaning or function. FREE MORPHEMES are morphemes that can stand alone as root words, such as *walk* or *dog*. BOUND MORPHEMES are morphological units that do not stand alone. They convey or alter meaning when attached to other morphemes. Prefixes and suffixes (e.g., pre-, -less), and inflectional endings (-ed, -ing) are examples of bound morphemes. MORPHOLOGY is composed of all the rules for making words, including rules for making plurals, possessives, and inflections in verbs. Content words carry the meaning in a sentence, and functional words join phrases and sentences. Generally, students with problems in this area may not use inflectional endings in their words, may not be consistent in their use of certain morphemes, or may be delayed in learning such morphemes as are used in irregular past tenses.

Syntax

SYNTAX RULES, commonly known as grammar, govern how morphemes and words are correctly combined to make sentences. Wood, (1976, p.115) describes six stages of syntax acquisition.

- Stages 1 and 2 (birth to about 2 years): Child is learning the semantic system.

- Stage 3 (ages 2 to 3 years): Simple sentences contain subject and predicate.

- Stage 4 (ages 2½ to 4 years): Elements such as question words are added to basic sentences (e.g., where); word order is changed to ask questions. The child begins to use and combine simple sentences and to embed words within the basic sentence.

- Stage 5 (about 3½ to 7 years): The child uses complete sentences that include word classes of adult language. The child is becoming aware of appropriate semantic functions of words and differences within the same grammatical class.

- Stage 6 (about 5 to 20 years): The child begins to learn complex sentences and sentences that imply commands, requests, and promises.

Semantics

SEMANTICS is language content: the linguistic meaning of morphemes, words, phrases, and sentences. As with syntax, Wood (1976) outlines stages of semantic development:

- Stage 1 (birth to about 2 years): The child is learning meaning while learning his first words. Sentences are one word, but the meaning varies according to the context. Therefore, *doggie* may mean "This is my dog," "There is a dog," or "The dog is barking."

- Stage 2 (about 2 to 8 years): The child progresses to two-word sentences about concrete actions. As more words are learned, the child forms longer sentences. Until about age seven, items are defined in terms of visible actions. The child begins to respond to prompts (e.g., *pretty/flower*); at about age eight, the child can respond to a prompt with an opposite (e.g., *pretty/ugly*)

SYNTAX RULES: govern how morphemes and words are correctly combined to make sentences

The child with a language disability manifests syntactic deficits by using sentences that lack length or complexity for a child that age. Such a child may have problems understanding or creating complex sentences and embedded sentences.

SEMANTICS: language content: the linguistic meaning of morphemes, words, phrases, and sentences

- **Stage 3 (begins at about age 8):** The child's word meanings relate directly to experiences, operations, and processes. Vocabulary is defined by the child's experiences, not the adult's. At about age twelve, the child begins to give dictionary definitions, and the semantic level approaches that of adults.

Semantic problems take the form of the following:

- Limited vocabulary

- Inability to understand figurative language or idioms; interprets literally

- Failure to perceive multiple meanings of words, changes in word meaning from changes in context, resulting in incomplete understanding of what is read

- Difficulty understanding linguistic concepts (e.g., before/after), verbal analogies, and such logical relationships as possessives, spatial, and temporal

- Misuse of transitional words such as *although*, *regardless*

Pragmatics

Commonly known as the speaker's intent, pragmatics are used to influence or control the actions or attitudes of others. COMMUNICATIVE COMPETENCE depends on how well one understands the rules of language and such social rules of communication as taking turns and using the correct tone of voice.

Pragmatic deficits are manifested by failures to respond properly to indirect requests after age eight (e.g., "Can't you turn down the TV?" elicits a response of "No" instead of "Yes" and the child turning down the volume). Children with these deficits have trouble reading cues that indicate the listener does not understand them. Whereas a person would usually notice this and adjust one's speech to the listener's needs, the child with pragmatic problems does not do this.

Pragmatic deficits are also characterized by inappropriate social behaviors such as interruptions or monopolizing conversations. Children may use immature speech and have trouble sticking to a topic. These problems can persist into adulthood, affecting academic, vocational, and social interactions.

Problems in language development often require long-term interventions and can persist into adulthood. Certain problems are associated with different grade levels.

Preschool and Kindergarten

The child's speech may sound immature. The child may not be able to follow simple directions and often cannot name such concepts as the days of the week and colors. The child may not be able to discriminate between sounds and the letters associated with the sounds. The child might substitute sounds and have

COMMUNICATIVE COMPETENCE: understanding the rules of language and such social rules of communication as taking turns and using the correct tone of voice

Pragmatic deficits are manifested by failures to respond properly to indirect requests. Pragmatic deficits are also characterized by inappropriate social behaviors such as interruptions or monopolizing conversations.

trouble responding accurately to certain types of questions. The child may play less with his peers or participate in nonplay or parallel play.

Elementary school

Problems with sound discrimination persist, and the child may have problems with temporal and spatial concepts such as before and after. As the child progresses through school, he or she may have problems making the transition from narrative to expository writing. Word retrieval problems may not be very evident because the child begins to devise strategies such as talking around the word he cannot remember or using fillers and descriptors. The child might speak more slowly, have problems sounding out words, and get confused with multiple-meaning words. Pragmatic problems such as failure to correctly interpret social cues and adjust to appropriate language, inability to predict consequences, and inability to formulate requests to obtain new information show up in social situations.

Secondary school

At this level, difficulties become more subtle. The child cannot use and understand higher-level syntax, semantics, and pragmatics. If the child has problems with auditory language, he may also have problems with short-term memory. Receptive and expressive language delays impair the child's ability to learn effectively. The child often cannot organize and categorize the information received in school. Problems associated with pragmatic deficiencies persist but, because the child is aware of them, he becomes inattentive, withdrawn, or frustrated.

Sample Test Questions and Rationale

(Rigorous)

1. Skilled readers use all but which one of these knowledge sources to construct meanings beyond the literal text:

   A. Text knowledge

   B. Syntactic knowledge

   C. Morphological knowledge

   D. Semantic knowledge

Answer: C. Morphological knowledge

The student is already skilled, so morphological knowledge is already in place.

(Rigorous)

2. Celia, who is in first grade, asked, "Where are my ball?" She also has trouble with passive sentences. Language interventions for Celia would target:

   A. Morphology

   B. Syntax

   C. Pragmatics

   D. Semantics

Answer: B. Syntax

Syntax refers to the rules for arranging words to make sentences.

Sample Test Questions and Rationale (cont.)

(Rigorous)

3. **Mr. Mendez is assessing his students' written expression. Which of these is not a component of written expression?**

   A. Vocabulary

   B. Morphology

   C. Content

   D. Sentence structure

Answer: B. Morphology

Morphology is correct. Vocabulary consists of words, content is made up of ideas, which are expressed in words, and sentences are constructed from words. Morphemes, however, are not always words. They may be prefixes or suffixes. Problems in this area would usually be considered problems with the mechanics of language, not expression.

SKILL 1.3 Cognition

Beginning with preoperational thought processes and moving to concrete operational thoughts, children go through patterns of learning. Eventually they begin to acquire the mental ability to think about and solve problems in their heads because they can manipulate objects and ideas symbolically. Even children who can use such symbols as words and numbers to represent objects and relations need concrete reference points. Children must be encouraged to use and develop the thinking skills that they possess in solving problems that interest them. The content of the curriculum must be relevant, engaging, and meaningful to the students.

The teacher of students with special needs must have a general knowledge of cognitive development. Although children with special needs have a cognitive development rate that may be different than other children, a teacher needs to be aware of some of the activities of each stage as part of the basis to determine what should be taught and when it should be taught.

The following information about cognitive development was taken from the Cincinnati Children's Hospital Medical Center Web site at *www.cincinnattichildrens.org.* Here are some common features indicating a progression from simple to more complex cognitive development:

Children (Ages 6–12)	Begin to develop the ability to think in concrete ways. Concrete operations are operations performed in the presence of the object and events that are to be used. Examples: how to combine (addition), separate (subtract or divide), order (alphabetize and sort and categorize), and transform objects and actions (change items such as 25 pennies = 1 quarter)
Adolescents (Ages 12–18)	Adolescents begin to develop more complex thinking skills, including abstract thinking, the ability to reason from known principles (form own new ideas or questions), the ability to consider many points of view according to varying criteria (compare or debate ideas or opinions), and the ability to think about the process of thinking.

What cognitive developmental changes occur during adolescence?

During adolescence (between twelve and eighteen years of age), the developing teenager acquires the ability to think systematically about all logical relationships within a problem. The transition from concrete thinking to formal logical operations occurs over time. Every adolescent progresses at varying rates in developing the ability to think in more complex ways. Each adolescent develops his or her own view of the world. Some adolescents may be able to apply logical operations to school work long before they are able to apply them to personal dilemmas. When emotional issues arise, they often interfere with an adolescent's ability to think in more complex ways. The ability to consider possibilities, as well as facts, may influence decision making in either positive or negative ways.

Some common features indicating a progression from simple to more complex cognitive development can be seen in early, middle, and late adolescence.

Early Adolescence

During early adolescence, the use of more complex thinking is focused on personal decision making in school and home environments, including the following:

- Begins to demonstrate use of formal logical operations in school work

- Begins to question authority and society standards

- Begins to form and verbalize thoughts and views on a variety of topics, usually more related to his or her own life, such as:

  - Which sports are better to play

  - Which groups are better to be included in

  - What personal appearances are desirable or attractive

  - What parental rules should be changed

Middle Adolescence

With some experience in using more complex thinking processes, the focus of middle adolescence often expands to include more philosophical and futuristic concerns, including the following:

- Often questions more extensively
- Often analyzes more extensively
- Thinks about and begins to form a code of ethics
- Thinks about different possibilities and begins to develop own identity
- Thinks about and begins to systematically consider possible future goals
- Thinks about and begins to make his or her own plans
- Begins to think long term
- Systematic thinking begins to influence relationships with others

Late Adolescence

During late adolescence, complex thinking processes are used to focus on less self-centered concepts and personal decision making, including the following:

- Develops idealistic views on specific topics or concerns
- Debates and develops intolerance of opposing views
- Begins to focus thinking on making career decisions
- Begins to focus thinking on emerging role in adult society
- Has increased thoughts about such global concepts as justice, history, politics, and patriotism

What encourages healthy cognitive development during adolescence?

Include adolescents in discussions about a variety of topics, issues, and current events.

Encourage adolescents to share ideas and thoughts with adults.

Encourage adolescents to think independently and develop their own ideas.

Help adolescents set their own goals.

Stimulate adolescents to think about possibilities of the future.

Compliment and praise adolescents for well-thought-out decisions.

Help adolescents reevaluate poorly made decisions for themselves.

SKILL 1.4 Physical development, including motor and sensory

The teacher must be aware of the physical stages of development and how the child's physical growth and development affect learning. Factors determined by the physical stage of development include the ability to sit and attend, the need for activity, the relationship between physical skills and self-esteem, and the degree to which physical involvement in an activity (as opposed to being able to understand an abstract concept) affects learning.

Children with physical impairments possess a variety of disabling conditions. Although significant differences exist among these conditions, so do similarities. Each condition usually affects one particular system of the body—either the cardiopulmonary system (blood vessels, heart, and lungs) or the musculoskeletal system (spinal cord, brain nerves). Some conditions develop during pregnancy, birth, or infancy because of known or unknown factors that may affect the fetus or newborn infant. Other conditions occur later because of injury (trauma), disease, or factors not fully understood.

In addition to motor disorders, individuals with physical disabilities may have such multi-disabling conditions as concomitant hearing impairments, visual impairments, perceptual disorders, speech defects, behavior disorders or mental handicaps, performance deficits, or deficits in emotional responsiveness.

The following are some characteristics that may present in individuals with physical disabilities and other health impairments:

- Lack of physical stamina; fatigue

- Chronic illness; poor endurance

- Deficient motor skills; normal movement may be prevented

- Physical limitations or impeded motor development; a prosthesis or an orthosis may be required

- Limited mobility and exploration of one's environment

- Limited self-care abilities

- Progressive weakening and degeneration of muscles

- Frequent speech and language defects; communication may be prevented; echolalia may be present

- Pain and discomfort throughout the body

- Emotional (psychological) problems that require treatment

- Need for social adjustments; may display maladaptive social behavior

- Need for long-term medical treatment, which may become a financial burden on the family

- Embarrassing side effects from certain diseases or treatment

- Erratic or poor attendance patterns, which lead to the child missing many skills and the parent or caregiver missing days of work

In 1981, the condition of autism was moved from the exceptionality category of Seriously Emotionally Disturbed to that of Other Health Impaired by virtue of a change in language in the original definitions under Public Law 94-142 ("Education of Handicapped Children." *Federal Register,* 1977). With IDEA, in 1990, autism was made into a separate exceptionality category.

Sample Test Question and Rationale

(Average)

1. **Muscular Dystrophy is a condition which affects the ________ system of the body.**

    A. cardiopulmonary

    B. musculoskeletal

    C. neurological

    D. All of the above

Answer: B. musculoskeletal

As the name implies, Muscular Dystrophy affects the musculoskeletal system.

COMPETENCY 2
CHARACTERISTICS OF STUDENTS WITH DISABILITIES

SKILL 2.1 Cognitive factors

"Mental retardation" is the term historically applied to overall developmental delays and disabilities in all academic and cognitive abilities. Children with this condition generally display significantly below average intellectual functioning on all cognitive measures, as well as deficits in at least two adaptive skills. These problems typically impact all aspects of the educational experience. The degree of cognitive impairment will have a profound impact on the choice of educational programming. In addition, a child with these generalized disabilities will probably need life-long assistance in some form. Characteristics with regard to the degree of cognitive impairment fall into four categories.

- Mild (IQ of 50-55 to 70) This level is sometimes referred to as "generalized learning disability" today in order to avoid the stigma often associated with the term "retardation"

    - Delays in most areas (communication, motor, academic)

    - Often not distinguished from normal children until of school age

    - Can acquire both academic and vocational skills; can become self-supporting

- Moderate (IQ of 35-40 to 50-55)

    - Only fair motor development; clumsy

    - Poor social awareness

    - Can be taught to communicate

    - Can profit from training in social and vocational skills; needs supervision, but can perform semiskilled labor as an adult

- Severe (IQ of 20-25 to 35-40)

    - Poor motor development

    - Minimal speech and communication

- Minimal ability to profit from training in health and self-help skills; may contribute to self-maintenance under constant supervision as an adult

- Profound (IQ below 20-25)

    - Gross retardation, both mental and sensor-motor

    - Little or no development of basic communication skills

    - Dependency on others to maintain basic life functions

    - Lifetime of complete supervision (institution, home, nursing home)

Sample Test Question and Rationale

(Rigorous)

1. **A child with intellectual disabilities who is fairly clumsy and possesses poor social awareness, but who can be taught to communicate and to perform semi-skilled labor and maintains himself under supervision, as an adult, probably belongs to which level of classification:**

    A. Mild

    B. Moderate

    C. Severe

    D. Profound

Answer: B. Moderate

Characteristics with regard to the degree of cognitive impairment fall into four categories.

- Mild (IQ of 50-55 to 70)
    - Delays in most areas (communication, motor, academic)
    - Often not distinguished from normal children until of school age
    - Can acquire both academic and vocational skills; can become self-supporting

- Moderate (IQ of 35-40 to 50-55)
    - Only fair motor development; clumsy
    - Poor social awareness
    - Can be taught to communicate
    - Can profit from training in social and vocational skills; needs supervision, but can perform semi-skilled labor as an adult

- Severe (IQ of 20-25 to 35-40)
    - Poor motor development
    - Minimal speech and communication
    - Minimal ability to profit from training in health and self-help skills; may contribute to self-maintenance under constant supervision as an adult

- Profound (IQ below 20-25)
    - Gross retardation, both mental and sensor-motor
    - Little or no development of basic communication skills
    - Dependency on others to maintain basic life functions
    - Lifetime of complete supervision (institution, home, nursing home)

SKILL 2.2 Affective and social-adaptive factors, including cultural, linguistic, gender, and socioeconomic factors

Although legal and educational definitions of the various disabilities state that they may NOT be due to cultural diversity or socioeconomic environment, these factors do impact children with disabilities in special ways. Quite often, students absorb the culture and social environment around them without deciphering the contextual meaning of the experiences. When provided with a diversity of cultural contexts, some students with exceptionalities cannot adapt and incorporate multiple meanings from cultural cues vastly different from their own socioeconomic backgrounds.

The educational experience for most students is a complex experience with a diversity of interlocking meanings and inferences. If one aspect of the complexity is altered, it affects other aspects, which may have an impact on how a student or teacher views an instructional or learning experience. With the current demographic profile of today's school communities, the complexity of understanding, interpreting, and synthesizing nuances from the diversity of cultural lineages can provide many communication and learning impediments that could hamper the acquisition of learning, especially for students with exceptionalities.

Teachers must create PERSONALIZED LEARNING COMMUNITIES where every student is a valued member of and contributor to the classroom experiences. In classrooms where sociocultural attributes of the student population are incorporated into the fabric of the learning process, dynamic interrelationships are created that enhance the learning experience and the personalization of learning.

Similarly, inclusion of students with exceptionalities into the general education classroom can be beneficial for advanced academic achievement as well as sociocultural development, provided proper accommodations for their special needs are made. Researchers continue to show that personalized learning environments increase learning for students, decrease drop-out rates among marginalized students, and decrease unproductive student behavior that can result from constant cultural misunderstandings or miscues between students.

Learning environments that help children with and without disabilities understand that both learning abilities and styles differ, and that each child has a place in and something to contribute to the group can prevent misunderstandings and intolerance of students with special needs. Promoting diversity of learning and cultural competency in the classroom creates a world of multicultural opportunities and learning. When students are able to step outside their comfort zones and share the world of a homeless student or empathize with an English language learner (ELL) who has just immigrated to the United States, is learning English

Sociocultural factors have a definitive impact on students' psychological, emotional, affective, and physiological development and on academic learning and future opportunities.

PERSONALIZED LEARNING COMMUNITIES: every student is a valued member of and contributor to the classroom experiences

When students with exceptionalities are provided with numerous academic and social opportunities to share cultural approaches to learning, everyone in the classroom benefits from bonding through shared experiences and an expanded viewpoint of a world experience that vastly differs from their own.

for the first time, and is still trying to keep up with the academic learning in an unfamiliar language, then students grow exponentially in social understanding and cultural connectedness.

Personalized learning communities provide supportive learning environments that address the academic and emotional needs of all students. As sociocultural knowledge is conveyed continuously in the interrelated experiences shared cooperatively and collaboratively in student groupings and individualized learning, the current and future benefits will continue to present the case and importance of understanding the whole child, inclusive of the social and cultural context.

Sample Test Question and Rationale

(Rigorous)

1. **Individuals with mild mental retardation can be characterized as:**

   A. Often indistinguishable from normal developing children at an early age

   B. Having a higher than normal rate of motor activity

   C. Displaying significant discrepancies in ability levels

   D. Uneducable in academic skills

Answer: A. Often indistinguishable from normal developing children at an early age

See rationale of the previous question.

SKILL 2.3 Genetic, medical, motor, sensory, and chronological age factors

Students with disabilities exhibit a wide range of characteristics that cut across disability categories. A number of factors influence the predominance of certain disabilities.

Genetic Factors

Genetics can play a large role in the characteristics of many disabilities. Various disabilities run in families and are more prevalent in certain gene pools. Dyslexia has a high incidence rate of 5 to 10 percent of school age children, and it is primarily genetically determined. Several genes have been independently identified as causative for dyslexia. In addition, the parent's age at time of conception can have an impact on the prevalence of disabilities.

Abnormal growth and development occurs when some of these genes or chromosomes are missing or damaged or if extra chromosomes exist. These abnormal genes are passed down from a parent, but sometimes they occur spontaneously for unknown reasons. Some common genetic disorders include Down Syndrome, Fragile X Syndrome, and Rett Syndrome.

Medical Factors

Many students with disabilities have medical problems that cause or aggravate their disability. These problems can include the following: heart problems, childhood cancer, diabetes, seizures, AIDS, traumatic brain disorders, blindness, limited mobility, hearing impairment, and other conditions that interfere with a student's academic functioning. ADD and ADHD are now considered medical problems, as well. ADD/ADHD can impact a wide range of learning and performance variables.

Gender

More boys are identified as having emotional and behavioral problems, especially hyperactivity and attention deficit disorder, autism, childhood psychosis, and problems with poor control (aggression, socialized aggression). Girls, on the other hand, have more problems with overcontrol (withdrawal and phobias). Problems with mental retardation and language and learning disabilities are much more prevalent in boys than in girls.

Chronological Characteristics

Educators must know the characteristics that are typical of all children as they progress through developmental stages. For example, when girls enter adolescence, they tend to experience affective or emotional disorders such as anorexia, depression, bulimia, and anxiety at twice the rate of boys. Students whose characteristics deviate from those of the normal population may be in need of special accommodations or services if their problems have an adverse impact on educational success. Often these students have needs that are of a physical, emotional, developmental, behavioral, and educational nature.

Motor Factors

The normal progression of learning demonstrated by a child is related to developmental growth in the areas of gross and fine motor abilities and language development. Teachers should be aware of the developmental milestones in motor and language skills that are normally achieved by children of various ages.

Sensory Factors

Students may experience sensory deficits in the areas of vision and hearing. Children with autism also often have sensory integration problems. Some can't handle noises, or certain touches or textures, and some crave certain sensory experiences. The sensory problems may involve any of the body's sensory systems—sight, hearing, touch, smell, taste, balance, and weight.

COMPETENCY 3
BASIC CONCEPTS IN SPECIAL EDUCATION

SKILL 3.1 **Definitions of all major categories and specific disabilities** *(as well as the incidence and prevalence of various types of disabilities)*

A table summarizing the classification of students with disabilities and the characteristics of each major classification is found in Skill 3.4. That classification system is used to help define both eligibility for special services and placement in special service programs. Many of the classifications are medical or physical in nature and the terminology is self explanatory (e.g., blindness). Other categories, particularly "Specific Learning Disability," include a wide range of disabilities, and it is important for the teacher to understand the terminology of these disabilities when applied to his or her students. Listed below are some of the most common specific learning disabilities teachers will encounter in their students with special needs.

SPECIFIC LEARNING DISABILITIES	
Central Auditory Processing Deficit (CAPD)	Students with CAPDs have normal hearing *physiologically*, but have deficits in the processing or auditory input. Such deficits impact both cognitive and linguistic functioning in both receptive and expressive modes. The symptoms sometimes are mistaken for ADHD because the child cannot adequately process instructions and information.
Communication Disorders	This group includes deficits in language processing, articulation, fluency, or voice.

Table continued on next page

Dyscalculia	Any serious disability in processing mathematical information, concepts or calculations, particularly when there are not corresponding disabilities in other verbal skills.
Dysgraphia	A serious deficit in the ability to carry out the motor or cognitive functions necessary to write. This may be a motor problem and/or a cognitive inability to plan and generate sentences. It is usually neurologically based.
Dyslexia	Although this term is not as widely used as it once was, it still refers to a reading disability that is based in problems learning to associate sounds and symbols (letters).
Nonverbal Learning Disabilities	These disabilities impact many areas of nonverbal problem solving. Although children with them can often "read" and memorize well, they have significant difficulty understanding what they read, as well as difficulty understanding nonverbal communication such as facial expressions and body language. As a result, both social competence and emotional well-being can be impacted. There may also be deficits in visual-spatial organization and motor control.
Pervasive Developmental Disorders Not Otherwise Specified (PDDNOS)	These disorders are very similar to autism and are sometimes referred to as "autism spectrum disorders." Though children with these disorders do not qualify as autistic, they have many of the same deficits in social and communication skills.

In addition to specific learning disabilities, special education teachers may often encounter the following diagnoses of children with special needs.

DIAGNOSES OF CHILDREN WITH SPECIAL NEEDS	
Attention Deficit Disorder (ADD) or Attention Deficit with Hyperactivity Disorder (ADHD)	Children with these disorders display serious inattention, distractibility, disorganization, and poor impulse control, often with constant movement or activity they cannot control. Typically, they do not show delayed cognition or mental retardation. These disorders can often accompany other medical or learning disorders, however, and further impact learning.
Asperger's Syndrome	Although the definition of this disorder is changing in some quarters, it usually refers to a type of autism involving most of the characteristics of autism, without cognitive delay or retardation. Children with this disorder have normal or above average cognitive abilities. It is often referred to as a "high functioning form of autism."
Cerebral Palsy	This is a neurological disorder that involves damage to the motor centers of the brain (during fetal development, or during or after birth) and results in tremors and muscle weakness or tension. Both gross and fine motor skills can be affected.

Table continued on next page

Developmental Disabilities	These disabilities result in significant delays in physical (e.g., Cerebral Palsy) or cognitive (mental retardation) abilities.
Tourette Syndrome	This is a seizure disorder (not epilepsy) that produces motor, vocal, and other tics (i.e., highly repetitive actions) over which the child has minimum control.

SKILL 3.2 The causation and prevention of a disability

Although we know the etiology of some disabilities (e.g., Down Syndrome, Cerebral Palsy), for some learning disabilities there is no currently identified cause. A wide range of possibilities make it almost impossible to pinpoint the exact cause. Listed below are some factors that can contribute to the development of a disability.

Problems in Fetal Brain Development

During pregnancy, the development of the brain can suffer disruptions that alter how the neurons form or interconnect. Throughout pregnancy, brain development is vulnerable to disruptions. If the disruption occurs early, the fetus may die, or the infant may be born with widespread disabilities and possibly mental retardation. If the disruption occurs later, when the cells are becoming specialized and moving into place, it may leave errors in the cell makeup, location, or connections. Some scientists believe that these errors may later show up as learning disorders.

Genetic Factors

Learning disabilities can run in families, which suggests a genetic link. For example, children who do not have certain reading skills, such as hearing the separate sounds of words, are likely to have a parent with a similar problem. A parent's learning disability can take a slightly different form in the child. Therefore, direct inheritance of specific learning disorders is unlikely.

Environment

Family environment may be another reason that learning disabilities appear to run in families. Parents with expressive language disorders may talk less to their children or their language may be muffled. In this case the lack of a proper role model for acquiring good language skills causes the disability.

Tobacco, Alcohol, and Other Drug Use

Many drugs taken by the mother pass directly to the fetus during pregnancy. Research shows that a mother's use of cigarettes, alcohol, or other drugs during pregnancy may have damaging effects on the unborn child. Mothers who smoke during pregnancy are more likely to have smaller birth weight babies. Newborns who weigh less than five pounds are more at risk for learning disorders.

Heavy alcohol use during pregnancy has been linked to Fetal Alcohol Syndrome (FAS), a condition resulting in low birth weight, intellectual impairment, hyper-activity, and certain physical defects.

Problems During Pregnancy or Delivery

Complications during pregnancy can also cause learning disabilities. The mother's immune system can react to the fetus and attack it as if it were an infection. This type of problem appears to cause newly formed brain cells to settle in the wrong part of the brain. In addition, during delivery, the umbilical cord can become twisted and temporarily cut off oxygen to the fetus, resulting in impaired brain functions.

Toxins in the Environment

New brain cells and neural networks are produced for a year after the child is born. These cells are vulnerable to certain disruptions.

Certain environmental toxins may lead to learning disabilities. Cadmium and lead are becoming a leading focus of neurological research. Cadmium is used in making some steel products. It can get into the soil and then into the foods we eat. Lead was once common in paint and gasoline and is still present in some water pipes.

Children with cancer who have been treated with chemotherapy or radiation at an early age can also develop learning disabilities. This type of disability is very prevalent in children with brain tumors who received radiation to the skull.

To prevent disabilities from occurring, information on the causes of disabilities should be widely available so that parents can take the necessary steps to safeguard their children from conception until the early years of life. While some of the causes of disability are unavoidable or incidental, many causes can be prevented.

Sample Test Questions and Rationale

(Average)

1. **Across America there is a toxic substance that widely contributes to the creation of disabilities in our children. What is it?**

   A. Children's aspirin

   B. Fluoride water

   C. Chlorine gas

   D. Lead

Answer: D. Lead

Lead poisoning is still a major factor influencing/causing disabilities. Today many homes in urban, suburban, and rural neighborhoods are still working to remove the lead paint in houses. In addition, toys and school supplies imported from countries with fewer governmental safeguards have been found to contain excessive amounts of lead. Teachers need to be vigilant when choosing supplies for their students.

(Average)

2. **____________ is an environmental reason for mild learning and behavioral disabilities:**

   A. Poverty

   B. Genetics

   C. Biochemical factors

   D. Maturational lag

Answer: A. Poverty

Included under environmental reasons for mild learning and behavior disabilities are factors relating to poverty, nutrition, toxins, language differences, sensory deprivation, emotional problems, and inadequate education. Although some environmental factors, e.g., toxins, cause organic dysfunction, the point of origin is outside the body (exogenous).

(Average)

3. **Parents are more likely to have a child with a learning disability if:**

   A. They smoke tobacco

   B. The child is less than 5 pounds at birth

   C. If the mother drank alcohol on a regular basis until she planned for a baby

   D. The father was known to consume large quantities of alcohol during the pregnancy

Answer: B. The child is less than 5 pounds at birth

Babies that are born weighing less than 5 pounds at birth are more likely to have a form of learning disability. The reasoning is that the babies may not have fully developed before birth.

SKILL 3.3 The nature of behaviors, including frequency, duration, intensity, and degrees of severity

In order to tackle the issue of behavior problems, educators usually start with a Behavior Intervention Plan (BIP). One of the first steps to developing a BIP entails taking a detailed FUNCTIONAL BEHAVIOR ASSESSMENT (FBA) summary, which must define behaviors in observable and measurable terms along four variables: frequency, duration, intensity, and degree of severity.

The FBA must note the frequency of the behaviors that have been identified. Frequency consists of how often a behavior occurs in a specified time block (e.g. morning, afternoon, evening). The activity during which the behavior typically occurs is also recorded. For example, does it occur during lunch, transitions, group time, or another time period? The data should indicate the frequency of the individual behaviors and note when it is less frequent and when the behavior is most likely to occur.

The FBA can help identify the following:

- When the behavior was first observed and key events at that time

- Any signs or cues from the student that help predict that the behavior will occur

- What happens just before the behavior that may trigger the behavior

- Settings, situations, and other variables that influence the behavior

These observations should include the following:

- Specific days or time of day

- Specific settings such as school, home, class, hallway, or bus

- Particular subject areas such as math or P.E.

- Type or length of assignment

- The manner of presenting instruction, feedback, or corrections

- The particular person presenting the information

Another variable that must be addressed is the duration of the behaviors. This variable entails measuring how long the behavior takes place by timing the behavior from start to finish and writing it down.

A third variable that must be measured is the intensity of the behavior. The FBA must have a scale that assesses whether the behavior is of low, medium, or high intensity. If the student is having a tantrum, is there a scale to measure the intensity of the tantrum? For example, a highly intense tantrum might include hitting the teacher or classmates, while a less intense tantrum may include property damage.

A fourth variable that is measured when assessing behavior is the degree of severity. All behaviors can be put into different categories depending on their impact. More severe behavior problems would involve physical violence and destruction

FUNCTIONAL BEHAVIOR ASSESSMENT (FBA): defines behaviors in observable and measurable terms along four variables: frequency, duration, intensity, and degree of severity

of property while less severe problems will involve screaming, yelling, and general disruption of class time.

The FBA may also include factors such as:

- When, where, and with whom the behavior is least likely to occur

- Specific skill deficits that interfere with the student's ability to behave as expected

- Whether the student is aware of expected behavior and understands the consequences of the behavior

- Whether the student has the skills necessary to behave as expected

- The apparent function of undesirable behavior (what the student gets, avoids, or escapes due to the behavior)

- Potential reinforcers for the student

Sample Test Questions and Rationale

(Easy)

1. **Duration is an appropriate measure to take with all of these behaviors EXCEPT:**

   A. Thumb sucking

   B. Hitting

   C. Temper tantrums

   D. Maintaining eye contact

   Answer: B. Hitting

   Hitting takes place in an instant. This should be measured by frequency.

(Average)

2. **All children cry, hit, fight, and play alone at different times. Children with behavior disorders will perform these behaviors at a higher than normal:**

   A. Rate

   B. Topography

   C. Duration

   D. Magnitude

   Answer: A. Rate

   Rate describes how often a behavior occurs.

SKILL 3.4 The classification of students with disabilities; labeling of students; ADHD; the implications of the classification process for the persons classified, etc.

The classification of student exceptionalities and disabilities in education is a categorical system; it organizes special education into categories. Within the categories are subdivisions that may be based on the severity or level of support services needed. Having a categorical system allows educators to differentiate and define types of disabilities, relate treatments to certain categories, and concentrate research and advocacy efforts. The disadvantage of the categorical system is the labeling of groups or individuals. Critics of labels say that labeling can place the emphasis on the label and not the individual needs of the child.

The following table summarizes the categories of disabilities and major characteristics of their definitions under IDEA.

CLASSIFICATION	CHARACTERISTICS
Autism*	Impairment in social interaction and communication accompanied by restricted repetitive and stereotyped patterns of behavior, interests, and activities, occurring before age three.
Deaf	Impairment in processing linguistic information with or without hearing aids that has an adverse impact on educational performance.
Deaf-blind	Hearing and visual impairments causing communication, developmental, and education problems too severe to be met in programs solely for deaf or blind children.
Hard of Hearing	Permanent or fluctuating hearing impairment that adversely affects educational performance but is not included in the definition of deafness.
Mentally Retarded	Significantly sub-average general intellectual functioning with deficits in adaptive behavior, manifested during the developmental period, and adversely affecting educational performance.
Multi-handicapped	Combination of impairments, excluding deaf-blind children, that cause educational problems too severe to be serviced in programs designed for a single impairment.
Orthopedically Impaired	Severe orthopedic impairment that adversely affects educational performance resulting from birth defects, disease (e.g., polio), or other causes (e.g., amputation, burns).
Other Health Impaired	Medical conditions such as heart conditions, tuberculosis, rheumatic fever, nephritis, asthma, sickle cell anemia, hemophilia, epilepsy, lead poisoning, leukemia, or diabetes. (IDEA listing). Other health conditions may be included if they are so chronic or acute that the child's strength, vitality, or alertness is limited.

Table continued on next page

Seriously Emotionally Disturbed (does not include children who are socially maladjusted unless they are also classified as seriously emotionally disturbed)	Schizophrenia, and conditions in which one or more of these characteristics is exhibited over a long period of time and to a marked degree: (a) inability to learn not explained by intellectual, sensory, or health factors, (b) inability to build or maintain satisfactory interpersonal relationships, (c) inappropriate types of behavior or feelings, (d) general pervasive unhappiness or depression, (e) tendency to develop physical symptoms or fears associated with personal or school problems.
Specific Learning Disability	Disorder in one or more basic psychological processes involved in understanding or in using spoken or written language that manifests itself in an imperfect ability to listen, think, speak, read, write, spell, or to do mathematical calculations. They cannot be attributed to visual, hearing, physical, intellectual, or emotional handicaps, or cultural, environmental, or economic disadvantage.
Speech Impaired	Communication disorder such as stuttering, impaired articulation, voice impairment, or language impairment adversely affecting educational performance.
Visually Handicapped (partially sighted or blind)	Visual impairment, even with correction, adversely affecting educational performance.

** Autism was added as a separate category of disability in 1990 under P. L. 101-476. This addition was not a change in the law but a clarification. The law previously covered students with autism, but now identifies them as a separate and distinct class entitled to the law's benefits. Autism is a developmental disability significantly affecting verbal and nonverbal communication and social interaction, generally evident before age three, that adversely affects a child's educational performance. Other characteristics often associated with autism are engagement in repetitive activities and stereotyped movements, resistance to environmental change or change in daily routines, and unusual responses to sensory experiences. The term does not apply if a child's educational performance is adversely affected primarily because the child has a serious emotional disturbance.*

It should also be noted that there is no classification for gifted children under IDEA. Funding and services for gifted programs are left up to the individual states and school districts. Therefore, the number of districts providing services and the scope of gifted programs varies among states and school districts.

Sample Test Questions and Rationale

(Average)

1. **Echolalia, repetitive stereotyped actions, and a severe disorder of thinking and communication are indicative of:**

   A. Psychosis

   B. Schizophrenia

   C. Autism

   D. Paranoia

Answer: C. Autism

The behaviors listed are indicative of autism.

Sample Test Questions and Rationale (cont.)

(Rigorous)

2. **Which of the following is typical of attention problems that a youngster with a learning disability might display?**

   A. Lack of selective attention

   B. Does not consider consequences before acting

   C. Unable to Control Own Actions or impulses

   D. Poor fine motor coordination

Answer: A. Lack of selective attention

Here are some of the characteristics of persons with learning disabilities: Disorder in one or more basic psychological processes involved in understanding or in using spoken or written language that manifests itself in an imperfect ability to listen, think, speak, read, write, spell, or to do mathematical calculations. They cannot be attributed to visual, hearing, physical, intellectual, or emotional handicaps, or cultural, environmental, or economic disadvantage.

(Average)

3. **In which of the following exceptionality categories may a student be considered for inclusion if his IQ score falls more than two standard deviations below the mean?**

   A. Mental retardation

   B. Specific learning disabilities

   C. Emotionally/behaviorally disordered

   D. Gifted

Answer: A. Mental Retardation

Only about 1 to 1.5% of the population fit the AAMD's definition of mental retardation. They exhibit significantly sub average general intellectual functioning with deficits in adaptive behavior, manifested during the developmental period, and adversely affecting educational performance.

SKILL 3.5 The influence of level of severity and presence of multiple exceptionalities on students with disabilities

Children who have multiple disabilities are an extremely heterogeneous population. Their characteristics are determined by the type and severity of their combined disabilities; therefore, they differ in their sensory, motor, social, and cognitive abilities. Although any number of combinations of disabilities is possible, major dimensions typically include mental retardation, neurological impairments, emotional disturbance, or deafness and blindness. Those whose impairments combine to form multiple disabilities often exhibit characteristics on a severe level. Low self-esteem and poor social skills often characterize this population. Youngsters with severe disabilities may possess profound language or perceptual-cognitive deprivations. Moreover, they may have extremely fragile physiological conditions. "It is important to understand that (with) the problem of severe/profound disabilities…It is the extent of the disabilities that results in the child's classification, not the type of disabilities" (Blackhurst & Berdine, 1985, pp. 473–474).

Some characteristics students with severe or profound multidisabilities have are:

- Often not toilet trained

- Frequently nonambulatory

- Aggressiveness toward others without provocation and antisocial behavior

- Markedly withdrawn or unresponsive to others

- No attention to even the most pronounced social stimuli

- Self-mutilation (head banging, biting, and scratching or cutting of self)

- Rumination (self-induced vomiting, swallowing vomitus)

- Self-stimulation (rocking, hand-flapping)

- Intense temper tantrums of unknown origin

- Excessive, pointless imitation, or the total absence of the ability to imitate

- Inability to be controlled verbally

- Extremely brittle medical existence (life-threatening conditions such as congenital heart disease, respiratory difficulties, metabolic disorders, central nervous system disorders, and digestive malfunctions)

COMPETENCY 4

THE INFLUENCE OF (AN) EXCEPTIONAL CONDITION(S) THROUGHOUT AN INDIVIDUAL'S LIFE SPAN

An exceptionality may have a positive, negative, or neutral effect throughout a child's life, depending on the characteristics of the exceptionality, available resources, and support system.

Early Childhood

Often the life of a child with an exceptionality will be different beginning at birth. The child may experience marked developmental delays in some areas and not in other areas. The child's exceptionality may have negative and positive effects on siblings. Some siblings may have feelings of embarrassment, resentfulness, or even guilt related to their sibling with a disability. Other siblings may gain insight, tolerance, and appreciation because of their experience with the sibling with the exceptionality.

The child with the exceptionality may require special diets, transportation, medical care, and other special services. These requirements may cause financial stress on the family.

School Age

Academic and social skills are crucial at this age. The goal during this age is to prepare the child to be an independent, productive citizen. A child with an exceptionality may or may not experience a difficult time interacting with others. If these skills are not taught, this deficiency may cause the child difficulty in developing relationships and future employment problems.

Having an exceptionality may or may not limit a child's academic ability. The goal of the educational system is to include students with exceptionalities in the general education curriculum as much as possible. The degree of inclusion in the curriculum is based on each student's ability.

During this time in life, the student and other concerned individuals collaborate to decide on the child's future and how the student will transition into the next phase of life. Depending on the characteristics of the child's exceptionality, it may be decided that the student will attend technical school, attend post-secondary education, or begin working.

Adult

An adult with an exceptionality may or may not lead a life that is different from any other adult. The adult may go to work every day and come home to take care of all of his or her own needs. Another adult with an exceptionality may live with a caregiver. Adults with exceptionalities have various living options, ranging from residential homes to a very restricted environment, such as institutions.

Many outside agencies provide services for those adults who may need assistance.

Some adults may still lack social skills to maintain a healthy work environment; therefore, job coaches, mentors, or outside agencies are needed to provide additional assistance or needed work skills.

Adults who lack social skills may also have difficulty finding mates and may never have families, while others may find mates and raise families of their own with no outside assistance.

DOMAIN II
LEGAL AND SOCIETAL ISSUES

PERSONALIZED STUDY PLAN

KNOWN MATERIAL/ SKIP IT

COMPETENCY 5
FEDERAL LAWS AND LEGAL ISSUES RELATED TO SPECIAL EDUCATION

Background

The U.S. Constitution does not specify protection for education. However, all states provide education, and thus individuals are guaranteed protection and due process under the Fourteenth Amendment. The basic source of law for special education is the Individuals With Disabilities Education Act (IDEA) and its accompanying regulations. IDEA represents the latest phase in the philosophy of educating children with disabilities. Initially, children with disabilities often did not go to school. When they did attend school, they were segregated into special classes in order to avoid disrupting the regular class. Their education usually consisted of simple academics and, later, training for manual jobs.

By the mid-1900s, advocates for children with disabilities argued that segregation was inherently unequal. By the time of P.L. 94-142, about half of the estimated eight million children with disabilities in the U.S. either were not being appropriately served in school or were excluded from schooling altogether. A disproportionate number of minority children were placed in special programs. Identification and placement practices and procedures were inconsistent, and parental involvement generally was not encouraged.

After segregation on the basis of race was declared unconstitutional in *Brown v. Board of Education*, parents and other advocates filed similar lawsuits on behalf of children with handicaps. The culmination of their efforts resulted in P.L. 94-142. This law and others such as the Rehabilitation Act of 1973, and The Americans With Disabilities Act of 1990, are basically civil rights laws that extend civil rights protections to the educational setting. Since school districts, individual schools, and teachers are all required to obey these laws, it is important to understand their implications for the manner in which special education services are delivered to children with disabilities.

SKILL 5.1 IDEA (2004)

Public Law (PL) 94-142 (Education for the Handicapped Act) was signed in 1975 and renamed Individuals with Disabilities Education Act (IDEA) in 1990. This law, in its various forms and revisions, lies at the foundation of all current special education practices. It was a culmination of many years' struggle to achieve equal educational opportunity for children and youth with disabilities.

The 1960s was an era when much national emphasis was placed upon the civil rights of the U.S. citizenry. Special education was supported by such leaders as President John F. Kennedy, Vice-President Hubert Humphrey, President Lyndon B. Johnson, and many more in Congress. Unlike rights legislation of a racial or an ethnic nature, the reform laws for persons with disabilities mostly enjoyed bipartisan support. From the late 1960s to the mid-1970s, much legislation and litigation from the courts included decisions supporting the need to assure an appropriate education to all persons, regardless of race, creed, or disabling conditions. Much of what was stated in separate court rulings and mandated legislation was brought together into what is now considered to be the "backbone" of special education, PL 94-142, which was formally signed into law by President Gerald R. Ford in 1975.

The philosophy behind these pieces of legislation is that education is to be provided to all children who meet age eligibility requirements. All children are assumed capable of benefiting from education. For children with severe or profound handicaps, education may be interpreted to include training in basic self-help skills, as well as vocational training and academics.

Although IDEA has been revised several times since its inception, its basic principles in all forms incorporate the concept of normalization. Within this concept, persons with disabilities have access to everyday patterns and conditions of life that are as close as possible or equal to their peers without disabilities. IDEA includes the following fundamental provisions:

1. **Free appropriate public education (FAPE):** Special Education services are to be provided at no cost to students or their families. The federal and state governments share any additional costs. FAPE also requires that education be appropriate to the individual needs of the students.

2. **Notification and procedural rights for parents:** These include a number of due process principles:

   A. Right to examine records and obtain independent evaluations.

   B. Right to receive a clearly written notice that states the results of the school's evaluation of the child and whether the child meets eligibility requirements for placement or continuation of special services.

C. Parents who disagree with the school's decision may request a due process hearing and a judicial hearing if they do not receive satisfaction through due process.

3. Identification and services to all children: States must conduct public outreach programs to seek out and identify children who may need services. This includes identifying students in the private as well as the public school setting.

4. Necessary related services: Developmental, corrective, and other support services that make it possible for a student to benefit from special education services must be provided. These may include speech, recreation, or physical therapy.

5. Individualized assessments: Evaluations and tests must be nondiscriminatory and individualized. Specifically, they must be conducted in the preferred language of the student.

6. Individualized Education Plans: Each student receiving special education services must have an Individualized Education Plan (IEP) developed in a meeting that includes a qualified representative of the local education agency (LEA), special education teacher(s), general education teacher(s), a person qualified to interpret assessment information, the parents, and the student (as appropriate). Others present at the meeting may include any personnel who provide services to the student, such as speech therapists or occupational therapists. The parents and/or the school may invite others to the meeting as needed. Note: It is important to remember that an IEP is a legal document that is binding on both the school and any teacher working with the child. See Skill 9.1 for details about the components of an IEP and the manner in which they can be used.

7. Least restrictive environment (LRE): There is no simple definition of LRE. LRE differs with the child's needs. LRE means that the student is placed in an environment that is not dangerous or overly controlling or intrusive. The student should be given opportunities to experience what other peers of similar mental or chronological age are doing. Finally, LRE is the environment that is the most integrated and normalized for the student's strengths and weaknesses. LRE for one child may be a regular classroom with support services, while LRE for another may be a self-contained classroom in a special school. The Council for Exceptional Children lists seven levels of service relevant to LRE: (Adapted from Deno, 1970).

CASCADE SYSTEM OF SPECIAL EDUCATION SERVICES	
Level 1	Regular classroom, including students with disabilities able to learn with regular class accommodations, with or without medical and counseling services
Level 2	Regular classroom with supportive services (i.e., consultation, inclusion)
Level 3	Regular class with part-time special class (i.e., itinerant services, resource room)
Level 4	Full-time special class (i.e., self-contained)
Level 5	Special stations (i.e., special schools)
Level 6	Homebound
Level 7	Residential (i.e., hospital, institution)

8. Advisory Boards: States are required to have advisory boards composed of individuals with disabilities, teachers and parents of students with disabilities to oversee compliance.

9. Early Intervention: Later forms of IDEA include provision for early intervention services and Individualized Family Service Plans (IFSP) for children 0-5 years of age.

10. Funds: IDEA supplies supplementary funds on a per child basis, and funds can be withheld in cases of noncompliance with the law.

IDEA has been updated several times. *Please see Skill 5.3 for the most updated information on IDEA.*

Supreme Court Cases Significant to the Development of P.L. 94-142

Brown v. Board of Education (1954)

While this case specifically addressed the inequality of separate but equal facilities on the basis of race, the concept that segregation was inherently unequal—even if facilities were provided—was later applied to handicapping conditions.

Pennsylvania Association for Retarded Citizens (PARC) v. Commonwealth of Pennsylvania (1972)

Special Education was guaranteed to children with mental retardation. The victory in this case sparked other court cases for children with other disabilities.

Mills v. Board of Education of the District of Columbia (1972)

The right to special education was extended to all children with disabilities, not just mentally retarded children. Judgments in PARC and Mills paved the way for P. L. 94-142.

Sample Test Questions and Rationale

(Rigorous)

1. **What legislation started FAPE?**

   A. Section 504

   B. EHCA

   C. IDEA

   D. Education Amendment 1974

   Answer: A. Section 504

   FAPE stands for Free Appropriate Public Education. Section 504 of the Rehabilitation Act in 1973 is the legislation that enacted FAPE. Since that time, it has been expanded and reauthorized in various forms of IDEA (Individuals with Disabilities Education Act).

(Average)

2. **What is true about IDEA? In order to be eligible, a student must:**

   A. Have a medical disability

   B. Have a disability that fits into one of the categories listed in the law

   C. Attend a private school

   D. Be a slow learner

   Answer: B. Have a disability that fits into one of the categories listed in the law

   To be eligible for services under IDEA, the student must have a disability that fits into one of the categories defined by the law. The disabilities are: Autism, Deaf, Deaf-Blind, Hearing Impaired, Mentally Retarded, Multiple Disabilities, Orthopedically Impaired, Other Health Impaired, Seriously Emotionally Disturbed, Specific Learning Disability, Speech Impaired, and Visually Impaired.

Sample Test Questions and Rationale (cont.)

(Average)

3. **According to IDEA 2004, students with disabilities are to do what:**

    A. Participate in the general education program to the fullest extent that it is beneficial for them

    B. Participate in a vocational training within the general education setting

    C. Participate in a general education setting for physical education

    D. Participate in a modified program that meets his/her needs

Answer: A. Participate in the general education program to the fullest extent that it is beneficial for them

Choices b, c, and d are all possible settings related to participating in the general education setting to the fullest extent possible. This still can mean that a student's LRE may restrict him/her to a separate program for the entire school day. Each child's LRE will depend upon his/her specific needs and abilities.

SKILL 5.2 Section 504

Section 504, a part of Public Law 93-112, was passed and signed into law in 1973. It is important because many children not covered under IDEA may be covered under Section 504. Currently Section 504 expands the older law by extending its protection to other areas that receive federal assistance, such as education. To be entitled to protection under Section 504, the individual must meet the definition of a person with a disability, which is any person who

1. Has a physical or mental impairment that substantially limits one or more of such person's major life activities

2. Has a record of such impairment

3. Is regarded as having such impairment

Major life activities include caring for one's self, performing manual tasks, walking, seeing, hearing, speaking, breathing, working, and learning.

The individual must also be otherwise qualified. This criterion has been interpreted to mean that the person must be able to meet the requirements of a particular program in spite of his or her disability. The person must be afforded reasonable accommodations by recipients of federal financial assistance. The usual remedy when a violation of Section 504 is proven is the termination of federal funding assistance.

Section 504 assists with the several categories of children that are not comprehensively covered for special education under IDEA. Children in these categories may meet the definition for disabled but are not eligible. For example, a child with an emotional disorder may not meet the criteria for intensity and degree. Others have medical conditions, but these conditions are not listed as disabilities. An example is the child with AIDS whose condition is not listed specifically in Other Health Impaired. (Refer to Skill 3.4 for definitions.)

Youth with social impairments do not qualify for special education under IDEA unless they have an emotional or behavioral disorder as well. There is controversy over whether to identify or even attempt to separate youth with social maladjustments from other youth who meet the definition of emotional/behavioral disturbance. Unlike slow learners, some of whom may qualify for compensatory services, these youngsters have no safety net of services.

Attention Deficit Disorder (ADD) is another category of children who require significant assistance in schools but for whom special education historically had no category. Recently, some states have included it under medical conditions. Youth who are addicted to drugs and alcohol are protected under IDEA only if they qualify for special education and related services under one of the disability categories such as emotional disturbance. These students, like other categories described, are at-risk, and, while they do not qualify for special education under IDEA, they are entitled to protection under Section 504 of the Rehabilitation Act or the Americans with Disabilities Act (ADA). See Skill 2.3 for more information about ADA.

Section 504 requires that schools not discriminate and provide reasonable accommodations in all programming aspects.

> *Section 504 assists with the several categories of children that are not comprehensively covered for special education under IDEA. Children in these categories may meet the definition for disabled but are not eligible.*

Sample Test Question and Rationale

(Average)

1. **What determines whether a person is entitled to protection under Section 504?**

    A. The individual must meet the definition of a person with a disability

    B. The person must be able to meet the requirements of a particular program in spite of his or her disability

    C. The school, business or other facility must be the recipient of federal funding assistance

    D. All of the above

Answer: D. All of the above

To be entitled to protection under Section 504, an individual must meet the definition of a person with a disability, which is: any person who (i) has a physical or mental impairment which substantially limits one or more of that person's major life activities, (ii) has a record of such impairment, or (iii) is regarded as having such an impairment.

Major life activities are: caring for oneself, performing manual tasks, walking, seeing, hearing, speaking, breathing, learning, and working. The person must also be "otherwise qualified", which means that the person must be able to meet the requirements of a particular program in spite of the disability. The person must also be afforded "reasonable accommodations" by recipients of federal financial assistance.

SKILL 5.3 Americans with Disabilities Act (ADA)

In 1990, Congress passed Public Law 101-336, the Americans with Disabilities Act, referred to as ADA. Like the Rehabilitation Act that preceded it, ADA (1990) bars discrimination in employment, transportation, public accommodations, and telecommunications in all aspects of life. However, ADA's protection is not limited to those receiving federal funding. This act gives protection to all people without regard to race, gender, national origin, religion, or disability. Children with disabilities, therefore, automatically qualify for protection under this act.

Title II and Title III are applicable to special education because they cover the private sector (such as private schools) and require access to public accommodations. New and remodeled public buildings, transportation vehicles, and telephone systems now must be accessible to the persons with disabilities. ADA also protects individuals with contagious diseases, such as AIDS, from discrimination.

The ADA is similar to the Rehabilitation Act in terms of who is protected under the act, but it does not require entities to be recipients of federal financial assistance.

Public Law 105-17 (IDEA '97)

In 1997, IDEA was revised and reauthorized as Public Law 105-17 as progressive legislation for the benefit of school age children with special needs, their parents, and those who work with these children. The 1997 reauthorization of IDEA made major changes in the areas of the evaluation procedures, parent rights, transition, and discipline.

The evaluation process was amended to require that members of the evaluation team look at previously collected data, tests, and information and use it when it is deemed appropriate. Previous to IDEA '97, an entire reevaluation had to be conducted every three years to determine if the child continued to be a child with a disability. This requirement was changed so that existing information and evaluations that would prevent unnecessary assessment of students and reduce the cost of evaluations could be considered.

In addition, eligibility was redefined to require evidence not only that the child has a disability, but also that the disability has a negative impact on the child's educational success or access to equal education.

Under the previous IDEA, an evaluation team did not need parent participation to make decisions regarding a student's eligibility for special education and related services. Under IDEA '97, parents were specifically included as members of the group making the eligibility decision.

Amendments to IEP requirements

The IEP was modified under IDEA '97 to emphasize the involvement of students with special needs in a general education classroom setting with the services and modifications deemed necessary by the evaluation team.

The Present Levels of Educational Performance (PLEP) was changed to require a statement of how the child's disability affects his or her involvement and progress in the general curriculum. IDEA '97 established that there must be a connection between the special education and general education curricula. For this reason, the PLEP had to include an explanation of the extent to which the student will not be participating with nondisabled children in the general education class and in extracurricular and nonacademic activities.

The IEP now had an established connection to the general education setting. General education teachers were required to attend IEP meetings, and IEPs had to

> The 1997 reauthorization of IDEA made major changes in the areas of the evaluation procedures, parent rights, transition, and discipline.

> IDEA '97 established that there must be a connection between the special education and general education curricula.

provide the needed test accommodations that would be provided on all state- and district-wide assessments of the student with special needs. IDEA '97's emphasis on raising the standards of those in special education placed an additional requirement of a definitive reason why a standard general education assessment would not be deemed appropriate for a child and how the child should then be assessed.

Schools were required to assure that paraprofessionals who worked with students with disabilities received training relevant to their placement.

IDEA '97 looked at how parents were receiving annual evaluations on their child's IEP goals and determined that this was not sufficient feedback for parents; it then required schools to make reports to parents on the progress of their children at least as frequently as they reported on the progress of their nondisabled peers.

The IEP was also modified to include a review of the student's transitional needs and services specifically:

- Beginning as early as age fourteen for some activities (IDEA 2004 changed the maximum age for all activities to sixteen), and annually thereafter, the student's IEP must contain a statement of his or her transition service needs under the various components of that IEP that focus upon the student's courses of study (e.g., vocational education or advanced placement)

- Beginning at least one year before the student reaches the age of majority under state law, the IEP must contain a statement that the student has been informed of the rights under the law that will transfer to him or her upon reaching the age of majority

Discipline

IDEA '97 broadened the schools' right to take a disciplinary action with children who have been classified as needing special education services and who knowingly possess or use illegal drugs or sell or solicit the sale of a controlled substance while at school or school functions.

Manifest determination review

Under IDEA '97, suspensions or disciplinary consequences could result in an alternative educational placement. This possibility was to be weighed by a manifest determination review, which is held by an IEP Team. Manifest determination reviews must occur no more than ten days after the disciplinary action. This review team has the sole responsibility of determining the following:

1. Does the child's disability impair his or her ability to understand the impact and consequences of the behavior under disciplinary action?

2. Did the child's disability impair the ability of the child to control the behavior subject to discipline?

Determination of the relationship between the student's disability and an inappropriate behavior could allow a change in placement to occur. However, other educational services specified in the IEP must continue in the new setting.

When no relationship between the inappropriate behavior and the disability is established, IDEA '97 used FAPE to allow that the relevant disciplinary procedures applicable to children without disabilities may be applied to the child with disabilities in the same manner in which they would be applied to children without disabilities.

Functional behavioral assessments (FBAs) and behavior intervention plans (BIPs) then became a requirement in many situations for schools to both modify and provide disciplinary consequences.

Finally, mediation was inserted as a new level of appeal before going to a hearing for disputes. States are required to pay for an impartial mediator to work to resolve disagreements with parents about the child's IEP or placement.

No Child Left Behind Act, PL 107-110 (2002)

NO CHILD LEFT BEHIND (NCLB), Public Law 107-110, was signed on January 8, 2002. It addresses accountability of school personnel for student achievement with the expectation that every child will demonstrate proficiency in reading, math, and science. The first full wave of accountability will be in twelve years when children who attended school under NCLB graduate, but the process to meet that accountability begins now. In fact, as students progress through the school system, testing will show if an individual teacher has effectively met the needs of the students. Through testing, each student's adequate yearly progress or lack thereof will be tracked.

NCLB affects regular and special education students, gifted students and slow learners, and children of every ethnicity, culture, and environment. NCLB is a document that encompasses every American educator and student.

Educators are affected as follows: elementary teachers (K–3) are responsible for teaching reading and using different, scientific-based approaches as needed; elementary teachers of upper grades will teach reading, math, and science; middle and high school teacher will teach to new, higher standards; sometimes, they will have to play catch up with students who did not have adequate education in earlier grades.

NO CHILD LEFT BEHIND: addresses accountability of school personnel for student achievement with the expectation that every child will demonstrate proficiency in reading, math, and science

NCLB affects regular and special education students, gifted students and slow learners, and children of every ethnicity, culture, and environment. NCLB is a document that encompasses every American educator and student.

Special educators are responsible for teaching students to a level of proficiency comparable to that of their nondisabled peers. This requirement will raise the bar of academic expectations throughout the grades. For some students with disabilities, the criteria for getting a diploma will be more difficult. Although a small percentage of students with disabilities will need alternate assessment, they will still need to meet grade appropriate goals.

In order for special education teachers to meet the professional criteria of this act, they must be highly qualified, that is certified or licensed in their area of special education, and show proof of a specific level of professional development in the core subjects that they teach. As special education teachers receive specific education in the core subject they teach, they will be better prepared to teach to the same level of learning standards as the general education teacher.

IDEIA (IDEA 2004)

The second revision of IDEA occurred in 2004. IDEA was reauthorized as the Individuals with Disabilities Education Improvement Act of 2004 (IDEIA 2004), commonly referred to as IDEA 2004 (effective July 1, 2005).

The intention was to improve IDEA by adding the philosophy and understanding that special education students need preparation for further study beyond the high school setting-teaching compensatory methods. Accordingly, IDEA 2004 provided a close tie to PL 89-10, the Elementary and Special Education Act of 1965, and stated that students with special needs should have maximum access to the general curriculum. Maximum access was defined as the access required for an individual student to reach his fullest potential. Full inclusion was not to be the only option by which to achieve this, and the act specified that skills should be taught to compensate students later in life in cases where inclusion was not the best setting.

IDEA 2004 added a new requirement for special education teachers on the secondary level, enforcing NCLB's highly qualified requirements in the subject area of their curriculum. The rewording in this part of IDEA states that they shall be no less qualified than teachers in the core areas.

Free and Appropriate Public Education (FAPE) was revised by mandating that students have maximum access to appropriate general education. Additionally, LRE placement for those students with disabilities must have the same school placement rights as those students who do not have disabilities. IDEA 2004 recognizes that, because of the nature of some disabilities, appropriate education may vary in the amount of participation and placement in the general education setting. For some students, FAPE will mean a choice of the type of educational institution they attend (private school for example). Any such choice must provide the special education services deemed necessary for the student through the IEP.

The definition of assistive technology devices was amended to exclude devices that are surgically implanted (i.e. cochlear implants) and clarified that students with assistive technology devices shall not be prevented from having special education services. Assistive technology devices may need to monitored by school personnel, but schools are not responsible for the implantation or replacement of such devices surgically. An example of this would be a cochlear implant.

The definition of child with a disability as the term used for children ages 3–9 with a developmental delay was changed to allow inclusion of Tourette Syndrome.

IDEA 2004 recognized that all states must follow the *National Instructional Materials Accessibility Standards*, which states that students who need materials in a certain form will get those at the same time their nondisabled peers receive their materials. Teacher recognition of this standard is important.

Changes in requirements for evaluations

The time allowed between the request for an initial evaluation and the determination of whether a disability is present has been changed to state that the determination must occur within sixty calendar days of the request. This change is significant; previously, it was interpreted to mean sixty school days. Parental consent is also required for evaluations and before the start of special education services.

No single assessment or measurement tool may now be used to determine special education qualification. Assessments and measurements used should be in *language and form* that will give the most accurate picture of the child's abilities.

IDEA 2004 recognized that a disproportionate representation of minorities and bilingual students exist and that preservice interventions that are *scientifically based on early reading programs, positive behavioral interventions and support, and early intervening services* may mean that some of those children do not need special education services. This understanding has led to a child not being considered to have a disability if he or she has not had appropriate education in math or reading. In addition, a child is not considered to have a disability if the reason for the delays is that English is a second language.

When determining a specific learning disability, the criteria may use not only a discrepancy between *achievement* and *intellectual ability*, but also whether or not the child responds to scientific research-based intervention. In general, children who may not have been found eligible for special education through testing but are known to need services (because of functioning, excluding lack of instruction) are still eligible for special education services. Because of this change, input for evaluation now includes state and local testing, classroom observation, academic achievement, and related developmental needs.

ELLs with Disabilities

Of growing concern to educators is the disproportionate rate of English language learners (ELLs) represented in classes of students with disabilities. Zehr (2001) reported that an estimated 184,000 of the nation's 2.9 million students (i.e., 6 percent) enrolled in programs for ELLs have disabilities, citing statistics from the U.S. Department of Education. Gurel (2004) reported that about 5 percent of the nation's school children have been identified with learning disabilities, though the percentage of ELLs has traditionally been higher over the years (Baca & Cervantes, 1989; Kretschmer, 1991 in Gurel, 2004).

The difficulty of accurate estimates stems from the fact that each state reports its ELLs who are served by special education differently (Robertson & Kushner, 1994 in Gurel, 2004). While it is true that the National Center for Educational Statistics (NCES); the No Child Left Behind Act (NCLB), 2002; and IDEA (1997) are all working to unify reporting criteria, there is still much work to be done in this area.

One way to serve the student with disabilities and the ELL student is to accurately assess their disability or limitation. How can teachers differentiate between ELLs with learning disabilities from those who are simply struggling with learning a second language? It is not easy. Many of the problems associated with second language learning are also identified as learning difficulties; for example, should processing difficulties, behavioral differences, reading difficulties, and expressive difficulties (Lock, R. H., & Layton, C. A., 2002) be associated with the difficulties of second language learning or learning difficulties? While some learning difficulties can be partially identified by observation over a period of time or by a lack of academic improvement (Gersten, R. & Baker, S. K., 2003), they are also typical of ELLs struggling with the complexities of language and a new school environment.

Therefore, it is of critical importance to assess the concerned student using a variety of testing procedures. Scribner, A. P. & Scribner, J. D. (2001) recommend the prereferral team be composed of specialists from different disciplines, including a special educator and a bilingual educator. Other team members would be a school representative, a general educator, a family member, and a community member. An interpreter should be provided to the family member if needed. The report drawn up should include much the same information as required for special education referral: a statement of the problem, potential sources of the problem, relevant background information, and a written plan with a follow-up schedule (Markowitz, J., Garia, S. B., Eichelberger, J. H., et al.1997; Olson, 1991).

Suggestions to achieve an accurate testing procedure are:

- Tests that are nondiscriminatory based on race or culture

- Tests conducted in both the student's primary language and English

- Identify student using observations from school, home, and community

- Alternative assessments combined with formal assessments

- Criterion-referenced assessments

- Curriculum-based assessments

- Portfolio of student's work

- Informal assessments: rubrics, dynamic assessment (test-teach-test), learning logs, self-evaluations

- Comparison of student's cultural teaching style (e.g., teacher-centered) with the school's teaching style (e.g., student-centered)

Teaching strategies for ELLs with disabilities

For most students, regardless of the disability or lack of English, it is the general classroom teacher who is responsible for their learning (NCLB, 2002). ESL, bilingual, and special education have produced a wealth of techniques that can be used by all teachers to the benefit of their students. There is little research on the combined fields of English language learning with learning disabilities, yet there are many similarities in the recommended teaching strategies. Gurel (2004) has organized these strategies into before, during and after instruction recognizing that there may be overlapping within the processes. Suggestions to teachers are:

Before Instruction	Plan relevant curricula
	Plan for universal design
	Plan thematic units
	Align curricula across grades and subjects
	Implement the ESL standards
	Collaborate with other professionals
	Create a print-rich environment
	Set high expectations
	Teach at the appropriate difficulty
	Write clear objectives
	Build on student strengths

Table continued on next page

During Instruction	Activate background knowledge Set students up to succeed Use active learning Use clinical teaching methods Teach in multiple modes Allow students to collaborate Use individual or small-group instruction Promote higher-order thinking skills Teach learning strategies Use graphic organizers Develop language in all content areas Focus on reading Incorporate technology Follow routines Provide clear instructions
After Instruction	Review frequently Use curriculum-based assessments Intervene at an early age Support the use of students' native language Extend the school year or offer summer school

Further reading on ELLs with disabilities

A major obstacle in working with ELLs with disabilities is the lack of guidelines dealing specifically with the two limitations. While both learning disabilities and teaching English to minorities or immigrants have been studied extensively, little research has been done on how to best integrate the two disciplines (Gersten & Baker, 2003; Ortiz, 1997 in Gurel 2004). The following suggestions for further reading are offered to those who seek more information.

- Aron, L.Y. & Loprest, P.J. (2007) *Meeting the Needs of Children with Disabilities*. Urban Institute Press.

- Echevarria, J. & Graves, A. (1998) *Sheltered Content Instruction: Teaching English-Language Learners with Diverse Abilities*. Allyn and Bacon.

- Gurel, Sarah M. (2004) *Teaching English Language Learners with Learning Disabilities: A Compiled Convergence of Strategies*. College of William and Mary. School of Education, Curriculum and Instruction.

- *http://learningdisabilities.about.com*

- *http://www.eric.ed.gov/*

- Zehr, Mary Ann (2008) "Bilingual Students with Disabilities Get Special Help." *Education Week*. Nov. 7, 2001. *http://www.edweek.org/ew/articles/2001/11/07/10clark.h21.html?print=1*

Changes in requirements for IEPs

Individualized Education Plans (IEPS) continue to have multiple sections. One section, *present levels of educational performance (PLEP)*, now addresses *academic achievement and functional performance*. Annual IEP goals must now address the same areas.

IEP goals should be aligned to state standards; therefore, short-term objectives are not required on every IEP. Students with IEPs must not only participate in regular education programs to the fullest extent possible, they must also show progress in those programs. Therefore, goals must be written to reflect academic progress.

For students who must participate in alternate assessment, there must be alignment to alternate achievement standards.

Significant change has been made in the definition of the IEP team. It now states that no less than one teacher from each of the areas of special education and regular education be present.

IDEA 2004 recognized that the amount of required paperwork placed upon teachers of students with disabilities should be reduced if possible. For this reason, some states will participate in a newly developed pilot program that uses multi-year IEPs. Individual student inclusion in this program will require consent by both the school and the parent.

SKILL 5.4 **Important legal issues** *(such as those raised by the following court cases: Rowley re: program appropriateness, Tatro re: related services, Honig re: discipline, Oberti re: inclusion)*

Significant Supreme Court Cases Involving Interpretation of IDEA

Following the passage of P.L. 94-142 and IDEA, questions have arisen over the interpretation of least restrictive environment and free, appropriate public education. The courts have been asked to judge the extent of a school district's obligation to provide support services and suspension procedures for students with disabilities. A brief description of some of the cases that the U.S. Supreme Court reviewed and the rulings are included in this section. These cases have addressed such issues as least restrictive environment, free and appropriate public education, transportation, suspension of exceptional education students, and provision of services in a private school setting.

Board of Education v. Rowley, 1982	This case concerned the interpretation of "Free and Public Education," and the lengths to which schools are required to go in order to provide it. Amy Rowley was a deaf elementary school student whose parents rejected their school district's proposal to provide a tutor and speech therapist services to supplement their daughter's instruction in the regular classroom. Her parents insisted on an interpreter, even though Amy was making satisfactory social, academic, and educational progress without one. They argued that although she was progressing well, there was a serious discrepancy between her level of achievement and her potential without the handicap. They held that the absence of an interpreter prevented her from reaching her full potential. In deciding in favor of the school district, the Supreme Court confirmed the act's requirement of a "basic floor of opportunity consistent with equal protection," but stated that this "basic floor" did not require "anything more than equal access." It explicitly ruled that schools are not required to "maximize the potential of handicapped children commensurate with the opportunity provided to other children." It further ruled that "if the child is being educated in the regular classrooms of the public education system, (services) should be reasonably calculated to enable the child to achieve passing marks and advance from grade to grade." Finally, the Court ruled that Amy did not need an interpreter, because "evidence firmly establishes that Amy is receiving an `adequate' education, since she performs better than the average child in her class and is advancing easily from grade to grade."
Irving Independent School District v. Tatro, 1984	IDEA lists health services as one of the related services that schools are mandated to provide to exceptional students. Amber Tatro, who had spina bifida, required the insertion of a catheter on a regular schedule in order to empty her bladder. The issue was specifically over the classification of clean, intermittent catheterization (CIC) as a medical service (not covered under IDEA) or a related health service, which would be covered. In this instance, the catheterization was not declared a medical service, but a related service necessary for the student to have in order to benefit from special education. The school district was obliged to provide the service. The Tatro case has implications for students with other medical impairments who may need services to allow them to attend classes at the school.
Smith v. Robinson, 1984	This case concerned reimbursement of attorney's fees for parents who win litigation under IDEA. At the time of this case, IDEA did not provide for such reimbursement. Following this ruling, Congress passed a law awarding attorney's fees to parents who win their litigation.
Honig v. Doe, 1988	Essentially, students may not be denied education or be excluded from school when their misbehavior is related to their handicap. The *stay put* provision of IDEA allows students to remain in their current educational setting pending the outcome of administrative or judicial hearings. In the case of behavior that is a danger to the student or others, the court allows school districts to apply their normal procedures for dealing with dangerous behavior, such as time-out, loss of privileges, detention, or study carrels. Where the student has presented an immediate threat to others, that student may be temporarily suspended for up to ten school days to give the school and the parents time to review the IEP and discuss possible alternatives to the current placement.

Table continued on next page

Oberti v. Board of Education of the Borough of Clementon School District, 1993	It was determined that IDEA requires school systems to supplement and realign their resources to move beyond those systems, structures, and practices that tend to result in unnecessary segregation of children with disabilities. The Act does *not* require states to offer *the same* educational experience to a child with disabilities as is generally provided for children without disabilities. To the contrary, states must address the unique needs of a disabled child, recognizing that that child may benefit differently from education in the regular classroom than other students. In summary, the fact that a child with disabilities will learn differently from his or her education within a regular classroom does not justify exclusion from that environment.

Sample Test Question and Rationale

(Rigorous)

1. How was the training of special education teachers changed by the No Child Left Behind Act of 2002?

   A. It required all special education teachers to be certified in reading and math

   B. It required all special education teachers to take the same coursework as general education teachers

   C. If a special education teacher is teaching a core subject, he or she must meet the standard of a highly-qualified teacher in that subject

   D. All of the above

Answer: C. If a special education teacher is teaching a core subject, he or she must meet the standard of a highly-qualified teacher in that subject

In order for special education teachers to be a student's sole teacher of a core subject, they must meet the professional criteria of NCLB. They must be highly qualified, that is certified or licensed in their area of special education, and show proof of a specific level of professional development in the core subjects that they teach. As special education teachers received specific education in the core subject they teach, they will be better prepared to teach to the same level of learning standards as the general education teacher.

COMPETENCY 6

THE SCHOOL'S CONNECTIONS WITH FAMILIES, PROSPECTIVE AND ACTUAL EMPLOYERS, AND COMMUNITIES OF STUDENTS WITH DISABILITIES

SKILL 6.1 Teacher advocacy for students and families

Learning about one's self involves identifying learning styles, strengths and weakness, interests, and preferences. For students with mild disabilities, developing an awareness of the accommodations they need will help them ask for necessary accommodations on a job and in postsecondary education. Students can also help identify alternative ways they can learn.

SELF-ADVOCACY involves effectively communicating one's own rights, needs, and desires and taking responsibility for making decisions that have an impact on one's life.

Developing self-advocacy skills in students who are involved in the transition process requires many elements. Helping the student to identify future goals or desired outcomes in transition planning areas is a good place to start. Self-knowledge is critical for the student in determining the direction that transition planning will take.

The role of the teacher in promoting self-advocacy should include encouraging the student to participate in the IEP process and other key parts of their educational development. Self-advocacy issues and lessons are effective when they are incorporated into the student's daily life. Teachers should listen to the student's problems and ask the student for input on possible changes that he or she may need. The teacher should talk with the student about possible solutions, discussing the pros and cons of certain actions. A student who self-advocates should feel supported and encouraged. Good self-advocates know how to ask questions and get help from other people. They do not let other people do everything for them.

Students need to practice newly acquired self-advocacy skills. Teachers should have students role play various situations, such as setting up a class schedule, moving out of the home, and asking for accommodations needed for a course.

The impact of transition planning on a student with a disability is very great. The student should be an active member of the transition team and the focus

---

SELF-ADVOCACY: effectively communicating one's own rights, needs, and desires and taking responsibility for making decisions that have an impact on one's life

The role of the teacher in promoting self-advocacy should include encouraging the student to participate in the IEP process and other key parts of their educational development.

of all activities. Students often think that being passive and relying on others to take care of them is the way to get action. Students should be encouraged to express their opinions throughout the transition process. They need to learn how to express themselves so that others listen and take them seriously. These skills should be practiced within a supportive and caring environment.

Sample Test Question and Rationale

(Easy)

1. **One of the most important goals of the special education teacher is to foster and create with the student:**

   A. Handwriting skills

   B. Self-advocacy

   C. An increased level of reading

   D. Logical reasoning

Answer: B. Self-advocacy

When a student achieves the ability to recognize his/her deficits and knows how to correctly advocate for his/her needs, the child has learned one of the most important life skills.

SKILL 6.2 Parent partnerships and roles

The discovery at birth or initial diagnosis of a child's disabling condition(s) has a strong impact upon the family unit. Though reactions are unique to individuals, the first emotion generally felt by the parent of a child with disabilities is shock, followed by disbelief, guilt, rejection, shame, denial, and helplessness. As parents finally accept the reality of their child's condition, many report feelings of anxiety or fearfulness about their personal ability to care for and rear an exceptional child. Many parents will doctor shop, hoping to find answers, while others will reject or deny information given them by health care professionals.

Role of the Family

The presence of a child with a disability within the family unit creates changes and possible stresses that will need addressing. Many will feel parenting demands greatly in excess of a nondisabled child's requirements. "A child (with a disability) frequently needs more time, energy, attention, patience, and money than the child (without a disability), and frequently returns less success, achievement, parent pride-inducing behavior, privacy, feelings of security and well-being" (Paul, 1981, p.6).

The family as a microcosmic unit in a society plays a vital role in many ways. The family assumes a protective and nurturing function, is the primary unit for social control, and plays a major role in the transmission of cultural values and mores. This role is enacted concurrently with changes in our social system at large.

Paradoxically, the parents who were formerly viewed as the cause of their children's disability are now expected to enact positive changes in their children's lives.

Siblings play an important role in fostering the social and emotional developments of a brother or sister with a disability. A wide range of feelings and reactions will evolve as siblings interact. Some experience guilt over being the normal child and try to overcompensate by being the successful, perfect child for their parents. Others react in a hostile, resentful manner toward the amount of time and care the disabled sibling receives and frequently create disruption as a way of obtaining parental attention.

The extended family, especially grandparents, can provide support and assistance to the nuclear family unit if they live within a manageable proximity; childcare services for an evening or a few days can provide a means of reprieve for heavily involved parents.

Parents as Advocates

Ironically, the possibility for establishing the partnership, which is now sought by educators with parents of children with disabilities, came about largely through the advocacy efforts of parents. The state compulsory education laws began in 1918 and were adopted across the nation with small variances in agricultural regions. However, because these children did not fit in with the general school curriculum, most continued to be turned away at the schoolhouse door, leaving the custodial services at state or private institutions as the primary alternative placement site for parents.

Educational policies reflected the litigation and legislation of the times, which overwhelmingly sided with the educational system and not with the family. After all, the educational policies reflected the prevailing philosophies of the times, such as Social Darwinism (i.e., survival of the fittest). Thus, persons with disabilities were set apart from the rest of society—literally out of sight, out of mind. Those with severe disabilities were placed in institutions, and those with moderate disabilities were kept at home to do family or farm chores.

Following the two world wars, the realization that disabling conditions could be incurred by a member of any family came to the forefront. Several celebrity families allowed stories to be published in national magazines about a family member with an identified disability, thus taking the entire plight of this family syndrome out of the closet.

The 1950s brought about the founding of many parent and professional organizations, and the movement continued into the next decade. Learning groups included the National Association of Parents and Friends of Mentally Retarded Children founded in 1950 and later called the National Association for Retarded Children, and now named the National Association of Retarded Citizens; the International Parents Organization in 1957, as the parents' branch of the Alexander Graham Bell Association for Parents of the Deaf in 1965. The Epilepsy Foundation of America was founded in 1967. The International Council for Exceptional Children had been established by faculty and students at Columbia University as early as 1922, and the Council for Exceptional Children recognized small parent organizations in the late 1940s.

During the 1950s, Public Law 85-926 brought about support for preparing teachers to work with children with disabilities so that these children might receive educational services.

The 1960s was the first period during which parents received tangible support from the executive branch of the national government. In 1960, the White House Conference on Children and Youth declared that a child should be separated from his family only as a last resort. This declaration gave vital support to parents' efforts toward securing a public education for their youngsters with disabilities.

Parents as Partners

Parent groups are a major component in assuring appropriate services for children with disabilities. They are coequal with special education and community service agencies. Their role is individual and political advocacy and sociopsychological support. Great advances in services for children with disabilities have been made through the efforts of parent advocacy groups, which have been formed to represent almost every type of disabling condition.

<h2 style="text-align:center;">Sample Test Question and Rationale</h2>

(Easy)

1. **Greg is a three-year-old boy who has recently survived a bout of meningitis. The pediatrician who treated Greg during his illness had to inform Greg's parents about some brain dysfunction which he had medically diagnosed. A reaction which would be anticipated upon learning of Greg's condition is:**

   A. Shock

   B. Disbelief

   C. Denial

   D. All of the above

Answer: D. All of the above

Although reactions are unique to individuals, the first emotions generally felt by the parents or guardians of a child with disabilities is shock, followed by disbelief, guilt, rejection, shame, denial and helplessness. As care-givers finally accept the reality of their child's condition, many report feeling anxiety or fear of their inability to care for the child. Many will doctor shop, hoping to find answers. Others will reject or refuse to believe information given by health care professionals.

SKILL 6.3 Public attitudes toward individuals with disabilities

Although the origin of special education services for youngsters with disabilities is relatively recent, the history of public attitude toward people with disabling conditions was recorded as early as the civilizations of ancient Greece and Rome. The Spartans practiced infanticide, the killing or abandonment of malformed or sickly babies. The ancient Greeks and Romans thought people with disabilities were cursed and forced them to beg for food and shelter. Those who could not fend for themselves were allowed to perish. Some with mental disabilities were employed as fools for the entertainment of the Roman royalty.

In the time of Christ, society thought that people with disabilities were suffering the punishment of God. Those with emotional disturbances were possessed by the devil, and, although early Christianity advocated humane treatment of those who were not normal physically or mentally, many remained outcasts of society, sometimes pitied and sometimes scorned.

During the Middle Ages, persons with disabilities were viewed within the aura of the unknown and were treated with a mixture of fear and reverence. Some were wandering beggars, while others were used as jesters in the courts. The Reformation, however, brought about a change of attitude. Individuals with disabilities were accused of being possessed by the devil, and exorcism flourished. Many innocent people were put in chains and cast into dungeons.

The early seventeenth century was marked by a softening of public attitude toward persons with disabilities. Hospitals began to provide treatment for those with emotional disturbances and mental retardation. A manual alphabet for those with deafness was developed, and John Locke became the first person to differentiate between persons who were mentally retarded and those who were emotionally disturbed.

In America, however, the colonists treated people with severe mental disorders as criminals, while those who were harmless were left to beg or treated as paupers. At one time, it was common practice to sell them to the person who would provide for them at the least cost to the public. When this practice was stopped, persons with mental retardation were put into poorhouses, where conditions were often extremely squalid.

The Nineteenth Century: The Beginning of Training

In 1799, Jean Marc Itard, a French physician, found a twelve-year old boy who had been abandoned in the woods of Averyron, France. His attempts to civilize and educate the boy, Victor, established many of the educational principles presently in use in the field of special education, including developmental and multi-sensory approaches, sequencing of tasks, individualized instruction, and a curriculum geared toward functional life skills.

Itard's work had an enormous impact upon public attitude toward individuals with disabilities. They began to be seen as educable. During the late 1700s, experts devised rudimentary procedures that could be used to teach those with sensory impairments (i.e., deaf, blind). This event was closely followed in the early 1800s by attempts to teach students with mild intellectual disabilities and emotional disorders (i.e., at that time referred to as the "idiotic" and "insane").

Throughout Europe, societies build schools for students with visual and hearing impairments, paralleled by the founding of similar institutions in the United States. In 1817, Thomas Hopkins Gallaudet founded the first American school for students who were deaf, known today as Gallaudet College in Washington, D.C., one of the world's best institutions of higher learning for those with deafness. Gallaudet's work was followed closely by that of Samuel Gridley, who was instrumental in founding the Perkins Institute for blind students in 1829.

The mid-1800s saw the further development of Itard's philosophy of education of students with mental disabilities. Around that time, his student, Edward Seguin, immigrated to the United States, where he established his philosophy of education for persons with mental retardation in a publication entitled *Idiocy and Its Treatment by the Physiological Method* in 1866. Seguin was instrumental in establishing the first residential school for individuals with retardation in the United States.

State legislatures began to assume responsibility for housing people with physical and mental disabilities. This institutional care was largely custodial. Institutions were often referred to as warehouses because of their deplorable conditions. Humanitarians such as Dorothea Dix helped relieve anguish and suffering in institutions for persons with mental illnesses.

1900–1919: Specific Programs

The early twentieth century saw the publication of the first standardized test of intelligence by Alfred Binet of France. The test was designed to identify educationally substandard children, but by 1916, the test was revised by the American Louis Terman, and the concept of the intelligence quotient (IQ) was introduced. Since then, the IQ test has come to be used as a predictor of both retarded (delayed) and advanced intellectual development.

At approximately the same time, Italian physician Maria Montessori was concerned with the development of effective techniques for early childhood education. Although she is known primarily for her contributions to this field, her work included methods of education for children with mental retardation, and the approach she developed is used in preschool programs today.

Ironically, the advancement of science and the scientific method led special education to its worst setback in modern times. In 1912, psychologist Henry Goddard published a study based on the Killikak family, in which he traced five generations of the descendants of a man who had one legitimate child and one illegitimate child. Among the descendants of the legitimate child were numerous mental defectives and social deviates. From this information, Goddard concluded that mental retardation and social deviation were inherited traits, and, therefore, mental and social deviates were a threat to society, an observation that he called the Eugenics Theory. Reinforcing the concept of retardation as hereditary deviance was a popular philosophy called *Positivism*, under which these unscientific conclusions were believed to be fixed, mechanical laws that were carrying mankind to inevitable improvement. Falling by the wayside was seen as the natural, scientific outcome for the defective person in society. Consequently, during this time, mass institutionalization and sterilization of persons with mental retardation and criminals were practiced.

Nevertheless, public school programs for persons with retardation gradually increased during this same period. Furthermore, the first college programs for preparing Special Education Teachers were established between 1900 and 1920.

1919–1949: Professional Personnel and Expansion of Services

As awareness of the need for medical and mental health treatment in the community was evidenced during the 1920s, halfway houses became a means for monitoring the transition from institution to community living. Outpatient clinics were established to provide increased medical care. Social workers and other support personnel were dispensed into the community to coordinate services for the needy. The thrust toward humane treatment within the community came to an abrupt halt during the 1930s and 1940s, primarily because of economic depression and widespread dissatisfaction toward the recently enacted social programs.

With increased public concern for people with disabilities came new research. John B. Watson introduced behaviorism, which shifted the treatment emphasis from psychoanalysis to learned behavior. He demonstrated in 1920 that Albert, an eleven-month old boy, learned maladaptive (or abnormal) behavior through conditioning. B.F. Skinner followed with a book entitled *Behavior of Organisms*, which outlined principles of operant (voluntary) behavior.

In 1922, the Council for Exceptional Children (first called the International Council for Exceptional Children) was founded. During the 1920s, many comprehensive statewide programs were initiated. The number of special education programs in public schools increased at a rapid rate until the 1930s, when the push for humane and effective treatment of people with disabilities began to diminish once again. The period of the Great Depression was marked by large-scale institutionalization and lack of treatment. Part of the cause was inadequately planned programs and poorly trained teachers. World War II did much to swing the pendulum back in the other direction, however, and inaugurated the most active period in the history of the development of special education.

1950–1969: The Parents, the Legislators, and the Courts Become Involved

The first two decades of the second half of this century were characterized by increased federal involvement in general education, gradually extending to special education. In 1950 came the establishment of the National Association of Retarded Children, later renamed the National Association of Retarded Citizens (NARC). It was the result of the efforts of concerned parents who felt the need for

> Two factors related to World Wars I and II helped improve public opinion toward persons with disabilities. The first factor was the intensive screening of the population of young men with physical and mental disabilities that were in the United States. Second, patriotism caused people to regard the enormous number of young men who returned from the wars with physical and emotional disabilities in a different light than they would have been regarded before that time. People became more sensitive to the problems of the veterans with disabilities, and this acceptance generalized to other groups in the population with special needs.

> The first two decades of the second half of this century were characterized by increased federal involvement in general education, gradually extending to special education.

an appropriate public education for people with disabilities. Increased media coverage exposed the miserable conditions in some of the institutions devoted to caring for people with disabilities, especially those with intellectual and emotional disabilities, and treatment consequently became more humane.

At about this time, parents of children with disabilities discovered the federal courts as a powerful agent on behalf of their children. The 1954 decision in the Brown v. the Topeka Board of Education case guaranteed equal opportunity rights to a free public education for all citizens, and the parents of children and youth with disabilities insisted that their children be included in that decision.

From this point on, the court cases and public laws enacted as a result of court decisions are too numerous to include in their entirety. Only those few that had the greatest impact on the development of special education as we know it today are listed. Collectively, they are part of a movement in U.S. Supreme Court history known as the Doctrine of Selective Incorporation, under which the states are compelled to honor various substantive rights under procedural authority of the Fourteenth Amendment.

Continuous passing of legislation, community agency involvement, and the media have brought individuals with disabilities increased social acceptance and awareness.

Sample Test Question and Rationale

(Average)

1. **Early nineteenth century is considered a period of great importance in the field of special education because principles presently used in working with exceptional students were formulated by Itard. These principles included:**

   A. Individualized instruction

   B. Sequence of tasks

   C. Functional life-like skills curriculum

   D. All of the above

Answer: D. All of the above

A French Physician, Jean Marc Itard, had found a boy abandoned in the woods of Aveyron, France. His attempts to civilize and educate the boy, Victor, established these principles, including developmental and multisensory approaches. At that time, students with mild intellectual sensory impairments, mild intellectual disabilities, and emotional disorders were referred to as 'idiotic" and "insane."

SKILL 6.4 Cultural and community influences on public attitudes toward individuals with disabilities

While society has progressed and many ideas are acceptable today that were not acceptable yesterday, having a disability still carries a stigma. Historically, people with disabilities have been ostracized from their communities. Until the 1970s, a large number of people with special needs were institutionalized at birth because the relatives did not know what to do, they felt embarrassed to admit they had a child with a disability, or they gave in to the cultural peer pressure to put their "problem" away. Sometimes this fear meant hiding a child's disability, which may even have led to locking a child in a room in the house. Perhaps the worst viewpoint society expressed before the 1970s and one that still prevails today is that the person with special needs cannot contribute to society.

Today, American society has exchanged the "must institutionalize" method for a "normalize" concept. Advocates have purchased houses in local communities and, in these houses, provide supervision or nursing care that allows people with disabilities to have "normal" social living arrangements. Congress passed laws that have given those with disabilities access to public facilities. American society has widened doorways, added special bathrooms, and made other accommodations for those with disabilities. The regular education classroom teacher is now learning to accept and teach students with special needs. America's film industry today rarely produces a movie or TV show without including someone with special needs. The concept of acceptance appears to be developing for those with physically noticeable handicaps.

But those with special needs who appear in such media as television and movies generally are those who rise above their label as disabled because of an extraordinary skill. Most people in the community are portrayed as accepting the disabled person when that special skill is noted. In addition, those who continue to express revulsion or prejudice towards the person with a disability often express remorse when the special skill is noted or peer pressure becomes too intense. This portrayal often ignores those who appear normal but who have learning and emotional disabilities and who often feel and suffer from the prejudices.

The most significant group any individual faces is the peer group. Pressure to appear normal and not "needy" in any area is intense from early childhood to adulthood. During the teen years when young people are beginning to express their individuality, the very appearance of walking into a special education classroom often brings feelings of inadequacy and labeling by peers that the student is "special." Being considered normal is the desire of all individuals with disabilities, regardless of the age or disability. People with disabilities today, as they did many years ago, measure their successes by how their achievements mask their disabilities.

Today, American society has exchanged the "must institutionalize" method for a "normalize" concept.

The most difficult cultural and community outlook on those who are disabled comes in the adult work world, where disabilities of persons can become highly evident and often cause difficulty in finding work and keeping their jobs. This place is particularly difficult for those who have not learned to self advocate or accommodate for their of special needs.

Sample Test Question and Rationale

(Rigorous)

1. **Acceptance of disabilities by parents and siblings is most influenced by:**

    A. Students obtain career training from elementary through high school

    B. Students acquire specific training in job skills prior to exiting school

    C. Students need specific training and supervision in applying skills learned in school to requirements in job situations

    D. Students obtain needed instruction and field-based experiences that help them to be able to work in specific occupations

Answer: C. Students need specific training and supervision in applying skills learned in school to requirements in job situations

The cultural influence on the family has the largest impact on their understanding of the disability.

SKILL 6.5 Interagency agreements

Nongovernmental agencies often deliver and coordinate agreements and involve community resources for the student and his or her family.

Special education teachers may need to inform parents about interagency agreements and the benefits of case managers so that they may better advocate for their children.

States such as California and Texas have implemented laws to govern and require cooperation among required services to best serve the parents and children with special needs. California's law (AB3632) goes a step beyond requiring cooperation of needed departmental resources such as Education, Health Services, Social Services, and Rehabilitation Services. It requires a sharing of information, personnel, and financial resources to provide a focused delivery that best meets the person's needs.

The stated purposes of interagency agreements is to provide the best services to a person with a disability so that they may receive an education that prepares them for living and working in an integrated community setting of their choice. These services may coordinate delivery of services in both the home and the school environment.

SKILL 6.6 Cooperative nature of the transition planning process

Transition planning is mandated in IDEA 1997. The transition planning requirements ensure that planning is begun at age fourteen (changed in 2004 to sixteen) and continues through high school. Transition planning and services focus on a coordinated set of student-centered activities designed to facilitate the student's progression from school to post-school activities. Transition planning should be flexible and focus on the developmental and educational requirements of the student at different grades and times.

Transition planning must focus on providing instruction and training in vocational programming when possible and where related services outside the school environment can be tied into making a student's transition successful. It is also possible that transition planning could provide job opportunities that may lead beyond the school years and to the ability to achieve what may be considered normal independence.

Most states, including Massachusetts and New York, often refer students finishing their school careers to their established departments for Vocational and Educational Services for Individuals with Disabilities (VESID), which coordinate the delivery of needed additional services beyond the secondary level of education. State departments such as these offer continued support in college environments and training schools and help those with disabilities find jobs.

Other community resources that can help with the transition to the "real world" environment and provide some continuity as the emerging adult leaves the protective school environment should be pointed out to the student and parent.

Transition planning is a student-centered event that necessitates a collaborative endeavor. Transition planning involves input from the following four groups:

1. The student

2. Parents

3. Secondary education professionals

4. Postsecondary education professionals

All these team members share the responsibility of making the student's transition a smooth one.

The student must play a key role in transition planning. This means asking the student to identify preferences and interests. The student should also attend

> *Transition planning must focus on providing instruction and training in vocational programming when possible and where related services outside the school environment can be tied into making a student's transition successful.*

meetings on transition planning. The degree of success experienced by the student in postsecondary educational settings depends on the student's degree of motivation, independence, self-direction, self-advocacy, and academic abilities developed in high school. Student participation in transition activities should be implemented as early as possible, no later than age sixteen.

In order to contribute to the transition planning process, the student should understand his learning disability and the impact it has on learning and work; implement achievable goals; present a positive self-image by emphasizing strengths, while understanding the impact of the learning disability; know how and when to discuss and ask for needed accommodations; be able to seek instructors and learning environments that are supportive; and establish an ongoing personal file that consists of school and medical records, individualized education program (IEP), résumé, and samples of academic work.

The primary function of parents during transition planning is to encourage and assist students in planning and achieving their educational goals. Parents also should encourage students to cultivate independent decision-making and self-advocacy skills.

The result of effective transition from a secondary to a postsecondary education program is a student with a learning disability who is confident, independent, self motivated, and striving to achieve career goals. This effective transition can be achieved if the team consisting of the student, parents, and professional personnel works to create and implement effective transition plans.

COMPETENCY 7

HISTORICAL MOVEMENTS/TRENDS AFFECTING THE CONNECTIONS BETWEEN SPECIAL EDUCATION AND THE LARGER SOCIETY

SKILL 7.1 Deinstitutionalization and community-based placements

The deinstitutionalization movement occurred simultaneously with efforts to treat individuals in their least restrictive environment. For many formerly institutionalized persons, semiprotected community settings could accommodate their needs. Another term, normalization, was coined when efforts were made for persons with disabilities to live their lives as close to the family setting as possible. Movement toward less restrictive environments culminated in establishing halfway residential houses, community residences (i.e., community group homes, foster family homes, apartment living), rehabilitation facilities, sheltered workshops, and vocational training programs.

The formation of local agencies and foundations assisted in the rehabilitation of these formerly institutionalized individuals. Services provided by these programs may differ somewhat from one locality to another; however, there is enough resemblance that generalities can be stated.

Rehabilitation facilities and sheltered workshops are particularly appropriate for individuals with severe disabilities. These facilities are geared toward slower-paced, intensive instruction in an effort to develop effective work habits, occupational skills, appropriate personal-social skills, and vocational interests. Some students can later receive vocational technical or on-the-job training in the community. In addition, these facilities are considered both a treatment and a training medium and generally have a variety of professionally trained counselors, evaluators, teachers, and supervisors. Sheltered workshops may provide employment for persons who can work productively in a protective, semicompetitive environment for at least a short period of time. These individuals would not be as likely to find successful experiences in a less restrictive, more competitive work setting.

Halfway residential houses are available in some communities for formerly institutionalized individuals who need support or supervision while receiving vocational training and other career development services elsewhere. Some of these facilities provide daily living and personal-social instruction, particularly if they are affiliated with a rehabilitative or sheltered workshop. A small staff may be available for individual and group counseling.

In some communities, group homes have been established that operate as much on the family concept as possible. The group home creates an environment that is more like family living than that of a large institution. It also provides a setting in which the variety of skills necessary for effective living can be pursued. Another type of alternative living unit is that of foster family homes. Most foster family arrangements are regulated by state and municipal licensing boards. In most cases, foster parents receive fees, but they do not usually receive training. Supervision of foster care homes is generally less rigorous than it is for group homes.

Apartment living arrangements, though not as prevalent or widely accepted at the present time as the group home concept, are rapidly gaining momentum. In this newer semi-independent living concept, the supervisor may live with the client, or clients may live together in a cluster of apartments in a separate part of the same building as the supervisor. As skills considered necessary for independent living are acquired and self-sufficiency is exhibited, clients are encouraged to move into apartments of their own. Periodic visits are made by supervisors to assure that the necessary level of self-care is maintained. The majority of clients who live in this type of arrangement attend a training program that helps them develop vocational and independent living skills. These clients remain a part of life-care and counseling programs but have work and leisure activities apart from agency staff supervising their living units.

SKILL 7.2 Inclusion

Inclusion is both a concept and a method of service delivery. It includes both indirect and direct services rendered by the special education teacher. With indirect services, the special education teacher consults with the regular classroom teacher about the type of instruction and instructional materials that would best meet the needs of a particular student. Through direct services, the special education teacher comes into the regular classroom and team-teaches with the general education teacher. The special education teacher works with individuals, small groups, and large groups of students who are experiencing similar educational difficulties.

Composite Scenario of an Inclusive Educational Setting

The following composite scenario provides a brief description of how regular and special teachers work together to address the individual needs of all of their students (ERIC Clearinghouse on Disabilities and Gifted Education, 1993).

Jane Smith teaches third grade at Lincoln Elementary School. Three days a week, she co-teaches the class with Lynn Vogel, a special education teacher. Their twenty-five students include four who have special needs because of disabilities and two others who currently need special help in specific curriculum areas. Each of the students with a disability has an IEP that was developed by a team that included both teachers. The teachers, paraprofessionals, and the school principal believe that these students have a great deal to contribute to the class and that they will achieve their best in the environment of a general education classroom.

All of the school personnel have attended in-service training designed to develop collaborative skills for teaming and problem solving. Mrs. Smith and the two professionals who work in the classroom also received special training on disabilities and how to create an inclusive classroom environment. The school's principal, Ben Parks, worked in special education many years ago and has received training on the impact of new special education developments and instructional arrangements on school administration. Each year, Mr. Parks works with the building staff to identify areas in which new training is needed. For specific questions that may arise, technical assistance is available through a regional special education cooperative.

Mrs. Smith and Miss Vogel share responsibility for teaching and supervising their paraprofessional. In addition to the time they spend together in the classroom, they spend two hours each week planning instruction, plus additional planning time with other teachers and support personnel who work with their students.

The teachers use their joint planning time to problem-solve and discuss the use of special instructional techniques for all students who need special assistance. Monitoring and adapting instruction for individual students is an ongoing activity. The teachers use curriculum-based measurement in systematically assessing their students' learning progress. They adapt curricula so that lessons begin at the edge of the students' knowledge, adding new material at the students' pace, and presenting it in a style consistent with the students' learning style. For some students, preorganizers or chapter previews are used to bring out the most important points of the material to be learned; for other students new vocabulary words may need to be highlighted or reduced reading levels may be required . Some students may use special activity worksheets, while others may learn best by using audiocassettes.

In the classroom, the teachers group students differently for different activities. Sometimes, the teachers and paraprofessionals divide the class, each teaching a small group or tutoring individuals. They use cooperative learning projects to help the students learn to work together and develop social relationships. Peer tutors provide extra help to students who need it. Students without disabilities are more than willing to help their friends' who have disabilities and vice versa.

While the regular classroom may not be the best learning environment for every child with a disability, it is highly desirable for all who can benefit. It provides contact with age-peers and prepares all students for the diversity of the world beyond the classroom.

Successful Inclusion

The following are activities and support systems that are commonly found where successful inclusion has occurred.

Attitudes and Beliefs

- The regular teacher believes that the student can succeed

- The school personnel are committed to accepting responsibility for the learning outcomes of students with disabilities

- School personnel and the students in the class have been prepared to receive a student with disabilities

Services and Physical Accommodation

- Services needed by the student are available (e.g., health, physical, occupational, or speech therapy)

- Adequate numbers of personnel, including aides and support personnel, are available

- Adequate staff development and technical assistance, based on the needs of the school personnel, are provided (e.g., information on disabilities, instructional methods, awareness and acceptance activities for students, and team-building skills)

- Appropriate policies and procedures for monitoring individual student progress, including grading and testing, are in place

Collaboration

- Special educators are part of the instructional or planning team

- Teaming approaches are used for problem solving and program implementation

- Regular teachers, special education teachers, and other specialists collaborate (e.g., co-teach, team teach, work together on teacher assistance teams)

Instructional Materials

- Teachers have the knowledge and skills needed to select and adapt curricula and instructional methods according to individual student needs

- A variety of instructional arrangements is available (e.g., team teaching, cross-grade grouping, peer tutoring, and teacher assistance teams)

- Teachers foster a cooperative learning environment and promote socialization

Sample Test Question and Rationale

(Easy)

1. **Students with disabilities develop greater self-images and recognize their own academic and social strengths when they are:**

   A. Included in the mainstream classroom

   B. Provided community based internships

   C. Socializing in the hallway

   D. Provided 1:1 instructional opportunity

Answer: A. Included in the mainstream classroom

When a child with a disability is included in the regular classroom it raises the expectations of the child's academic performance and their need to conform to "acceptable peer behavior." These expectations can help the child succeed, assuming he/she has the capacity to do so in that setting. Care should be taken, however, not to expect a child to succeed in a setting that is not appropriate for him/her.

SKILL 7.3 Application of technology

The reauthorization of IDEA 2004 provided funding to expand the use of technology in the IEP process. IDEA also provided funding to improve the use of technology by children with disabilities in the classroom, and it supported the use of technology with universal design principles and assistive technology devices to maximize accessibility to the general education curriculum for children with disabilities.

Each public agency must make sure that assistive technology devices or services are available to children with disabilities if needed as a part of the child's special education, related services, or supplementary aids and services. On a case-by-case basis, the use of school-purchased assistive technology devices in a child's home or in other settings is required if the child's IEP team determines that the child needs access to those devices in order to receive a free appropriate public education (FAPE).

Before the passing of IDEA 2004, the Assistive Technology Act of 1998 was passed to provide financial assistance to states so that they could maintain a permanent, comprehensive statewide program of technology-related assistance for individuals with disabilities. It was designed to increase the availability and funding for assistive technology devices and services. In addition, its goals were to:

- Increase the involvement of individuals with disabilities and their family members in decisions related to the provision of assistive technology devices and services

- Increase the awareness of laws that facilitate the availability of assistive technology devices and services

- Facilitate the change of laws to obtain increased availability or provision of assistive technology devices and services

- Increase the likelihood that individuals with disabilities will be able to obtain and maintain possession of assistive technology devices

SKILL 7.4 Transition

See also Skill 6.6

The importance of the transition of youth with disabilities from school to work or other community life was recognized by the mandate in IDEA for transition goals and objectives in these students' IEPs. With the enactment of this law, IDEA (P.L. 101-476), transition services became a right.

Halpern (1992) reviewed the transition movement of the 1980s and early 1990s as it related to preparation for work and its emergence from two movements that preceded it—the work/study movement of the 1960s and the career education movement during the 1970s. A discussion about this progression follows in this section. In reality, transition occurs throughout a person's life on both vertical and horizontal levels. An example of vertical transition is from one grade to the next. An example of horizontal transition is from regular classroom to resource room and vice versa (Ysseldyke, Algozzine & Thurlow, 1992).

Work/Study Movement

WORK/STUDY PROGRAM: an integrated academic, social, and vocational curriculum that included appropriate work experience

During the 1960s, a popular approach emerged that addressed the WORK/STUDY PROGRAM. This program was conducted cooperatively between the public schools and local office of state rehabilitation agencies. The general goal of these programs was to create an integrated academic, social, and vocational curriculum that included appropriate work experience. Programs were to be designed in such a way that students with mild disabilities would become prepared for eventual community adjustment. Cooperative agreements between the schools and the rehabilitation agency were made in order to administer these programs.

Many secondary level teachers taught half a school day and assumed the role and duties of work coordinator for the other half. This arrangement facilitated the eventual referral of these students by the schools to become clients of the rehabilitation agency.

Career Education Movement

With the near demise of the cooperative work/study program, a new movement called career education came into being during the 1970s. Whereas the work/study movement emphasized delivery of services within a specific type of inter-agency agreement, the career education movement focused on the integration of readiness for a life career throughout a student's education, from kindergarten through grade twelve. Career education had its inception in 1970, when Sidney Marland, then the Commissioner of Education, declared career education a top priority of the U.S. Office of Education. Career education was targeted for the general populace of students and did not mention students with disabilities. In 1974, the Office of Career Education was established within the U.S. Office of Education. Public Law 95-207, the Career Education Implementation Incentive Act, was passed in 1977. This act specifically mentioned people with disabilities as an appropriate target population for services.

In 1976, the Division of Career Development was approved as a twelfth division of the Council for Exceptional Children (CEC). Though Public Law 95-207 was repealed by Congress in 1982, CEC had already endorsed the concept of career education through a position paper in 1978.

CAREER EDUCATION provides the opportunity for children to acquire, in the least restrictive environment possible, the academic, daily living, personal-social and occupational knowledge, and specific vocational work skills necessary for attaining their highest levels of economic, personal, and social fulfillment. The individual can obtain this fulfillment through work, both paid and unpaid, and in a variety of other societal roles and personal life styles including his or her pursuits as a student, citizen, family member, and participant in meaningful leisure time activities. (Position Paper, 1978, cited in Halpern, 1992, p. 205).

Transition

The transition movement emerged in the publication of a position paper from the Office of Special Education and Rehabilitation Services (OSERS) (Will, 1984). The transition model has also become known as a bridge model that describes three types of services or bridges needed to facilitate the transition from school to work.

1. Transition without special services: This type refers to the use of generic services available to anyone in the community. Postsecondary education in vocation and community colleges are examples.

2. Transition with time-limited services: This refers to specialized, short-term services where the presence of a disability is usually required to qualify a person for access to the service. An example is vocational rehabilitation.

3. Transition with ongoing services: This has become known through federally supported demonstration projects. An example is supported employment. The Individuals with Disabilities Education Act (IDEA), and its revisions in 1997 and 2004, contain several initiatives in the area of transition, including the requirement that all IEPs address transition goals and objectives no later than the student's sixteenth birthday and at age fourteen or younger when appropriate.

Comparisons of the three movements

The work/study movement was restricted to secondary education and primarily served students with mild mental retardation. It required interagency collaboration. The career education movement was oriented to both elementary and secondary education, available to students with and without disabilities, implemented in both regular and special education environments, and designed for a general education curriculum. The transition movement provides the broadest focus on the types of adult service agencies that need to be directly involved in the partnerships with schools in order to facilitate the movement from school to work.

Congress defined TRANSITION SERVICES as: A coordinated set of activities for a student, designed within an outcome-oriented process, that promotes movement from school to post-school activities, including post-secondary education, vocational training, integrated employment, supported employment, continuing and adult education, adult services, independent living, and community participation. The coordinated set of activities is based upon the individual student's needs, taking into account the student's preferences and interests. This set of activities should include instruction, community experiences, the development of employment and other post-school adult living objectives, and, when appropriate, acquisition of daily living skills and functional vocational evaluation.

Continuation into the 1990s: Goals 2000

Effective education and transition into adulthood was highlighted in President Bush's 1990 State of the Union message. The six stated goals to be met by the year

TRANSITION SERVICES: coordinated set of activities for a student, designed within an outcome-oriented process, that promotes movement from school to post-school activities, including post-secondary education, vocational training, integrated employment, supported employment, continuing and adult education, adult services, independent living, and community participation

2000 had emerged from collaboration with the National Governor's Association. The goals are:

- Every American child must start school prepared to learn, sound in body and sound in mind

- The high school graduate rate in the U.S. must increase to no less than 90 percent

- All students in grades four, eight, and twelve will be tested for progress in critical subjects

- American students must rank first in the world in achievement in mathematics and science

- Every adult must be a skilled, literary worker and citizen, able to compete in a global economy

- Every school must be drug free and offer a disciplined environment conducive to learning

Many of these goals have either clear or potential relevance for transition programs that are of concern to us. We are concerned about functional illiteracy, and approximately 20 percent of the entire adult American population is unable to perform basic math calculations or read at a rudimentary level of effectiveness. We are concerned about high school dropouts, and approximately 30 percent of all American students drop out of school (Halpern, 1992, p. 208).

The following concerns were stated by Halpern, 1992, p. 208:

- Should vocational apprenticeship programs, such as those found in Germany, be developed as a strong and viable alternative to the college preparation programs that are the cornerstone of high schools in our country?

- Should the federal government get into the business of determining and measuring minimum education competencies? (Education is not in our country's Constitution as a national function. It is governed by the states.)

- Can all students be educated together, or is some sort of tracking system desirable? (If so, the tracking system must be nondiscriminatory.)

- Should schools be the instruments of social reform, or should they stick to the business of education?

- What should be the role of parents in dealing with the education of their children?

Sample Test Question and Rationale

(Average)

1. **Vocational training programs are based on all of the following ideas except:**

   A. Students obtain career training from elementary through high school

   B. Students acquire specific training in job skills prior to exiting school

   C. Students need specific training and supervision in apply skills learned in school to requirements in jog situations

   D. Student obtain needed instruction and field-based experiences that help them to be able to work in specific occupations

Answer: A. Students obtain career training from elementary through high school

Vocational education programs or transition programs prepare students for entry into the labor force. They are usually incorporated into the work-study at the high school or post-secondary levels. They are usually focused on job skills, job opportunities, skill requirements for specific jobs, personal qualifications in relation to job requirements, work habits, money management, and academic skills needed for specific jobs.

SKILL 7.5 Advocacy

> **ADVOCACY:** support and representation in communication and negotiation

ADVOCACY is support and representation in communication and negotiation. Advocacy has played a significant role in changes in law as it pertains to special education.

Historical Movement of Advocacy and Special Education

Initially, parents were the advocates for their own exceptional children. Gradually, parents started to ask other parents to attend IEP meetings as advocates. Because many things are discussed at IEP meetings and the topics are often emotional, it is hard to remember and respond to everything. Parent advocates listen and take notes so that the child's parent can later review the discussions of the IEP meeting. An advocate might also ask questions, explain information regarding the disability or the particular child, or voice the need for additional or changed services.

Current Special Education Advocacy

The range of advocates for a student with a disability has widened. An advocate could be the student's parent, another parent, a teacher, an educational staff member from another school, an educational consultant, a representative from an agency that works with exceptional individuals, a community member, a lawyer, a medical professional, or even the student.

In addition to attending the IEP meeting, advocates can also provide premeeting activities such as organizing information on the student (e.g., educational history and medical history), as well as familiarizing parents and students with the procedures of how the school district works.

The first priority of an effective advocate is to build a positive working relationship with the school that will result in the best possible educational program for the student. While the goal is to gain a free and appropriate public education (FAPE), the requests of an advocate should be practical and realistic.

Often the presence of an advocate is an effort to facilitate communication and make changes in a student's educational program. It may also be a step to avoid possible due process.

Parent and Professional Advocacy Activity and Parent Organization

There have always been, and will always be, exceptional children with special needs, but special education services have not always been in existence to provide for these needs. Private schools and state institutions were primary sources of education for individuals with disabilities in earlier years.

The Tenth Amendment to the U.S. Constitution leaves education as an unstated power and, therefore, vested in the states. As was the practice in Europe, government funds in America were first appropriated to experimental schools to determine whether students with disabilities actually could be educated.

During the mid-twentieth century, legislators and governors in control of funds, faced with evidence of need and the efficacy of special education programs, refused to expend funds adequately, thus creating the ultimate need for federal guidelines in PL 94-142 to mandate flow-through money. Concurrently, due process rights and procedures were outlined, based on litigation and legislation enacted by parents of children with disabilities, parent organizations, and professional advocacy groups. "Public support in the form of legislation and appropriation of funds has been achieved and sustained only by the most arduous and persevering efforts of individuals who advocate for exceptional children" (Hallahan & Kauffman, 1986 p. 26).

Parents, professionals, and other members of advocacy groups and organizations finally succeeded in bringing astounding data about the population of youth with disabilities in our country to the attention of legislators. Among the findings revealed, Congress noted that:

1. More than eight million children with disabilities were in the United States, and more than half were not receiving an appropriate education.

2. More than one million children with disabilities were excluded from the educational system, and many other children with disabilities were enrolled in regular education classes where they were not benefiting from the educational services provided because of their undetected conditions.

3. Because of inadequate educational services within the public school systems, families were forced to seek services outside the public realm. Years of advocacy effort resulted in the current laws and court decisions mandating special education at a federal level.

SKILL 7.6 Accountability and meeting educational standards

With the passing of the No Child Left Behind legislation in 2002, special education students and teachers must meet a higher standard of accountability. No Child Left Behind is designed to change the culture of America's schools by closing the achievement gap, giving more flexibility, providing parents with more options, and teaching students based on what is effective.

No Child Left Behind is designed to change the culture of America's schools by closing the achievement gap, giving more flexibility, providing parents with more options, and teaching students based on what is effective.

Under the act's accountability provisions, states must describe how they will close the achievement gap and make sure all students, including those who are disadvantaged, achieve academic proficiency. They must produce annual state and school district report cards that inform parents and communities about state and school progress. Schools that do not make progress must provide supplemental services, such as free tutoring or after-school assistance; take corrective actions; and, if still not making adequate yearly progress after five years, make dramatic changes in the way the school is run.

In an effort to ensure that states and schools are meeting educational standards, the No Child Left Behind legislation requires that each school prepare an annual district report card and give it to parents. The report cards provide information on how each school performed on state assessments. The report cards must state student performance in terms of three levels—basic, proficient, and advanced. Achievement data should be broken out by student subgroups according to race, ethnicity, gender, English language proficiency, migrant status, disability status, and low-income status. The report cards should also indicate which schools need improvement, corrective action, or restructuring.

The report cards also present information on the percentage of students not tested; graduation rates for secondary school students; performance of school districts on adequate yearly progress measures; professional qualifications of teachers in the state, including the percentage of teachers in the classroom with only emergency or provisional credentials; and the percentage of classes in the state that are not taught by highly qualified teachers, including a comparison between high- and low-income schools.

IDEA 2004 added new language that ensures that children with disabilities are taught by highly qualified teachers and receive research-based instruction. IDEA 2004 also includes new requirements that schools provide high-quality, intensive preservice preparation and professional development for all staff that work with children with disabilities.

DELIVERY OF SERVICES TO STUDENTS

PERSONALIZED STUDY PLAN

KNOWN MATERIAL/ SKIP IT

PAGE	COMPETENCY AND SKILL	
85	**8:** **Background knowledge**	☐
	8.1: Conceptual approaches underlying service delivery	☐
	8.2: Placement and program issues	☐
	8.3: Integrating best practices, multidisciplinary research, and professional literature into the educational setting	☐
101	**9:** **Curriculum and instruction and their implementation across the continuum of educational settings**	☐
	9.1: The Individualized Family Service Plan (IFSP) and the Individualized Education Program (IEP) process	☐
	9.2: Instructional development and implementation	☐
	9.3: Teaching strategies and methods	☐
	9.4: Instructional format and components	☐
	9.5: Career development and transition issues	☐
	9.6: Technology for teaching and learning in special education settings	☐
142	**10:** **Assessment**	☐
	10.1: Use of assessment for screening, diagnosis, placement, and the making of instructional decisions	☐
	10.2: Procedures and test materials	☐
	10.3: How to select, construct, conduct, and modify informal assessments	☐
154	**11:** **Structuring and managing the learning environment**	☐
	11.1: Structuring the learning environment	☐
	11.2: Classroom management techniques	☐
	11.3: Behavior management strategies	☐
172	**12:** **Professional roles**	☐
	12.1: Specific roles and responsibilities of teachers	☐
	12.2: Influence of teacher attitudes, values, and behaviors on the learning of exceptional students	☐
	12.3: Communicating with parents, guardians, and appropriate community collaborators	☐

COMPETENCY 8
BACKGROUND KNOWLEDGE

> **SKILL 8.1** **Conceptual approaches underlying service delivery to students with disabilities** *(including cognitive, constructivist, psychodynamic, behavioral, sociological, ecological, therapeutic [speech/language, physical, and occupational], and medical approaches)*

Services for students with disabilities may employ a variety of educational approaches. Because each student represents a unique combination of needs, the combination of services provided to the child per his IEP is also unique. Even students with similar services (for example, speech and language therapy) may have different amounts of therapy time and different goals and objectives.

The COGNITIVE APPROACH TO SPECIAL EDUCATION emphasizes measurable outcomes of a student's learning. It is often associated with Bloom's taxonomy of higher level thinking (knowledge, comprehension, application, analysis, and synthesis) and Haladyna's learning processes of understanding, problem solving, critical thinking, and creativity.

Special educators are encouraged to include learning that extends beyond initial knowledge and comprehension.

The CONSTRUCTIVIST APPROACH TO SPECIAL EDUCATION is based heavily upon observations by Piaget and Vygotsky and uses student experience and experimentation to gain new knowledge rather than a presentation by the teacher. Many exceptional students learn well from a hands-on approach and may benefit from a constructivist component in the classroom.

The SOCIOLOGICAL APPROACH TO SPECIAL EDUCATION takes into account the value of education from different cultures. If a child's sociological background is different than the prevailing culture where he lives, he may be perceived as needing special education. Care should be taken to avoid assigning special education labels that result from sociological differences and not disabilities.

The ECOLOGICAL APPROACH TO SPECIAL EDUCATION emphasizes understanding the child in his or her life context. It recognizes that the effect of a disability is influenced by the child's family, background, and culture and the entire environment surrounding the child throughout life. Students who receive special needs labels early or who come from environments where little emphasis is placed on

COGNITIVE APPROACH TO SPECIAL EDUCATION: emphasizes measurable outcomes of a student's learning

CONSTRUCTIVIST APPROACH TO SPECIAL EDUCATION: uses student experience and experimentation to gain new knowledge rather than a presentation by the teacher

SOCIOLOGICAL APPROACH TO SPECIAL EDUCATION: takes into account the value of education from different cultures

ECOLOGICAL APPROACH TO SPECIAL EDUCATION: emphasizes understanding the child in his or her life context

educational experiences are often viewed differently by educators. This view in itself can affect the child's learning, as can family and social background. It is important to take this background into consideration when making the determination of special education needs.

The THERAPEUTIC APPROACH TO SPECIAL EDUCATION addresses delays and disabilities in the following areas:

- Speech and language therapy

- Physical therapy (gross motor function such as walking, climbing, running, jumping)

- Occupational therapy (fine motor function such as handwriting, using buttons and zippers, and manipulating objects such as puzzle pieces)

- Vision therapy (such as visual tracking)

- Art therapy

> **THERAPEUTIC APPROACH TO SPECIAL EDUCATION:** addresses delays and disabilities with supportive services such as speech and language therapy, physical therapy, occupational therapy, etc.

Learning Theories

Student learning is affected by many factors, including student learning style, how material to be learned is presented, and student background knowledge or experiences. Several educational learning theories have implications for classroom practices. Piaget's observations about stages of development have implications for both theories of learning and strategies for teaching. Piaget recorded observations on the following four learning stages:

- Sensory motor stage (from birth to age 2)

- Preoperation stages (ages 2 to 7 or early elementary)

- Concrete operational (ages 7 to 11 or upper elementary)

- Formal operational (ages 7 to 5 or late elementary/high school)

Piaget believed children passed through this series of stages to develop from the most basic forms of concrete thinking to sophisticated levels of abstract thinking.

Some of the most prominent learning theories in education today have been influenced by brain-based learning research and the emergence of Multiple Intelligence Testing. Supported by recent brain research, brain-based learning approaches suggest that knowledge about the way the brain retains information enables educators to design the most effective learning environments. Caine, et al (2005) cite twelve principles that relate knowledge about the brain to teaching practices. These twelve principles are:

> *Some of the most prominent learning theories in education today have been influenced by brain-based learning research and the emergence of Multiple Intelligence Testing.*

1. The brain is a complex adaptive system

2. The brain is social

3. The search for meaning is innate

4. We use patterns to learn more effectively

5. Emotions are crucial to developing patterns

6. Each brain perceives and creates parts and whole simultaneously

7. Learning involves focused and peripheral attention

8. Learning involves conscious and unconscious processes

9. We have at least two ways of organizing memory

10. Learning is developmental

11. Complex learning is enhanced by challenge (and inhibited by threat)

12. Every brain is unique

Educators can use these principles to design methods and environments in their classrooms to maximize student learning. The last principle listed (Every brain is unique) is particularly relevant to teachers of students with special needs.

The MULTIPLE INTELLIGENCE THEORY, developed by Howard Gardner, suggests that students learn in (at least) seven different ways:

1. Visually/spatially

2. Musically

3. Verbally

4. Logically/mathematically

5. Interpersonally

6. Intrapersonally

7. Bodily/kinesthetically

The most current form of constructivist learning theory recommends allowing students to construct learning opportunities. For constructivist teachers, the belief is that students create their own reality of knowledge and how to process and observe the world around them. Students are constantly constructing new ideas that serve as frameworks for learning and teaching. This approach is based in part

Many students with disabilities find it particularly difficult to learn in a nonpreferred style, so identifying the preferred style can be crucial to the accommodations needed for a student with disabilities.

MULTIPLE INTELLIGENCE THEORY: suggests that students learn in (at least) seven different ways

The constructivist learning theory recommends allowing students to construct learning opportunities.

on the work of Piaget, who maintained that children build their mental schemata by working and interacting with both the environment and other learners. The constructivist model comprises the following four components:

1. Learner creates knowledge

2. Learner constructs and makes meaningful new knowledge to existing knowledge

3. Learner shapes and constructs knowledge by life experiences and social interactions

4. In constructivist learning communities, the student, teacher, and classmates establish knowledge cooperatively on a daily basis

Constructivist learning for students is dynamic and ongoing. For constructivist teachers, the classroom becomes a place where students are encouraged to interact with the instructional process by asking questions and posing new ideas to old theories. The use of cooperative learning that encourages students to work in supportive learning environments using their own ideas to stimulate questions and propose outcomes is a major aspect of a constructivist classroom, as is a hands-on learning approach.

Cognitive approaches to teaching often emphasize teaching metacognitive strategies in order "to help the learner gain understanding about how knowledge is constructed and about the conscious tools for constructing that knowledge."

Cognitive approaches to teaching often emphasize teaching metacognitive strategies in order "to help the learner gain understanding about how knowledge is constructed and about the conscious tools for constructing that knowledge" (Joyce and Weil 1996). The cognitive approach to learning involves the teacher's understanding that teaching the student to process his or her own learning and mastery of skill provides the greatest learning and retention opportunities in the classroom. Students are taught to develop concepts and teach themselves skills in problem solving and critical thinking. The student becomes an active participant in the learning process and the teacher facilitates that conceptual and cognitive learning process.

Social and behavioral theories look at the social interactions of students in the classroom that instruct or have an impact on learning opportunities. The psychological approaches behind both theories are subject to individual variables that are learned and applied either proactively or negatively in the classroom. The stimulus of the classroom can promote effective learning or evoke behavior that is counterproductive for both students and teachers. Students are social beings that normally gravitate to action in the classroom, so teachers must be cognizant in planning classroom environments that provide both focus and engagement to maximize learning opportunities.

Sample Test Questions and Rationale

(Rigorous)

1. An educational implication of cognitive learning stages is the importance given to:

   A. Defining behavior

   B. Modifying behavior

   C. Assessing entry-level skills

   D. Knowing the ages of the students

Answer: C. Assessing entry-level skills

According to Cognitive Learning Theory, because learning is sequential, prerequisite skills must be attained before moving on to the next level.

(Rigorous)

2. Advocates of cognitive learning stages support the idea that behavior is:

   A. Variable

   B. Predictable

   C. Learned

   D. Practical

Answer: B. Predictable

Piaget's observations about stages of development have implications for both theories of learning and strategies for teaching. Piaget recorded observations on the following four learning stages: sensory motor stage (from birth to age 2); pre-operation stages (ages 2 to 7 or early elementary); concrete operational (ages 7 to 11 or upper elementary); and formal operational (ages 7-15 or late elementary/high school). Piaget believed children passed through this series of stages to develop from the most basic forms of concrete thinking to sophisticated levels of abstract thinking.

SKILL 8.2 **Placement and program issues** *(such as early intervention; least restrictive environment; inclusion; role of Individualized Education Program [IEP] team; due process guidelines; categorical programs; continuum of educational and related services; related services and their integration into the classroom, including roles of other professionals; accommodations, including access to assistive technology; transition of students into and within special education placements; community-based training; postschool transitions)*

Identification

Identification of a student's learning problem occurs when comparisons are made between a given student's academic and behavioral characteristics and those of the peer population. Teachers hold expectations for student behaviors, and those who exhibit actions that differ are singled out.

Students with disabilities are identifiable by academic and social behaviors that deviate significantly from those of their classmates. The longer it takes to identify these students, the further they fall behind their age-mates in school.

Federal legislation requires that sincere efforts be made to help the child learn in the regular classroom.

TEACHER ASSISTANCE TEAMS: make professional suggestions about curricular alternatives and instructional modifications

All children and youth exhibit behaviors that deviate from normative expectations at times. But overall, it is the intensity of the behavior, the degree to which it is shown, and the frequency and length of time that it persists or has occurred that is significant. Behavior rating scales, checklists, inventories, and sociograms are used to determine whether a particular behavior is occurring and to what extent.

Intervention

Once a student is identified as being at-risk academically or socially, remedial interventions are attempted within the regular classroom. Federal legislation requires that sincere efforts be made to help the child learn in the regular classroom.

In some states, school-based teams of educators are formed to solve learning and behavior problems in the regular classroom. These informal problem-solving teams have a variety of names that include concepts of support (school support teams, student support teams), assistance (teacher assistant teams, school assistance teams, or building assistance teams), and appraisal (school appraisal teams) (Pugach & Johnson 1989b).

Regardless of what the teams are called, their purpose is similar. Chalfant, Pysh, and Moultrie (1979) state that TEACHER ASSISTANCE TEAMS are created to make professional suggestions about curricular alternatives and instructional modifications. These teams may be composed of a variety of participants, including regular education teachers, building administrators, guidance counselors, special education teachers, and the student's parent(s). The team composition varies based on the type of referral, the needs of the student, and availability of educational personnel and state requirements (Georgia Department of Education 1986).

Instructional modifications are tried in an attempt to accommodate the student in the regular classroom. Effective instruction is geared toward individual needs and recognizes differences in how students learn. Modifications are tailored to individual student needs. Some strategies for modifying regular classroom instruction shown in the table below are effective with at-risk students with disabilities and students without learning or behavior problems.

STRATEGIES FOR MODIFYING CLASSROOM INSTRUCTION	
Strategy 1	Provide active learning experiences to teach concepts. Student motivation is increased when students can manipulate, weigh, measure, read, or write using materials and skills that relate to their daily lives. In addition, retention is better when new learning is related to existing knowledge.

Table continued on next page

Strategy 2	Provide ample opportunities for guided practice of new skills. Frequent feedback on performance is essential to overcome student feelings of inadequacy. Peer tutoring and cooperative projects provide non-threatening practice opportunities. Individual student conferences, curriculum-based tests, and small group discussions are three useful methods for checking progress.
Strategy 3	Provide multisensory learning experiences. Students with learning problems sometimes have sensory processing difficulties; for instance, an auditory discrimination problem may cause misunderstanding about teacher expectations. Lessons and directions that include visual, auditory, tactile, and kinesthetic modes are preferable to a single sensory approach. Such an approach also helps students with learning disabilities that impact abstract learning.
Strategy 4	Present information in a manner that is relevant to the student. Particular attention to this strategy is needed when a cultural or economic gap exists between the lives of teachers and students. Relate instruction to a youngster's daily experience and interests.
Strategy 5	Provide students with concrete illustrations of their progress. Students with learning problems need frequent reinforcement for their efforts. Charts, graphs, and check sheets provide tangible markers of student achievement.

Referral

Referral is the process through which a teacher, a parent, or some other person formally requests an evaluation of a student to determine eligibility for special education services. The decision to refer a student may be influenced by the following:

- Student characteristics, such as the abilities, behaviors, or skills (or lack thereof) that students exhibit.

- Individual differences among teachers in their beliefs, expectations, or skills in dealing with specific kinds of problems.

- Expectations for assistance with a student who is exhibiting academic or behavioral learning problems.

- Availability of specific kinds of strategies and materials.

- Parents' request for referral or opposition to referral.

- Institutional factors that may facilitate or constrain teachers in making referral decisions. Fewer students are referred when school districts have complex procedures for referral, psychological assessments are backlogged for months, special education classes are filled to capacity, or principals and other administrators do not fully recognize the importance of special services.

Everyone must clearly understand referral procedures, and they must be coordinated among all school personnel. All educators must to be able to identify characteristics typically exhibited by special needs students. Also, the restrictiveness of special service settings must be known and the appropriateness of each clearly understood. The more restrictive special education programs tend to group students with similar disabilities for instruction. Last, the specialized services afforded through equipment, materials, teaching approaches, and specific teacher-student relations should be clearly understood.

Evaluation

If instructional modifications in the regular classroom have not proven successful, a student may be referred for multidisciplinary evaluation. The evaluation is comprehensive and includes:

- Norm and criterion-referenced tests (e.g., IQ and diagnostic tests)

- Curriculum-based assessment

- Systematic teacher observation (e.g., behavior frequency checklist)

- Samples of student work

- Parent interviews

The purpose of the evaluation is twofold: to determine eligibility for special education services and to identify a student's strengths and weaknesses in order to plan an individual education program.

The purpose of the evaluation is twofold: to determine eligibility for special education services and to identify a student's strengths and weaknesses in order to plan an individual education program.

The wording in federal law is very explicit about the manner in which evaluations must be conducted and about the existence of due process procedures that protect against bias and discrimination. Provisions in the law include the following:

- The testing of children in their native or primary language unless it is clearly not feasible to do so

- The use of evaluation procedures selected and administered to prevent cultural or ethnic discrimination

- The use of assessment tools validated for the purpose for which they are being used (e.g., achievement levels, IQ scores, adaptive skills)

- Assessment by a multidisciplinary team using several pieces of information to formulate a placement decision

Furthermore, parental involvement must occur in the development of the child's educational program. According to the law, parents must:

- Be notified before initial evaluation or any change in placement by a written notice in their primary language describing the proposed school action, the reasons for it, and the available educational opportunities

- Consent, in writing, before the child is initially evaluated

Parents may then:

- Request an independent educational evaluation if they feel the school's evaluation is inappropriate

- Request an evaluation at public expense if a due process hearing decision is that the public agency's evaluation was inappropriate

- Participate on the committee that considers the evaluation, placement, and programming of the student

All students referred for evaluation for special education should have on file the results of a relatively current vision and hearing screening. This will determine the adequacy of sensory acuity and ensure that learning problems are not due to a vision and/or hearing problem.

Eligibility

Eligibility is based on criteria defined in federal law or state regulations, which vary from state to state. Evaluation methods correspond with eligibility criteria for the special education classifications. For example, a multidisciplinary evaluation for a student being evaluated for intellectual disabilities would include the individual's intellectual functioning, adaptive behavior, and achievement levels. Other tests are based on developmental characteristics exhibited (e.g., social, language, and motor).

Eligibility for services in behavior disorders requires documented evidence of social deficiencies or learning deficits that are not because of intellectual, sensory, or physical conditions. Therefore, any student undergoing multidisciplinary evaluation for this categorical service is usually given an intelligence test, diagnostic achievement tests, and social and/or adaptive inventories. Results of behavior frequency lists, direct observations, and anecdotal records collected over an extended period often accompany test results.

Additional information frequently used when making decisions about a child's eligibility for special education include the following:

- Developmental history
- Past academic performance
- Medical history or records
- Neurological reports
- Classroom observations
- Speech and language evaluations

- Samples of student work
- Parent interviews
- Home visits
- Discipline reports
- Personality assessment

A student evaluated for learning disabilities is given reading, math, and spelling achievement tests; an intelligence test to confirm average or above average cognitive capabilities; and tests of written and oral language ability. Tests need to show a discrepancy between potential and performance. Classroom observations and samples of student work (such as impaired reading ability or impaired writing ability) also provide indicators of possible learning disabilities.

If considered eligible for special education services, the child's disability should be documented in a written report stating specific reasons for the decision.

Three-year reevaluations (triennials) of a student's progress are required by law and determine the growth and changing needs of the student. During the reevaluation, continued eligibility for services in special education must be assessed using a range of evaluation tools similar to those used during the initial evaluation. All relevant information about the student is considered when making a decision about continued eligibility or whether the student no longer needs the service and is ready to begin preparing to exit the program. If the student is deemed ready to exit the program, planning for the transition must occur.

Individual Education Plan

Before placement can occur, the multidisciplinary team must develop an Individualized Education Plan (IEP), a child-centered educational plan that is tailored to meet individual needs. IEPs acknowledge each student's requirement for a specially designed educational program.

The following three purposes are identified by Polloway, Patton, Payne, and Payne (1989):

1. IEPs outline instructional programs. They provide specific instructional direction, which eliminates any pulling together of marginally related instructional exercises.

2. IEPs function as the basis for evaluation.

3. IEPs facilitate communication among staff members, teachers, and parents, and, to some extent, between teachers and students.

Development of the IEP follows initial identification, evaluation, and classification. The educational plan is evaluated and rewritten at least annually. An IEP is a binding legal document, and both the school system and the teacher are responsible for seeing that its conditions are met. An IEP also follows the child from school to school when the child moves. *For more detail on the contents of the IEP, see Skills 5.2 and 9.1.*

Placement

The law defines Special Education and identifies related services that may be required if Special Education is to be effective. By law, placement in a Special Education delivery service must be the student's least restrictive environment. Special Education services occur at a variety of levels, some more restrictive than others. The largest number of students (those with mild disabilities) is served in settings closest to normal educational placements. Service delivery in more restrictive settings is limited to students with severe or profound disabilities, who comprise a smaller population within special education. The exception is correctional facilities, which serve a limited and restricted populace.

One way to organize the options for placement of special education students is shown on the Cascade System of Special Education Services (Deno, 1970), shown with Skill 5.1. The multidisciplinary team must be able to match the needs of the student with an appropriate placement in the cascade system of services. According to Polloway, et al. (1994), two assumptions are made when we use the cascade of services as a guide to place students. First, a child should be placed in an educational setting as close to the regular classroom as possible, and placed only as far away from this least restrictive environment as necessary to provide an appropriate education.

Second, program exit should be a goal. A student's placement may change when the team obtains data suggesting the advisability of an alternative educational setting. As adaptive, social, cognitive, motor, and language skills are developed, the student may be placed in a lesser restrictive environment. The multi-disciplinary team is responsible for monitoring and recommending placement changes when appropriate.

Due Process

"Due process is a set of procedures designed to ensure the fairness of educational decisions and the accountability of both professionals and parents in making these decisions" (Kirk, et al, 2003, p. 66).

These procedures serve as a mechanism by which the child and his family can voice their opinions or concerns and sometimes dissensions. Due process safeguards exist in all matters pertaining to identification, evaluation, and educational placement.

Due process occurs in two realms: substantive and procedural. Substantive due process is the content of the law (e.g., appropriate placement for special education students). Procedural due process is the form through which substantive due process is carried out (i.e., parental permission for testing). IDEA contains many items of both substantive and procedural due process.

1. A due process hearing may be initiated by parents of the Local Education Agency (LEA) as an impartial forum for challenging decisions about identification, evaluation, or placement. Either party may present evidence, cross-examine witnesses, obtain a record of the hearing, and be advised by counsel

or by individuals having expertise in the education of individuals with disabilities. Findings may be appealed to the State Education Agency (SEA), and, if still dissatisfied, either party may bring civil action in a state or federal district court. Hearing timelines are set by legislation.

2. Parents may obtain an independent evaluation if there is disagreement about the educational evaluation performed by the LEA. The results of such an evaluation (1) must be considered in any decision made with respect to the provision of a free, appropriate public education for the child, and (2) may be presented as evidence at a hearing. Further, the parents may request this evaluation at public expense (1) if a hearing officer requests an independent educational evaluation, (2) if the decision from a due process hearing is that the LEA's evaluation was inappropriate. If the final decision holds that the evaluation performed is appropriate, the parent still has the right to an independent educational evaluation, but not at public expense.

3. Written notice must be provided to parents prior to a proposal or refusal to initiate or make a change in the child's identification, evaluation, or educational placement and must include:

   A. A listing of parental due process safeguards

   B. A description and a rationale for the chosen action

   C. A detailed listing of components (e.g., tests, records, reports) that were the basis for the decision

   D. Assurance that the language and content of notices were understood by the parents

4. Parental consent must be obtained before evaluation procedures can occur unless a state law specifies otherwise.

5. Sometimes parents or guardians cannot be identified to function in the due process role. When this occurs, a suitable person must be assigned to act as a surrogate. The LEA makes this assignment in full accordance with legislation.

As the due process procedure is followed, multidisciplinary teams make a series of major decisions. A typical chain of events that occurs as decisions are made is outlined in the figure below. Multidisciplinary teams are composed of persons from various disciplines. Team members include teachers (regular and special education), building and district administrators, school psychologists, school social workers, parents, and medical experts.

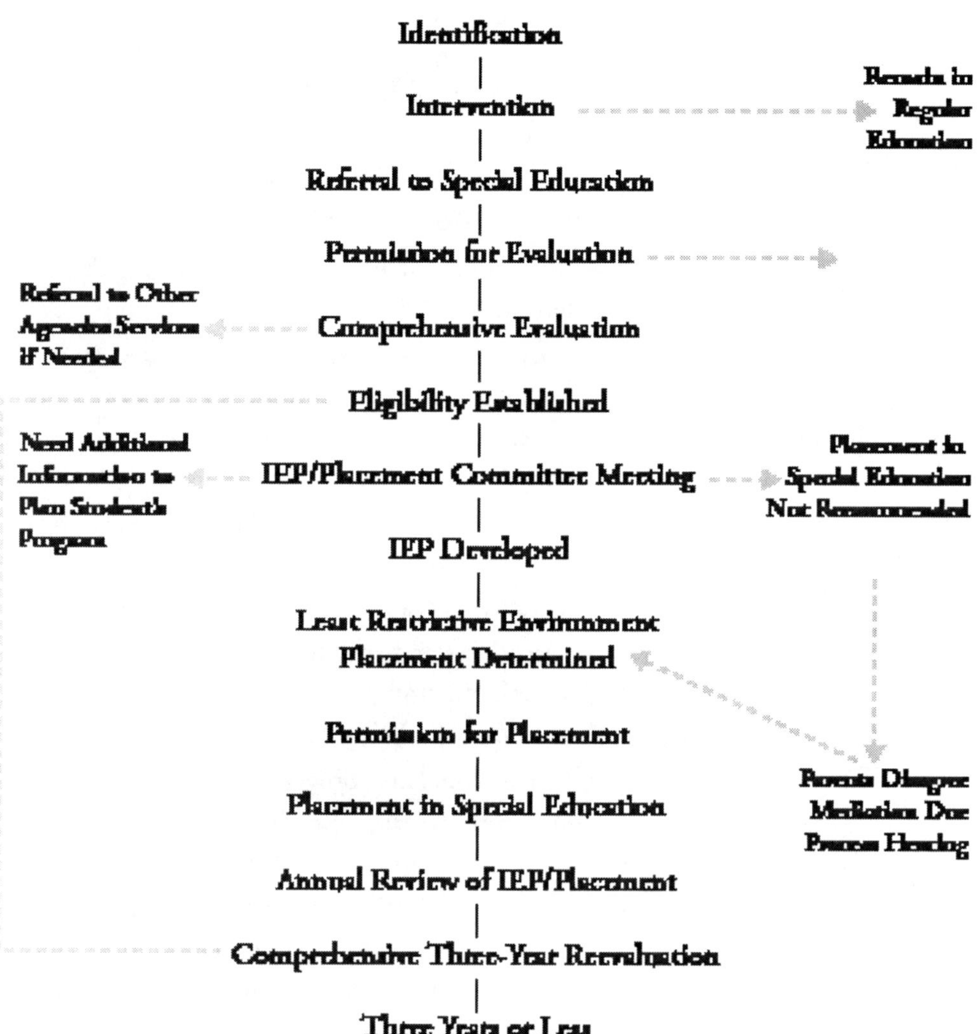

From: Georgia Department of Education

Sample Test Questions and Rationale

(Rigorous)

1. **Which components of the IEP are required by law?**

   A. Present level of academic and functional performance; statement of how the disability affects the student's involvement and progress; evaluation criteria and timeliness for instructional objective achievement; modifications of accommodations

   B. Projected dates for services initiation with anticipated frequency, location and duration; statement of when parent will be notified; statement of annual goals

   C. Extent to which child will not participate in regular education program; transitional needs for students age 16

   D. All of the above

Answer: D. All of the above

According to IDEA, each IEP must contain the following:

- A statement of the present levels of educational performance of the child

- A statement of annual goals, including short-term instructional objectives

- A statement of the specific educational services to be provided to the child, and the extent to which the child will be able to participate in regular educational programs

- The projected date for initiation and anticipated duration of such services

- Appropriate objective criteria and evaluation procedures and schedules for determining, on at least an annual basis, whether instructional objectives are being achieved

- Instructional and program accommodations and supports that must be provided throughout the educational settings and, specifically, in state and district mandated testing

- A clear rationale for any placement that involves nonparticipation in any part of the general education classroom

- Transition services, as appropriate and needed

Sample Test Questions and Rationale (cont.)

(Rigorous)

2. **What does the section of the IEP entitled "Present Levels" or "Present Levels of Educational Performance" address?**

   A. Academic achievement and functional performance

   B. English as a second language

   C. Functional performance

   D. Academic achievement

Answer: A. Academic achievement and functional performance

Individualized Education Plans (IEPS) continue to have multiple sections. One section, present levels, now addresses academic achievement and functional performance. Annual IEP goals must now address the same areas.

(Average)

3. **Which of the following must be provided in a written notice to parents when proposing a child's educational placement?**

   A. A list of parental due process safeguards

   B. A list of family services available through the school

   C. A list of persons responsible for the child's education

   D. A list of academic subjects the child has passed

Answer: A. A list of parental due process safeguards

Written notice must be provided to parents prior to a proposal or refusal to initiate or make a change in the child's identification, evaluation, or educational placement. Notices must contain:

- A listing of parental due process safeguards

- A description and a rationale for the chosen action

- A detailed listing of components (e.g., tests, records, reports) that were the basis for the decision

- Assurance that the language and content of the notices were understood by the parents

SKILL 8.3 Integrating best practices, multidisciplinary research, and professional literature into the educational setting

In the education field, best practice is a term usually associated with work that is serious, thoughtful, and informed by current research in teaching and learning. Based on multidisciplinary research, some of the best practices that can be used in the educational setting include problem and project based learning; higher order thinking; active, student-centered learning; collaboration; application of skill and knowledge; and student engagement. In special education, best practices also include a variety of additional tasks, such as aligning instruction with the IEP or 504 Plan and modifying various aspects of the educational environment and/or instruction to meet the special needs of the student.

The current educational reform efforts suggest that many teaching methods based on constructivist principles advance learning in students with special needs more effectively than teaching-by-telling. The social aspect of learning by collaboration and an individual's need to explore and experiment are best directed through instruction based on constructivist theory.

Some of the constructivist-based strategies recognized as best practice include student-centered instruction, experiential and holistic learning, authentic experiences, reflective exercises, social interactions that scaffold learning, collaborative grouping, problem-oriented activities, integrated thematic units, and hands-on learning activities.

Using a mixture of these methods throughout the school year creates a balance of activities for students. These methods also help create a supportive classroom environment. In such an environment, students make choices, take risks comfortably, hold themselves accountable, express themselves in a number of ways, and establish a community of learners.

The most effective teaching environments are student-centered classrooms with an abundance of project-based activities and opportunities for collaboration and scaffolding support for learning strategies and skills. In order to promote problem solving and close the gap between inert knowledge and knowledge application, teachers must anchor instruction within an authentic context that will mirror real-life problems.

Another best practice occurs when teachers build a community of learners. Communities take part in activities together with a shared understanding about what they are doing and what it means to them. Members of the community have a chance to expand both the individual's and the group's knowledge, participate in decision making, take risks without fear of failure, develop expertise, experience a variety of activities, and work on tasks with others.

In special education, best practices include a variety of tasks, such as aligning instruction with the IEP or 504 Plan and modifying various aspects of the educational environment and/or instruction to meet the special needs of the student.

One of the best practices used by technology-integrating teachers is focusing on the curriculum objectives and student disabilities or needs first and then deciding when and if to use technology to help students meet these objectives.

Differentiated instruction is a best practice designed for general education, but it has many implications for teaching students with special needs, whether in the general education classroom or a more restrictive setting, such as a resource room or substantially separate classroom. When using differentiated instruction, a teacher analyzes student differences and needs as a basis for planning lessons that both align with standards and take into account each student's needs. *More detail about differentiated instruction can be found in Skill 9.3.*

Sample Test Question and Rationale

(Easy)

1. **Which of the following teaching activities is LEAST likely to enhance observational learning in students with special needs?**

   A. A verbal description of the task to be performed, followed by having the children immediately attempt to perform the instructed behavior

   B. A demonstration of the behavior, followed by an immediate opportunity for the children to imitate the behavior

   C. A simultaneous demonstration and explanation of the behavior, followed by ample opportunity for the children to rehearse the instructed behavior

   D. Physically guiding the children through the behavior to be imitated, while verbally explaining the behavior

Answer: A. A verbal description of the task to be performed, followed by having the children immediately attempt to perform the instructed behavior

Students are given verbal instructions only. The children are not given a chance to observe or see the behavior so that they can imitate it. Some of the students may have hearing deficiencies, or specific learning disabilities that require hands on or multisensory presentations.

COMPETENCY 9
CURRICULUM AND INSTRUCTION AND THEIR IMPLEMENTATION ACROSS THE CONTINUUM OF EDUCATIONAL SETTINGS

Instructional alternatives to help students with learning problems may be referred to as compensatory techniques, instructional adaptations, accommodations, or modifications. A problem-solving approach to determining what modifications should be made centers around the following:

1. The requirements of the course (often state or local standards and objectives)

2. The requirement(s) that the student is not meeting

3. Factors interfering with the student's meeting the requirements

4. Identification of possible modifications or accommodations

Many of the adaptations and modifications helpful to students with disabilities can be seen in terms of Cummins' (1994) analysis of the cognitive demands of a task or lesson. Such adaptations can be designed to either lighten the cognitive burden of a task or make it easier for the student to carry that burden. Cummins' work with students with limited English proficiency (LEP) led him to analyze tasks in terms of two variables: amount of context and cognitive demand. Lessons or tasks that have a lot of context for a student will be easier for that student than tasks with little or no context. The more context, the easier the task.

COGNITIVE DEMAND is a measure of how much information must be processed quickly. A cognitively demanding task requires processing lots of information all at once or in rapid succession and is more demanding or difficult. Cognitively undemanding tasks or lessons present only single pieces of information or concepts to process, and they separate tasks or lessons into discrete, small steps. When making changes to accommodate students with special needs, it is helpful to focus on changes that will move the task or lesson from a cognitively demanding, low-context arena to one of high context and reduced cognitive demand.

Adaptations or changes designed to help the student(s) meet the requirements of a class or standard can take place in a number of areas of curriculum and setting. The following are some of the primary areas in which a special education teacher may need to make changes: the learning environment, methods of instruction and presentation, materials and texts, lesson content, assessment and testing, use of assistive technology, and staff collaboration.

Adapting the overall instructional environment

The teacher can modify the classroom instructional environment in several ways.

Individual student variables

Some students with disabilities benefit from sitting close to the teacher or away from windows. Others (with ADHD, for example) might benefit from wiggle seats or fiddle objects, still others from an FM system or cubicles that reduce distractions. Seating that reduces distractions serves also to reduce the cognitive load of lessons by removing the need for the students to block distractions themselves.

> **COGNITIVE DEMAND:** a measure of how much information must be processed quickly

Classroom organization

Many students with learning disabilities benefit from a highly structured environment in which physical areas (e.g., supplies, reading, math, writing) are clearly labeled and a schedule for the day prominently displayed. Individual schedule charts can be useful if some students follow different schedules, such as leaving periodically for a resource room or specialized therapy. Such schedules reduce the cognitive load required to simply get through the day and provide increased context for the student navigating the daily routine.

The teacher can also vary grouping arrangements (e.g., large group, small group, peer tutoring, or learning centers) with student needs in mind. Five basic types of grouping arrangements are typically used in the classroom, outlined in the following paragraphs.

Large group with teacher

Examples of appropriate activities include show and tell, discussions, watching plays or movies, brainstorming ideas, and playing games. In general education classrooms, science, social studies, and most content area subjects are taught in large groups. The advantage of large-group instruction is that it is time-efficient and prepares students for higher levels of secondary and postsecondary education settings. However, with large groups, instruction cannot be as easily differentiated or tailored to individual student needs or learning styles. Mercer and Mercer (1985) recommend the following guidelines for effective large-group instruction:

- Keep instruction short, ranging from five to fifteen minutes for first grade to seventh grade; five to forty minutes for grades eight to twelve

- Use questions to involve all students, use lecture-pause routines, and encourage active participation among the lower-performing students

- Incorporate visual aids to promote understanding and maintain a lively pace

- Break up the presentation with different rates of speaking, giving students a "stretch break," varying voice volume, etc.

- Establish rules of conduct for large groups and praise students who follow the rules

When students with special needs are included in large group instruction, care must be taken to conduct the activity with their needs in mind. For example, if a particular student may have a limited recall or understanding of a subject, it can be useful to ask the student a concrete question or let the student answer before anyone else so his or her answer is not "taken" by someone else. Choral responses regarding key points can help provide context and support for students with some disabilities, as well.

Small group instruction

Small group instruction usually includes five to seven students and is recommended for teaching basic academic skills such as math facts or reading, and for introducing many abstract content area concepts. This model is especially effective for students with learning problems. Composition of the groups should be flexible to accommodate different rates of progress through instruction. Some of the advantages of teaching in small groups are that the teacher is better able to tailor the instruction to the special needs of certain students, provide feedback, monitor student progress, and give more individual attention and praise. With small groups, the teacher must provide a steady pace for the lesson, provide questions and activities that allow all to participate, and include lots of positive praise. Small groups can also make differentiated instruction easier and more practical.

One student with teacher

One-to-one tutorial teaching can be used to provide extra assistance to individual students. Such tutoring may be scheduled at set times during the day or provided as the need arises. The tutoring model is typically found more often in elementary and resource classrooms than in secondary settings and is particularly effective for students with certain disabilities.

Peer tutoring

In an effective peer tutoring arrangement, the teacher trains the peer tutors and matches them with students who need extra practice and assistance. In addition to academic skills, the arrangement can help both students work on social skills such as cooperation and self-esteem. Both students may be working on the same material or the tutee may be working to strengthen areas of weakness. The teacher determines the target goals, selects the material, sets up the guidelines, trains the student tutors in the rules and methods of the sessions, and monitors and evaluates the sessions. Care must be taken, however, to avoid the appearance that some students are smarter than others and that the "smarter" students have more work because of the "slower" students. It can be very helpful if the teacher can find something that allows the tutee in one situation to act as tutor in another.

Cooperative learning

Cooperative learning differs from peer tutoring in that students are grouped in teams or small groups and the methods are based on teamwork, individual accountability, and team reward. Individual students are responsible for their own learning and share of the work as well as the group's success. As with peer tutoring, the goals, target skills, materials, and guidelines are developed by the teacher. Teamwork skills may also need to be taught. By focusing on team goals, all members of the team are encouraged to help each other as well as improve their individual performance. When students with disabilities are included in such cooperative teams, it is imperative that the teacher arrange the tasks so that there is something substantive and important for each member of the group to contribute.

Classroom management

The teacher can vary grading systems, reinforcement systems, and even the rules to accommodate the varying needs of the students. Early teaching and practice of daily classroom routines can be particularly helpful to students with certain learning disabilities or emotional problems. It may be helpful to pay extra attention to the transitions between tasks, lessons, or parts of the day. Some students benefit from having clear stimuli (e.g., a bell, hand signal, or flag) to signal changes and transitions. Attention and time spent on such routines early in the year can pay big dividends in classroom management later in the year. The specific techniques required will depend upon the needs of the students.

See Skills 11.1 and 11.2 for more information on classroom management.

Methods of presentation of subject matter

The teacher can vary the method of presentation of new material in many ways depending upon the specific needs of the students. In general, subject matter should be presented in a fashion that helps students organize, understand, and remember important information. Students with learning disabilities will often benefit from hands-on, multimodal presentation and interaction with new concepts and materials. It is helpful if the goal of the lesson and the most important points are clearly stated at the start. Students with learning disabilities also benefit from material that is presented one concept at a time (this reduces cognitive demand). Advance organizers and other instructional devices can

- Connect information to what is already known (increases context)

- Make abstract ideas more concrete (reduces cognitive demand)

- Capture students' interest in the material

- Help students organize the information and visualize the relationships (increases context and reduces demand)

Organizers can be visual aids—such as diagrams, tables, charts, and guides—or verbal cues that alert students to the nature and content of the lesson. Organizers may be used:

- Before the lesson to alert the student to the main point of the lesson, establish a rationale for learning, and activate background information

- During the lesson to help students organize information, keep focused on important points, and aid comprehension

- **At the close of the lesson** to summarize and remember important points

Examples of organizers include the following:

- Question and graphic-oriented study guide.

- Concept diagramming: Students brainstorm a concept and organize information into three lists (always present, sometimes present, and never present).

- Semantic feature analysis: Students construct a table with examples of the concept in one column and important features or characteristics in the opposite column. This table can involve words, pictures, or even concrete objects, as necessary to meet the individual student's needs.

- Semantic webbing: The concept (in word, picture or object) is placed in the middle of the chart or chalkboard and relevant information is placed around it. Lines show the relationships. Color coding and letting students physically attach string or pipe cleaners to make the web can increase context and make the conceptual relationships more concrete.

- Memory (mnemonic) devices.

- Diagrams, charts, and tables.

More information on instructional design and presentation can be found in Skills 9.2 and 9.3.

Instructional materials

In many school systems the textbooks and primary instructional materials have been chosen by the school, though the teacher may also be able to select additional materials. Although specialized materials for certain special needs (e.g., large print or CDs for students with visual disabilities or dyslexia) may be available, it is usually necessary for the teachers to modify instructional materials and texts for their students with special needs. It may be necessary to enlarge the print on a worksheet or text not available in large print, or to provide additional diagrams or rearrange text on the page for students with organizational difficulties. Students with certain visual or writing difficulties may not be able to copy math problems from a book, or may need larger numbers or space for their work.

Though the specific modifications will depend upon individual student needs, one of the most common requirements will be finding or revising text for learners who cannot read at grade level or who have difficulty comprehending what they read in content areas such as science and social studies. The most common specific learning disabilities involve reading difficulties. In order for such students to have equal access to the grade level curriculum in content areas, it is often necessary to revise printed material so students can access it at their reading comprehension level. Whether selecting published materials or revising them for the students, these guidelines should be followed in order to increase context, reduce cognitive demand, and provide content material that students with learning disabilities can access.

- Avoid complex sentences with many relative clauses

- Avoid the passive tense

- Try to make the topic sentence the first sentence in a paragraph

- Make sure paragraphs have a concluding sentence that restates the topic sentence in another way

- Use simple, declarative sentences that have only one main idea or concept at a time

- Use simple, single syllable, concrete words rather than more complex words (e.g., "an arduous journey" should be "a hard trip")

- Eliminate nonessential information in favor of the main concepts necessary to teach

- Try to use only one tense in all the sentences

- Add diagrams and illustrations whenever possible and deliver information through labels rather than complete sentences

- Whenever possible, include multisensory elements and multimodalities in the presentation

- Avoid unfamiliar names and terms that will "tie up" the students' cognitive efforts (e.g., while the student is trying to figure out how to read the name "Aloicious" he or she will miss the point of the sentence; change the name to "Al")

Methods of practice and retention

Many of the common review and practice methods used in general education classrooms are suitable for students with special needs. Others will need modification. Each daily lesson should begin with a review of the important facts, rules, and concepts of the previous lesson. The review may incorporate questions from the teacher, a brief quiz, checking homework, and feedback on homework. On the basis of the students' responses to the questions, the teacher can adjust the instruction of the lesson to go over areas that were not mastered or retained.

Reviews of the lesson can also be in the in the form of a synopsis and teacher questioning at the end of the lesson to see whether the students have learned the material. At the beginning of the next day, if the teacher sees that the students responded correctly at the end of the previous lesson, but not in the day-after review, they may need to work on retention strategies. Students with certain learning disabilities may need to "over learn" new material—that is, additional practice and review may be necessary for them. The teacher may need to alter the amount or content of material to be practiced (limit it to the most essential concepts or skills, for example), the time allowed for practice, or the methods used. Some students may have disabilities that impact their ability to recall information, for example, and their practice may need to involve recognition rather than recall. Many students with learning disabilities need heavy teacher scaffolding support when a skill or concept is first introduced. They may also need a more gradual reduction of scaffolding than their peers without disabilities in order to retain the information.

Homework provides review opportunities for independent practice. Review should be done on a daily basis, with weekly and monthly cumulative reviews to provide information on retention of knowledge and opportunities to "over learn" the materials. It may be necessary to modify the homework assigned to students with learning disabilities. In many cases students with certain learning or emotional disabilities cannot handle the same level of homework as students without disabilities. In addition, parents may or may not have the skills necessary to help practice the highly specialized lessons some children with learning disabilities need (e.g., specialized phoneme awareness practice).

Students can also review and practice skills in peer tutoring, cooperative learning arrangements, and individual student seatwork. When errors are observed, teachers should find opportunities to teach the materials again. By immediately correcting the errors, the student is not inadvertently reinforced for the wrong process. Opportunities to reteach can also appear in student questions about present material that refer back to previous material.

Lesson content

Although the content of the curriculum is usually dictated by state or local standards, the teacher of students with special needs will often need to modify the content through differentiated instruction in order for the students to access it. Modifications in curriculum are sometimes required by a student's IEP (*see Skill 9.1*). In addition, student learning disabilities may require the teacher to modify the lesson content so as to reduce the cognitive demands on the student. *More detailed information on using differentiated instruction to do this is provided in Skill 9.3.*

Assessment

Teachers of students with special needs will frequently find it necessary to modify their assessment techniques and procedures in order to accurately assess the students' knowledge and skills. This section lists common kinds of accommodations and modifications needed in special education. *More detail on assessment in general can be found in the sections on Skills 10.1, 10.2, and 10.3.*

Because certain disabilities can interfere with performance on an assessment, it is often necessary for the teacher to break down the task or skill and test each part separately. Many of the common accommodations and modifications in testing are designed to separate the specific skill or knowledge being tested from some other ability or skill impacted by a disability. For example, when testing a student with dyslexia on retention of a concept in science, it would be inappropriate to use a reading/writing assessment. The student's response to a written test would be confounded by the inability to read the test or to compose readable written responses. In such cases an oral exam might more accurately assess the student's science knowledge.

Accommodations or modifications in assessment usually fall into the following categories:

- **Setting:** Changes in the location of the testing, such as separate seating or room, special lighting of noise buffers, adaptive furniture, small group or one-to-one testing.

- **Timing and scheduling:** Changes in the duration or time of the test, such as allowing extra time or an absence of time limits, frequent breaks, or scheduling the test at a time of day when a student functions best (for example, when he or she has had specific medication).

- **Presentation of test:** Changes in how the test is given to a student, such as oral testing, large print or Braille, sign language, colored overlays or special paper, etc. This would also include allowing the teacher to clarify directions or read the test to the student.

- **Student responses:** Changes in how the student is allowed to respond to the test, such as allowing oral responses, multiple choice rather than essay, dictating open responses, use of assistive devices such as computer keyboards, spell checkers, writing software, etc.

In many cases such accommodations and modifications will be specified in a student's IEP, and the teacher is legally responsible to see that the required accommodations are made both in classroom assessments and in district wide testing.

SKILL 9.1 The individualized family service plan (IFSP) and the individualized education program (IEP) process

IFSP (INDIVIDUALIZED FAMILY SERVICE PLAN): an IDEA-mandated legal document meant to summarize relevant assessments and diagnoses, determine needed services, and provide a structure for the implementation of those services for children from birth to age three

IEP (INDIVIDUALIZED EDUCATION PLAN): an IDEA-mandated legal document meant to summarize relevant assessments and diagnoses, determine needed services, and provide a structure for the implementation of those services for school-age children aged three to twenty-one

The IFSP (for children, birth to age threee) and the IEP (for school age children, age three to twenty-one) are both mandated by the IDEA. They are legal documents meant to summarize relevant assessments and diagnoses, determine needed services, and provide a structure for the implementation of those services.

The IFSP focuses on a child's family as a whole in the context of daily life and preparation for school. It is designed for children who are diagnosed with a disability or a developmental delay or who are determined to be "at risk" for a delay or disability. The plan is developed when someone close to the child (parent, doctor, social worker, etc.) brings their concerns to the state health department and a team of specialists, parents, and family members meets to evaluate the child's needs.

The IFSP usually includes statements of the child's levels of cognitive, language, communication, physical, and emotional functioning, as well as diagnoses of any specific problems. The plan also lists needed services and methods by which these services will be delivered. The IFSP often leads to IEP development when the child enters school.

An IEP is the document that forms the basis for special services and instruction in the educational setting. An IEP is developed when someone (e.g., parent, teacher, specialist) asks for a meeting to consider the child's needs. Typical "team" members at a meeting include parents (and sometimes parent advocates), a general education teacher familiar with state standards, any special education teachers involved, specialists who can test or interpret tests for the team, and a representative of the school district. The child may also be present, especially in secondary education.

If the team determines that the child is eligible for special education services, an IEP is written. According to IDEA, each IEP must contain the following:

- A statement of the present levels of educational performance of the child

- A statement of annual goals, including short-term instructional objectives

- A statement of the specific educational services to be provided to the child, and the extent to which the child will be able to participate in regular educational programs

- The projected date for initiation and anticipated duration of such services

- Appropriate objective criteria and evaluation procedures and schedules for determining, on at least an annual basis, whether instructional objectives are being achieved

- Instructional and program accommodations and supports that must be provided throughout the educational settings and, specifically, in state- and district-mandated testing

- A clear rationale for any placement that involves nonparticipation in any part of the general education classroom

- Transition services, as appropriate and needed

All teachers and staff who interact with a child on an IEP are required to follow the dictates of the IEP. In addition to goals and objectives, the IEP will specify what accommodations or instructional modifications are to be provided to the child. Accommodations usually concern access to the curriculum. A child with accommodations to access the curriculum will follow the same grade level standards and goals as general education students and be graded on the same scale. Modifications usually refer to changes that significantly alter the standards, content, instructional level, or performance level required of the student. This means the student will be graded differently than grade peers. Whatever terminology is used, these distinctions are important, and it is the teacher's responsibility to be familiar with all aspects of the IEP, so as to ensure compliance with it.

Sample Test Question and Rationale

(Rigorous)

1. **The minimum number of IEP meetings required per year is:**

    A. As many as necessary

    B. One

    C. Two

    D. Three

Answer: B. One

P. L. 99-457 IDEA (1986) requires at least an annual IEP meeting.

SKILL 9.2 Instructional development and implementation *(e.g., instructional activities, curricular materials and resources, working with classroom and support personnel, tutoring options)*

Teaching was once seen as developing lesson plans, teaching, going home early, and taking the summer off. However, the demands of a classroom involve much more than grading papers. National and state learning standards must be taken into account because not only will the teacher and students be measured by the students' scores at the end of the year, the school will also be graded. Teachers must be knowledgeable about state and local standards and skilled at structuring their own classes in ways that will meet those frameworks.

On the large scale, the teacher must think about the scope of his or her plans for the day, the week, the unit, the semester, and the year. The teacher must decide on the subject matter for the unit, semester, and year, making certain that it is appropriate to the age of the students, relevant to their real lives, and in their realm of anticipated interest. Should the teacher introduce politically controversial issues or avoid them? He or she must make these decisions deliberatively on the basis of feedback from students and, at the same time, keep sight of his or her objectives.

The chosen curriculum should introduce information in a cumulative sequence and not introduce too much new information at a time. Review difficult material and practice to aid retention. New vocabulary and symbols should be introduced one at a time, and the relationships of components to the whole should be stressed. Students' background information should be recalled to connect new information to the old. Finally, teach strategies or algorithms first and then move on to tasks that are more difficult.

Creating Goals and Objectives

The teacher must be very skilled at writing academic objectives that fall within the guidelines of the state and local expectations. In addition, these objectives must be measurable so that, when the unit or semester is complete, he or she can know for sure whether or not goals have been met. Once long range goals have been identified and established, the teacher must ensure that all goals and objectives are in conjunction with student ability and needs. Some objectives may be too basic for a higher level student, while others cannot be met with a student's current level of knowledge. There are many forms of evaluating student needs to ensure that all goals set are challenging, yet achievable.

The choice of instructional strategy depends primarily on the needs of the students. Teachers should check student cumulative files for reading level and prior subject area achievement. This analysis provides a basis for goal setting but shouldn't be the only method used. Depending on the subject area, a basic skills test, reading level evaluations, writing samples, and interest surveys can all be useful in determining if all goals are appropriate. Informal observation throughout the year should be used to verify these more quantitative analyses. Finally, the teacher must take into consideration the student's level of motivation.

When students with disabilities are involved, information from their individualized education program or individualized family service plans (*see Skill 10.1*) can give the teacher guidelines on what type of instructional modifications are recommended for a particular child. Interviews with the student, when possible, and the student's family, as well as interest inventories can help the teacher select instructional strategies that students identify as helping them learn best. Interest inventories can be teacher-made, commercially prepared, or on computer programs. The teacher can construct a class profile from these inventories.

From the profiles, the teacher should be able to determine learning styles—whether the student is a visual, an auditory, or a kinesthetic learner. With a group of primarily visual learners, for example, a lecture would probably not be very effective unless it were accompanied by visual aids. Students also have preferences for certain types of materials over others, such as manipulative materials over worksheets. The cognitive level of the students will also affect the type of strategy employed.

Students who have difficulty with abstract concepts will need hands-on, concrete instruction strategies to help them make the transition from concrete to semi-concrete to abstract concepts. Using Cuisenaire rods to develop knowledge of fractions is an example of this method. In many classrooms, student abilities will vary and a differentiated form of instruction will be helpful.

A teacher may adapt an objective provided by the state or district in order to meet the needs of their student population. For example, a teacher might adapt the objective *"State five causes of World War II"* to require a higher level of cognitive demand or abstract thought by saying, *"State five causes of World War II and explain how they contributed to the start of the war."* The objective could be modified for a lower level of cognitive demand by saying, *"From a list of causes, pick three that specifically caused World War II." (See Skill 9.3 for more detail on differentiated instruction.)*

The type of task also influences choice of instructional strategy. Teaching a mnemonic device is effective in helping students remember the names of the planets in order, whereas an outline is more useful for reviewing a history chapter. Other factors influencing choice of strategy involve students' frustration level, motivation, and attitude towards the task. The need for supervision and assistance, the ability to work independently or in groups, and variations in time needed to complete the task also affect choice of strategy.

When organizing and sequencing objectives, remember that skills are building blocks. A taxonomy of educational objectives, such as that provided by Bloom (1956), can be helpful in constructing and organizing objectives. Simple, factual knowledge of material is low on this cognitive taxonomy and should be worked with early in the sequence (for example, memorizing definitions or famous quotes). Eventually, objectives should be developed to include higher level thinking such as comprehension (i.e., being able to use a definition); application (i.e.,

When organizing and sequencing objectives, remember that skills are building blocks. A taxonomy of educational objectives, such as that provided by Bloom, can be helpful in constructing and organizing objectives.

being able to apply the definition to other situations); synthesis (i.e., being able to add other information); and evaluation (i.e., being able to judge the value of something).

Emergent Curriculum

EMERGENT CURRICULUM describes the projects and themes that classrooms embark on that have been inspired by the children's interests. This approach can be useful in overall curriculum design. Teachers use all the tools of assessment available to discover as much as they can about their students, and then continually assess the students throughout the unit or semester. As the teachers get to know the students, they listen to what their interests are and create a curriculum in response to what they learn from observations of their own students.

Webbing is a recent concept related to the idea of emergent curriculum. The two main uses are planning and recording curriculum. PLANNING WEBS are used to generate ideas for activities and projects for the children from an observed interest such as rocks. Teachers can work together to come up with ideas and activities for the children and to record them in a web format. Activities can be grouped by different areas of the room or by developmental domains. For example, clusters fall either under areas such as dramatic play or science areas or around domains such as language, cognitive, and physical development. Either configuration works; being consistent in each web is important. This format will work as a unit, weekly, or monthly program plan. Any new activities that emerge throughout the unit can also be added to the web. The record will serve in the future to plan activities that emerge from the children's play and ideas.

Lesson Plan Development

Lesson plans are important in guiding instruction in the classroom. Incorporating the nuts and bolts of a teaching unit, the LESSON PLAN outlines the steps of teacher implementation and assessment of the teacher's instructional effectiveness and student learning success. Teachers are able to objectify and quantify learning goals and targets in terms of incorporating effective performance-based assessments and projected criteria for identifying when a student has learned the material presented. All components of a lesson plan—including the unit description, learning targets, learning experiences, explanation of learning rationale, and assessments—must be present to provide both quantifiable and qualitative data to ascertain whether student learning has taken place and whether effective teaching has occurred for the students.

EMERGENT CURRICULUM: projects and themes that classrooms embark on that have been inspired by the children's interests

PLANNING WEBS: used to generate ideas for activities and projects for the children from an observed interest such as rocks

LESSON PLAN: outlines the steps of teacher implementation and assessment of the teacher's instructional effectiveness and student learning success

Effective lesson plans will generally include the following in some form:

- Quizzes or reviews of the previous lesson

- Step-by-step presentations with multiple examples

- Guided practice and feedback

- Independent practice that requires the student to produce faster, increasingly independent (reduced scaffolding) responses

A typical format for a written lesson plan describing what is being taught and how the students will be able to access the information would include the following items:

1. **Unit description:** Describes the learning and classroom environment.

   A. **Classroom characteristics:** Describe the physical arrangements of the classroom and the student grouping patterns for the lesson being taught. Classroom rules and consequences should be clearly posted and visible.

   B. **Student characteristics:** Demographics of the classroom that include student number, gender, and cultural and ethnic backgrounds and students with IEPs.

2. **Learning goals, targets, and objectives:** What are the expectations of the lessons? Are the learning goals appropriate to the state learning standards and district academic goals? Are the targets appropriate for the grade level and subject content area and inclusive of a multicultural perspective and global viewpoint?

3. **Learning experiences for student:** How will student learning be supported using the learning goals?

   A. What prior knowledge or experiences will the students bring to the lesson? How will you check and verify that student knowledge?

   B. How will you engage all students in the classroom? How will students who have been identified as marginalized in the classroom be engaged in the lesson unit?

   C. How will the lesson plan be modified for students with IEPs, and how will independent education students be evaluated for learning and processing the modified lesson targets?

   D. How will the multicultural aspect be incorporated into the lesson plan?

   E. What interdisciplinary connections will be used to incorporate other subject areas?

   F. What types of assessments and evaluations will be used to test student understanding and processing of the lesson plan?

   G. How will students be cooperatively grouped to engage in the lesson?

4. **Rationales for learning experiences:** Provide data on how the lesson plan addresses student learning goals and objectives. Address whether the lesson provides accommodations for students with IEPs and provides support for marginalized students in the classroom.

5. **Assessments:** Construct pre- and post-assessments that evaluate student learning as it correlates to the learning goals and objectives. Do the assessments include a cultural integration that address the cultural needs and inclusion of students? Do assessments incorporate accommodations needed by students with special needs?

In designing lesson plans teachers should keep the following principles in mind:

Vary assignments

A variety of assignments on the same content allows students to match learning styles and preferences with the assignment. If all assignments are writing assignments, for example, students who are hands-on or visual learners are at a disadvantage unrelated to the content base itself. *See Skill 9.3 for more information on how to vary learning tasks.*

Cooperative learning

COOPERATIVE LEARNING activities allow students to share ideas, expertise, and insight in a non-threatening setting. The focus tends to remain on positive learning rather than on competition.

Structured environment

Some students need and benefit from clear structure that defines the expectations and goals of the teacher. The student knows what is expected and when and can work and plan accordingly.

Clearly stated assignments

Assignments should be clearly stated along with the expectation and criteria for completion. Reinforcement and practice activities should not be a guessing game for the students. Many students with special needs benefit from written, step by step instructions and printed rubrics they can use to check off their tasks as they proceed. The exception is, of course, those situations in which a discovery method is used.

Independent practice

INDEPENDENT PRACTICE involving application and repetition is necessary for thorough learning. These activities should always be within the student's abilities to perform successfully without assistance. Students with special needs often benefit from STAGED INDEPENDENT PRACTICE, where the teacher provides scaffolding to start, then gradually fades out the support until the student is working as independently as possible.

Repetition

Very little learning is successful with a single exposure. Learners generally require multiple exposures to the same information for learning to take place. However, this repetition does not have to be dull and monotonous. Varied assignments can provide repetition of content or skill practiced without repetition of specific activities. This method helps keep learning fresh and exciting for the student.

Overlearning

As a principle of effective learning, OVERLEARNING recommends that students continue to study and review after they have achieved initial mastery. The use of repetition in the context of varied assignments offers the means to help students pursue and achieve overlearning. Many students with learning and memory disabilities will have some form of overlearning prescribed in their IEPs.

Lesson Plan Collaboration

According to Walther-Thomas et al (2000), ongoing professional development that provides teachers with opportunities to create effective instructional practice is vital and necessary. "A comprehensive approach to professional development is perhaps the most critical dimension of sustained support for successful program implementation." The inclusive approach incorporates learning programs that include all stakeholders in defining and developing high quality programs for students. The figure below shows how an integrated approach of stakeholders can provide the optimal learning opportunity for all students.

Figure 1: Integrated Approach to Learning

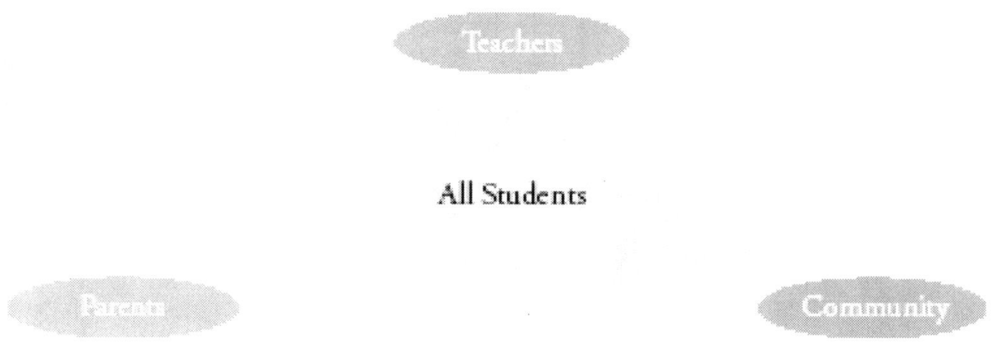

STAGED INDEPENDENT PRACTICE: an approach to student activities in which the teacher provides scaffolding to start, then gradually fades out the support until the student is working as independently as possible

OVERLEARNING: a principle of effective learning that recommends students continue to study and review after they have achieved initial mastery

---

In this integrated approach to learning, teachers, parents, and community support become joint contributors to student learning. The focus and central core of the school community is triangular as a representation of how effective collaboration can work in creating success for student learners. The goal of student learning and achievement now becomes the heart of the school community.

For teachers, having a collaborative approach to instruction fosters for students a deeper appreciation of learning, subject matter, and knowledge acquisition. Implementing a consistent approach to learning from all stakeholders helps create equitable educational opportunities for all learners.

Research has shown that educators who collaborate become more diversified and effective in implementing curriculum and assessing effective instructional practices. Gaining additional insight into how students learn and modalities of differing learning styles can increase a teacher's capacity to develop effective instruction methods. Teachers who team teach or have daily networking opportunities can create a portfolio of curriculum articulation and inclusion for students.

People in business are always encouraged to network in order to further their careers. The same can be said for teaching. If English teachers get together and discuss what is going on in their classrooms, those discussions make the whole much stronger than the parts. Even if no formal opportunities for such networking exist, schools or even individual teachers should develop them and seek them out.

Sample Test Question and Rationale

(Rigorous)

1. **The Integrated approach to learning utilizes all resources available to address student needs. What are the resources?**

   A. The student, his/her parents, and the teacher

   B. The teacher, the parents, and the special education team

   C. The teacher the student, and an administrator to perform needed interventions

   D. The student, his/her parents, the teacher and community resources

Answer: D. The student, his/her parents, the teacher and community resources

The integrated response encompasses all possible resources including the resources in the community.

> **SKILL 9.3** **Teaching strategies and methods** *(e.g., modifications of materials and equipment, learning centers, facilitated groups, study skills groups, self-management, cooperative learning, diagnostic-prescriptive method, modeling, skill drill, guided practice, concept generalization, learning strategy instruction, and direct instruction)*

No two students are alike. It follows, then, that no students learn alike. To apply a one-dimensional instructional approach and a strict tunnel vision perspective of testing is to impose learning limits on students. All students have the right to an education, but there cannot be a singular path to that education. A teacher must acknowledge the variety of learning styles and abilities among students within a class (and, indeed, the varieties from class to class) and apply multiple instructional and assessment processes to ensure that every child has appropriate opportunities to master the subject matter, demonstrate such mastery, and improve and enhance learning skills with each lesson.

It has been traditionally assumed that a teacher will use direct instruction in the classroom. The amount of time devoted to it will vary according to the age of the class as well as other factors. Lecturing can be very valuable because it's the quickest way to transfer knowledge to students and they can learn note-taking and information-organizing skills in this way. However, teachers should be very cautious about using very much lecture in a class of any age. In the first place, the attention span even of senior high school students is short when they are using only one sense—the sense of hearing. Teachers should limit the use of lecture compared to other methods and limit the length of all lectures.

Students' attitudes and perceptions about learning are powerful factors influencing academic focus and success. When instructional objectives center on students' interests and are relevant to their lives, effective learning is more likely to occur. If a student thinks a task is unimportant, he or she will not put much effort into it. If students think they lack the ability or resources to successfully complete tasks, even attempting the tasks becomes too great a risk. Not only must teachers understand the students' abilities and interests, they must also help students develop positive attitudes and perceptions about tasks and learning.

> *A teacher must acknowledge the variety of learning styles and abilities among students within a class (and, indeed, the varieties from class to class) and apply multiple instructional and assessment processes to ensure that every child has appropriate opportunities to master the subject matter, demonstrate such mastery, and improve and enhance learning skills with each lesson.*

Differentiated Instruction

In recent years, increasing emphasis has been put on incorporating at least some principles of differentiated instruction into classrooms with students of mixed ability. Tomlinson (2001) states that teachers must first determine where the students are with reference to an objective, then tailor specific lesson plans and learning activities to help each student learn as much as possible about that objective. The effective teacher seeks to connect all students to the subject matter through multiple techniques with the goal that each student will relate to one or more techniques and excel in the learning process. Differentiated instruction encompasses modifying curriculum in several areas.

Content

What is the teacher going to teach? Or, perhaps better put, what does the teacher want the students to learn? Differentiating content means that students have access to aspects of the content that pique their interest, with a complexity that provides an appropriate challenge to their intellectual development, but does not go beyond their frustration level. When students with special needs are included in a classroom, this often means modifying a lesson plan so that it has several levels. One common way to structure such levels is outlined below.

MULTI-LEVEL LESSON PLAN

Basic Level

A basic level might address the content of the objective at a cognitively less demanding level (e.g., knowledge, the lowest level on Bloom's taxonomy). Example: The student or student group matches names to planets on a diagram, or they correctly define key vocabulary.

Moderate Level

A moderate level could address the content at a higher level than basic, but still a fairly low level (e.g., comprehension). Example: After learning that the Earth orbits the sun due to the Sun's greater gravity, challenge the student or student group to give other examples of objects orbiting others and explain why in their own words.

Mastery Level

A mastery level might address the objective at the level most students should reach given state standards (e.g., analysis). Example: The student or student group compares two planets based on a set of variables.

Advanced Level

An advanced level would address the objective at a higher level aimed at gifted students who can go beyond the required curriculum (e.g., the highest level on Bloom, evaluation). Example: The student or student group is given a real or fictional theory of planetary movement and asked to evaluate its accuracy in light of the facts they have learned in the unit.

Process

The classroom management techniques where instructional organization and delivery are maximized for the diverse student group. These techniques should include dynamic, flexible grouping activities, where instruction and learning occur as whole-class, teacher-led activities; and in a variety of small group settings, such as teacher-guided small group, peer learning and teaching (while teacher observes and coaches), or independent centers or pairs. Such techniques should also include strategies for anchor activities and smooth transitions from activity to activity.

Product

The expectations and requirements placed on students to demonstrate their knowledge or understanding. The type of product expected from each student should reflect that student's own capabilities. When working with students with special needs, the student's IEP will provide guidelines on the best way to assess the student's progress and any testing accommodations that must be made. *(See Skill 9.4 for common testing accommodations.)*

Alternative Assessments

In ALTERNATIVE ASSESSMENT, students create an answer or a response to a question or task. In traditional, inflexible assessments, students choose a prepared response from among a selection of responses, such as matching, multiple-choice, and true or false. When implemented effectively, an alternative assessment approach will exhibit the following characteristics, among others:

ALTERNATIVE ASSESSMENT: a question or task that requires a student-created answer

- Requires higher-order thinking and problem solving

- Provides opportunities for student self-reflection and self-assessment

- Uses real world applications to connect students to the subject

- Provides opportunities for students to learn and examine subjects on their own and collaborate with their peers

- Encourages students to continue learning beyond the requirements of the assignment

- Clearly defines objective and performance goals

- Allows students to demonstrate their knowledge using their individual strengths rather than through a "one size fits all" method

Teachers are learning the value of giving assessments that meet the individual abilities and needs of students. After the teacher has provided instruction, discussion, questioning, and practice, rather than assigning one task to all students, he or she asks students to generate tasks that will show their knowledge of the information presented. Students are given choices and, thereby, have the opportunity to demonstrate more effectively the skills, concepts, or topics that they as individuals have learned. For example, following a unit on the life of a famous historical figure, students might choose from among "tests" such as a traditional written report, a poster illustrating important events and contributions of the individual, a timeline of event, a cause and effect web or diagram analyzing the individual's contributions, a skit or oral presentation, a comic book style summary, etc. It has been established that student choice increases student originality, intrinsic motivation, and higher mental processes.

Preparing Students for Test-taking Situations

Test taking is not a pleasant experience for many students with behavioral or learning disabilities. They may lack study skills, experience anxiety before or during a test, or have problems understanding and differentiating the task requirements for different tests. Details in Skill 9.4 outline common accommodations students may need for tests, and alternative assessments (above) can also help, but the teacher can help students learn to cope with tests in other ways, as well.

Some of the ways that teachers can help students be more successful test takers include the following lessons throughout instruction:

- Help students get used to timed tests with timed practice tests.

- Provide study guides before tests.

- Make tests easier to read by leaving ample space between the questions.

- Modify multiple choice tests by reducing the number of choices, reforming questions to yes-no, or using matching items.

- Modify short-answer tests with cloze (fill-in) statements, or provide a word bank of facts or choices from which the student may choose.

- Essay tests can be modified by using partial outlines for the student to complete, allowing additional time, or test items that do not require extensive writing.

- When practicing test-taking skills, the teacher can gradually reduce the amount of scaffolding or context for students who are successful, enabling them to eventually be successful on more standard tests. Some students with special needs, however, will continue to need accommodations.

Sample Test Questions and Rationale

(Easy)

1. Teaching techniques that stimulate active participation and understanding in the mathematics class include all but which of the following?

   A. Having students copy computation facts for a set number of times

   B. Asking students to find the error in an algorithm

   C. Giving immediate feedback to students

   D. Having students chart their progress

   Answer: A. Having students copy computation facts for a set number of times

   Copying does not stimulate participation or understanding.

(Easy)

2. The social skills of students with mental retardation disabilities are likely to be appropriate for children of their mental age, rather than chronological age. This means that the teacher whose class contains children with these disabilities will need to do all of the following except:

   A. Model desired behavior

   B. Provide clear instructions

   C. Expect age appropriate behaviors

   D. Adjust the physical environment when necessary

   Answer: C. Expect age appropriate behaviors

   Age appropriate in this example refers to the student's mental age or functioning level, not his/her chronological age.

SKILL 9.4 Instructional format and components *(e.g., small- and large-group instruction, facilitated group strategies, functional academics, general academics with focus on special education, ESL and limited English proficiency, language and literacy acquisition, self-care and daily living skills, prevocational and vocational skills)*

Grouping Students

Several methods of grouping students are discussed in Skill 11.1. As noted in that Skill section, small group instruction is excellent for teaching basic skills such as math, reading, and writing, and it is particularly effective with students with learning disabilities. Some students' IEPs will, in fact, require small group instruction for some or all subjects. When using small group instruction, it is necessary to determine the criteria for assigning students to each group.

In past classroom practices, it was common for students to be grouped according to ability. This practice is sometimes referred to as tracking or homogenous grouping. For example, students who found math challenging would be in the "low" math group, average math students would be in the "grade-level" math group, and excelling math learners would make up the "advanced" group. Some form of this type of grouping is often used in differentiated instruction. However, this type of grouping can lead to problems with students' self-concept and motivation in class.

Students who found themselves in the low group would feel ashamed or stupid, and the label associated with these students is that they were difficult, incapable, or slow learners. At the same time, students in the advanced group may feel superior and boast their successes in front of other students and feel stressed over the need to perform.

In summary, this type of grouping typically leads to a combination of feelings including resentment, stress, inferiority, and failure—feelings that do not enhance learning. This is not to say that teachers can never group students by ability. If care is taken in the structure and naming of groups, and if groupings vary so a particular child is not always in a group with the same children, these disadvantages can be avoided.

However, teachers often find that heterogeneous grouping (grouping by mixed abilities) allows all students to feel success without the negative effects of homogenous groups. In mixed groups, students can learn from more advanced students, while advanced students still have opportunities to excel in an activity. Cooperative learning is an excellent setting for heterogeneous groups because students work together to solve problems or complete activities while benefiting from all learning abilities. In this setting, all students feel they are successful in their learning, and feelings of confidence, friendship, and achievement are developed.

Procedures for Promoting Positive and Productive Small Group Interactions

Cooperative learning situations, as practiced in today's classrooms, grew out of research conducted by several groups in the early 1970s. Cooperative learning situations can range from very formal applications such as STAD (student teams-achievement divisions) and CIRC (cooperative integrated reading and composition) to less formal groupings known variously as "group investigation," "learning together," or "discovery groups."

Grouping students by ability typically leads to a combination of feelings including resentment, stress, inferiority, and failure—feelings that do not enhance learning.

Cooperative learning as a general term is now firmly recognized and established as a teaching and learning technique in American schools.

Since cooperative learning techniques are so widely used in the schools, it is necessary to orient students in the skills by which cooperative learning groups can operate smoothly and, thereby, enhance learning. Students who cannot interact constructively with other students will not be able to take advantage of the learning opportunities provided by the cooperative learning situations and will furthermore deprive their fellow students of the opportunity for cooperative learning.

These skills form the hierarchy of cooperation in which students first learn to work together as a group, so they may then proceed to levels at which they may engage in simulated conflict situations. In this cooperative setting, teachers and students can constructively investigate different points of view.

To teach cooperative skills, the teacher should

- Ensure that students see the need for the skill

- Ensure that students understand what the skill is and when it should be used

- Set up practice situations and encourage mastery of the skill

- Ensure that students have the time and the needed procedures for discussing (and receiving feedback on) how well they are using the skill

- Ensure that students persevere in practicing the skill until the skill seems a natural action

A further goal of cooperative learning techniques is to establish and enhance mutual respect for other students. Cooperative learning can promote positive social goals when used effectively as a teaching and learning tool. When the teacher promotes interaction of students among ethnic and social groups, students tend to respond positively by forming friendships and having enhanced respect for other sociological groups. Thus, the teacher who effectively manages cooperative learning groups has not only promoted cognitive learning but has also promoted desirable behaviors in terms of mutual respect for all students.

Sample Test Question and Rationale

(Rigorous)

1. **Which type of grouping arrangement would be MOST effective for teaching basic academic skills such as math facts or reading?**

   A. Large group with teacher

   B. Peer tutoring

   C. Small group instruction

   D. Cooperative learning

Answer: C. Small group instruction

Small group instruction usually includes 5 to 7 students and is recommended for teaching basic academic skills such as math facts or reading. This model is especially effective for students with learning problems. Large-group instruction is time efficient and prepares students for higher levels of secondary and post-secondary education settings. However, with large groups, instruction cannot be as easily tailored to high or low levels of students. Peer tutoring is not appropriate for teaching basic concepts. Peer tutoring can be effective in practice and review where the teacher trains the peer tutors and matches them with students who need extra practice and assistance. Cooperative learning differs from peer tutoring in that students are grouped in teams or small groups, and the methods are based on teamwork, individual accountability, and team reward. This approach is appropriate for discovery type lessons, rather than specific instruction in introductory concepts.

SKILL 9.5 Career development and transition issues as related to curriculum design and implementation for students with disabilities according to the criteria of ultimate functioning

Career development is the complex process of acquiring the knowledge, skills, and attitudes necessary to create a plan of choosing and being successful in a particular career field. Career development typically has four stages. The stages of career development are awareness, exploration, preparation, and placement.

Career Awareness

Career awareness activities focus on introducing students to the broad range of career options. First students must be provided with current, in-depth information about careers. This information includes job-related skills, necessary education and training, and a description of typical duties, responsibilities, and tasks. Students must be instructed on how to access the variety of available resources, such as Internet, professional magazines, newspapers, and periodicals. Guest speakers and career fairs are provided so that students can speak with and interview workers with firsthand experiences.

Career Exploration

Career exploration focuses on learning about careers through direct, hands-on activities. This stage is also important for gaining insight into the characteristics of these occupations as well as personal interests and strengths. These activities can be provided through in-school and work-based experiences. In-school activities include contextual learning activities, simulated work experiences, and career fairs. Work-based experiences range from non-paid to paid activities. These activities include job shadowing, mentors, company tours, internship, service learning, cooperative education, and independent study.

Career Preparation

Career preparation provides students with the specific academic and technical knowledge and skills needed for success in a particular occupation. This preparation may include career and technical education programs or postsecondary education. They include the core activities of career assessments (formal and informal) and work-readiness skills (soft-skills development, computer competency, and job search skills). Community organizations, employers, and professional organizations are also available to provide trainings and insight on accommodations that may be provided for students with special needs.

Career Placement

Students transitioning from high school need to work collaboratively with involved parents, teachers, and guidance counselors to enter either the workplace or postsecondary education successfully. Placement should depend on the student's aptitude, skills, experiences, and interest.

Essential Domains of Transition Planning for Students with Disabilities

One of the requirements of a student's IEP is that transition services be included. Transition services will be different for each student. Transition services must take into account the student's interests and preferences. Evaluation of career interests, aptitudes, skills, and training may be considered.

The transition activities that have to be addressed, unless the IEP team finds it uncalled for, are instruction, community experiences, and the development of objectives related to employment and other post-school areas.

Instruction

The instruction part of the transition plan deals with school instruction. The student should have a portfolio completed upon graduation. Students should research and plan for further education and training after high school. Education can be in a college setting, technical school, or vocational center. Goals and objectives created for this transition domain depend upon the nature and severity of the student's disability, the student's interests in further education, plans made for accommodations needed in future education and training, and identification of postsecondary institutions that offer the requested training or education.

Community experiences

This part of the transition plan investigates how the student uses community resources. Resources entail places for recreation, transportation services, agencies, and advocacy services. It is essential for students to deal with the following areas:

- Recreation and leisure: movies, YMCA, religious activities

- Personal and social skills: calling friends, religious groups, going out to eat

- Mobility and transportation: passing a driver's license test or using Dial-A-Ride

- Agency access: using a phone book and making calls

- System advocacy: have a list of advocacy groups to contact

- Citizenship and legal issues: for example, registering to vote

Development of employment

This segment of the transition plan investigates becoming employed. Students should complete a career interest inventory. They should have chances to investigate different careers. Many work skill activities can take place within the classroom, home, and community. Classroom activities may concentrate on

employability skills, community skills, mobility, and vocational training. Home
and neighborhood activities may concentrate on personal responsibility and daily
chores. Community-based activities may focus on part-time work after school and
in the summer, cooperative education or work-study, individualized vocational
training, and volunteer work.

Daily living skills

This segment of the transition plan is also important, although it may not be
included in all IEPs, depending upon the needs of the student. For some students
with disabilities, however, living away from home can be an enormous undertak-
ing. Numerous skills are needed to live and function as an adult. In order to live
as independently as possible, a person should have an income; know how to cook,
clean, shop, pay bills, and get to a job; and have a social life. Some living situations may entail independent living, shared living with a roommate, supported
living, or group homes. Areas that may need to be looked into include personal
and social skills, living options, income and finances, medical needs, community
resources, and transportation.

Resources to help students function effectively in a variety of environments

Vocational training is an important element in transition programs. One of the
first steps in determining the appropriate vocational program entails performing a
functional vocational evaluation. This evaluation gives information about a
student's aptitudes, interests, and skills in relation to employment. It concentrates
on practical skills related to a specific job or goal that a student has. It entails
information that is collected through situational assessments while the student is
on the job. These assessments may include surveys, observations, interviews, and
other methods. The information obtained during the evaluation is used to define
the transition activities needed for the students.

It also provides information on the student's strengths and weaknesses in the vocational area. It includes suggestions regarding potential career paths and training
programs that are deemed appropriate for the student, makes the preparation for
vocational education more precise, and minimizes the possibility that the student
might enter an ill-suited vocational program that doesn't reflect the student's likes
or strengths.

Vocational educators that have knowledge of vocational training and job requirements can help provide career information to students. They can also help develop
realistic assessment activities for students to determine if they have the aptitude or
skills necessary to complete a particular program.

One of the first steps in determining the appropriate vocational program entails performing a functional vocational evaluation.

The transitional plan in the IEP should reflect appropriate vocational training that appeals to the student's aptitude, skills, strengths, and preferences. It should be based on decisions involving a variety of people, including the student, the family, teachers, vocational educators, and other interested parties.

Sample Test Question and Rationale

(Rigorous)

1. **A transition or vocational curriculum approach focuses on:**

   A. Remediation of basic academic skills

   B. Preparation for functioning in society as adults

   C. Preparation for the world of work

   D. Daily living and social skills

Answer: B. Preparation for functioning in society as adults

A transition or vocational curriculum approach focuses upon what students need to learn that will be useful to them and prepare them for functioning in society as adults. Life preparation includes not only occupational readiness, but also personal-social, and daily living skills.

SKILL 9.6 Technology for teaching and learning in special education settings *(e.g., integrating assistive technology into the classroom; computer-assisted instruction; augmentative and alternative communication; adaptive access for microcomputers; positioning and power mobility for students with physical disabilities; accessing and using information technology; use of productivity tools; technology for sensory disabilities; and voice-activated, speech-synthesis, speech recognition, and word-prediction software)*

ASSISTIVE TECHNOLOGY DEVICE: any item, piece of equipment or product system, whether acquired commercially off the shelf, modified, or customized that is used to increase, maintain or improve functional capabilities of children with disabilities

IDEA provides the following definition of an ASSISTIVE TECHNOLOGY DEVICE:

"Any item, piece of equipment or product system, whether acquired commercially off the shelf, modified, or customized that is used to increase, maintain or improve functional capabilities of children with disabilities."

IDEA 2004 clarified that assistive technology "does not include a medical device that is surgically implanted, or the replacement of such device."

Almost anything can be considered assistive technology if it can be used to increase, maintain, or improve the functioning of a person with a disability.

Some areas in which assistive technology (AT) may be used:

- Communication
- Hearing
- Vision
- Environmental management
- Academic concepts related to reading, writing, or using numbers

- Body movement
- Leisure activities
- Memory
- Work or vocational skills

AT devices can increase the following for a person with a disability:

- Level of independence
- Quality of life
- Productivity

- Performance
- Educational/vocational options
- Success in regular education settings

A variety of AT devices are available to address the functional capabilities of students with disabilities. Zabala (2000) identified AT devices in fourteen major areas.

Academic and Learning Aids

Academic and learning aids are electronic and nonelectronic aids such as calculators, spell checkers, portable word processors, and computer-based software solutions that assist the student in academic areas.

Reading

AT solutions that address difficulty with reading may include:

- **Colored overlays:** Overlays that alter the contrast between the text and background are helpful for students with perceptual difficulties. It may be necessary to experiment to determine the best color or combination of colors for a student.

- **Reading window:** A simple, no-tech solution for students who have difficulty with tracking. A "frame" is constructed from tag board or cardboard, allowing the student to see one line of text at a time as he or she moves down the page.

- **Spell checker or talking dictionary:** Students type in words they are having difficulty reading and the device will say the word for them.

- **Auditory textbooks:** Students who have difficulty reading traditional print texts may use audio-taped texts or texts on CDs to follow along as the text is read aloud. Textbooks on tape or CD are available to students with disabilities through Recordings for the Blind and Dyslexic, as are specialized CD players that allow the student to key in pages, headings, or chapters to access specific text quickly. Some even allow the student to insert electronic bookmarks.

- **Talking word processing programs:** Low-cost software applications that provide speech output of text displayed on the computer monitor. Some programs highlight the text as it is read.

Spelling

AT is available to support spelling in handwritten and computer-generated text.

- **Personal word list or dictionary:** Students maintain a list of commonly misspelled words for personal reference; can be handwritten or computer generated.

- **Hand-held spell checker:** Students type in words, and a list of correctly spelled words that closely approximate the misspelled word is provided. Some models offer speech feedback.

- **Word processing program with spell check:** Most word processing programs offer a spell check feature in which misspelled words are underlined.

- **Talking word processing program with spell check:** These programs are helpful for students who cannot visually identify the correct word on a traditional spell check program. The talking feature allows the student to "listen" for the correct spelling of the word.

Writing

AT to support writing includes a number of low and high tech options.

- **Alternative paper:** For students with fine motor difficulties, modifying the writing paper may be appropriate. One solution is to provide paper with bold lines. Another solution is to use a tactile paper that has a raised line that the student can actually feel. Some students benefit from using graph paper, placing one letter in each box, to improve legibility. Graph paper can also be used for math problems, to assure that the numbers are in alignment.

- **Pencil grips:** This is an inexpensive alternative that gives the student with fine motor difficulties a larger and more supportive means of grasping a pencil.

- **Adapted tape recorder:** Students who have difficulty with writing may be allowed to tape record some of their assignments. Adapted tape recorders can also be used to record class lectures for students who have difficulty taking notes. Tape recorders with an index feature allow the student to mark key points on a tape for later reference.

- **Portable word processor:** For students with significant writing difficulties, a portable word processor can provide an alternative to using pencil and paper. These devices use a full size keyboard and allow the student to type in texts. Files can be stored in the device to be uploaded to a computer at a later time. Advantages over a traditional computer or laptop are the economical price, portability, and long battery life.

- **Talking word processor software:** These programs provide feedback by reading aloud what the student has typed in, allowing the student to hear what he has written. This type of multisensory feedback assists the student in identifying and correcting errors.

- **Word prediction software:** This type of software is beneficial for students who have difficulty with spelling and grammar. As the first letter, or letters of a word are typed in, the computer predicts the word the student is typing. This type of technology is beneficial to students who type slowly, as it reduces the number of keystrokes needed to complete a word.

- **Outlining and webbing software:** This type of software assists students who have difficulty organizing thoughts and planning. Webbing programs allow for graphic diagrams to give the student a visual representation of what is needed to complete the writing task.

- **Voice recognition software:** This type of software has gained in popularity in recent years due to its wide commercial applications. Voice recognition allows the student to "speak" into the computer, and the spoken word is translated into written text on the computer screen.

Math

To support students with difficulties in math, both low tech and high tech options are available.

- **Calculators:** Students who have difficulty performing math calculations can benefit from the use of a calculator. Adapted calculators may have larger buttons or larger display screens that are useful for students with physical disabilities. Talking calculators are available for students with visual impairments.

- **On-screen electronic worksheets:** For student with physical disabilities who have difficulty with writing, worksheets can be produced in an on-screen format, allowing the student to use a computer screen to answer the questions.

- **Manipulatives of all types:** Students who have difficulty acquiring or retaining math concepts often benefit from objects designed to provide a kinesthetic or visual illustration of the concept. These low tech aids include such things as place value blocks, fraction strips, geared clocks, play money, etc.

Aids for Daily Living

Devices to assist with self-help skills in activities such as eating, bathing, cooking, dressing, toileting, and home maintenance include:

- **Adapted eating utensils:** These are low tech aides to assist students with feeding themselves. Adapted utensils may include forks, spoon, and knives with an enlarged handle to allow a better grasp or with straps or cuffs for attaching the utensils to the hand for stability. Electronic devices to assist with eating are also available for students with more severe physical disabilities.

- **Adapted drinking aids:** Adaptations to cups and glasses include modified handles or positioning aids to stabilize the cup on a table or wheelchair tray. Some drinking utensils may have tops or modified rims to prevent spillage.

- **Self-care aids:** Students may need assistance to complete self-care tasks such as dressing, grooming, and toileting. Dressing aids include items such as adapted sock aids for putting on and taking off socks, zipper grips for pulling zippers up and down, no-tie curly laces for shoes, and button hooks to assist in buttoning. Grooming aids include adapted handles on brushes, combs, and toothbrushes. Toileting aids could include adapted toilet seats and safety rails for transferring on and off the toilet.

Assistive Listening Devices and Environmental Aids

Assistive listening devices and environmental aids are electronic and nonelectronic aids such as amplification devices, closed captioning systems, and environmental alert systems that assist a student with a hearing impairment to access information that is typically presented through an auditory modality.

- **Assistive listening devices:** These devices amplify sound and speech and are appropriate for a student with a hearing impairment. Personal amplification systems are portable and can be used in different environments. These systems consist of a transmitter that transmits the sound to the student's receiving unit. Personal sound field systems consist of a transmitter and a receiver, along with a portable speaker. Sound field systems can also be installed in entire rooms.

- **Text telephones (TTY):** Students with hearing impairments may use the TTY keyboard to type messages over the telephone. Some TTYs have answering machines and some models offer a print-out of the text.

- **Closed captioning devices:** Modern televisions are equipped with closed captioning options that present the text on the television screen.

- **Environmental aids:** These can included adapted clocks, notification systems, pagers, and warning devices. Visual alert systems may be configured to alert the student of a doorbell, telephone ringing, or smoke detector sounding. Personal pagers may have vibrating and text messaging options.

- **Real-time captioning:** This may be used to caption speech, such as class lectures and presentations, to a text display. A computer with specialized software and a projection system are needed for this type of software.

Augmentative Communication

Augmentative communication consists of electronic and nonelectronic devices and software solutions that provide a means for expressive and receptive communication for students with speech and language impairments.

- **Object-based communication displays:** Low tech solutions that use actual objects to represent daily activities. The student selects or touches the object to communicate a want or need.

- **Picture communication boards and books:** Low tech solutions that use pictures to represent messages. The pictures are organized according to categories, or activities in the student's day.

- **Alphabet boards:** Students who are able to spell but have limited language can use an alphabet board to communicate. The student touches the letters to spell out words, phrases, or sentences.

- **Talking switches:** This devices allow for recording of one or two messages. The student activates the switch to "say" the message. A picture may be used in conjunction with the device.

- **Voice output devices (low tech):** Multiple messages can be recorded on these devices. Messages are recorded and accessed by the student to communicate wants and needs. The low tech models can range in capacity from one to up to sixty-four messages. Pictures are used on the device as a representative of each message.

- **Voice output devices (middle tech):** On these devices, the messages are represented by picture symbols. These devices have the capacity to store multiple messages on multiple levels.

- **Voice output devices (high tech):** High tech voice output devices are very sophisticated pieces of technology that allow the student to use a computer generated voice to speak for him or her. Some devices uses paper-based displays, while others are computer-generated (dynamic) displays. Some offer a keyboard to allow the student to type in messages as well.

- **Integrated communication solutions:** Several software-based applications are available that use a laptop computer in conjunction with a voice output system.

Computer Access and Instruction

These are input and output devices, alternative access aids, modified or alternative keyboards, switches, special software, and other devices and software solutions that assist a student with a disability to use a computer.

- **Adaptive pointing devices:** Hand-held pointers, hand splints, and mouth sticks can assist the student with physical disabilities to access a computer without the use of hands.

- **Keyboard adaptations:** The computer keyboard can be adapted for students with physical disabilities. Keyguards are devices that cover the computer keyboard and allow access through holes that keep the student from hitting more than one key at a time.

- **Alternative keyboards:** Alternative keyboards may be enlarged for students who need larger targets, or they could be mini keyboards for students with limited movement.

- **Touch screens:** Touch screens allow access to the computer by touch, rather than by using the keyboard or mouse. This is another area of assistive technology that has shown a lot of growth in recent years, due to the wide commercial usage of touch screen products.

- **On-Screen keyboards:** For students who have difficulty using a traditional keyboard, an on-screen keyboard allows the student to write using a mouse, switch, or a scanning system.

- **Mouse alternatives:** Mouse alternatives include trackballs, joysticks, and track pads and are appropriate for students who have difficulty using a traditional mouse.

- **Adaptive output:** Text and graphics on the computer screen can be enlarged for students with visual impairments. Text displayed can also be read aloud by the use of screen reading applications. Printers that print Braille from text typed on the computer are also available for students with visual impairments.

Environmental Controls

Environmental controls are devices such as switches, environmental control units, and adapted appliances that are used by a student with a physical disability to increase independence. These devices allow the student to use alternate devices, such as switches to control items such as lights, televisions, and door locks.

Mobility Aids

Mobility aids are aids that increase personal mobility, such as wheelchairs, walkers, canes, crutches, and scooters.

Prevocational and Vocational Aids

Prevocational and vocational aids are aids and adaptations that are used to assist a student in completing prevocational and vocational tasks, such as picture-based task analysis sheets, adapted knobs, adapted timers, and adapted watches.

Recreation and Leisure Aids

Recreation and leisure aids are aids such as adapted books, switch adapted toys, and leisure computer-based software applications that are used by a student with a disability to increase participation and independence in recreation and leisure activities.

- Game and puzzle adaptations: Games and puzzles may be adapted by the addition of knobs to the pieces, by using card holders, and by using grabbing devices to pick up the pieces.

- Book adaptations: Adaptations to books may include enlarging the text, providing an audio version to read along, or adding pictures or tactile symbols for non-readers.

- Switch-adapted toys: Toys that run on batteries may be adapted to be operated by the use of a switch, thus providing the student with limited physical movement the ability to play with the toy.

Seating and Positioning

Adaptive seating systems and positioning devices provide students with appropriate positioning to enhance participation and access to the curriculum. Seating and positioning systems may included seat inserts for wheelchairs, standers, and adaptive chairs, as well as inflated "pillows" or "wiggle seats" for helping children with ADHD remain seated.

Visual Aids

Visual aids include magnifiers, talking calculators, Braille writers, adapted tape players, screen reading software applications, and Braille note-taking devices that assist a student with a visual impairment to access and produce information in a print format.

- **Braille writer:** A portable device for producing Braille. Students type in text on the keyboard, using the six key entry method. A copy of the text in Braille is embossed on the paper inserted into the Braille writer.

- **Electronic Braille writer:** A updated version of the Braille writer, the electronic Braille writer is lightweight and offers the option of the text being read aloud to the student. A Braille copy of the text can also be printed out.

- **Closed circuit television (CCTV):** Assists students with visual impairments by enlarging text and graphics. The page to be read is placed on the base under the camera. The image is displayed on a monitor, with an appropriate level of magnification for the student. Foreground and background colors can be altered for the individual student.

- **Text enlargement software:** Software is available to increase the size of the text and graphics displayed on the computer monitor.

- **Screen reading software:** Screen reading software may also be of benefit to students with visual impairments. These applications allow the computer to read the text aloud.

A student with a disability may require AT in a variety of categories. For example, a student may use an augmentative communication device to supplement communication skills, adaptive switch toys to participate in leisure activities, and an adapted keyboard for accessing software applications on the classroom computer.

AT devices are not limited to specific disability areas. For example, a student with an attention deficit may require an assistive listening device to focus attention on the teacher's voice. Students with various types of disabilities may benefit from audio-recorded materials that were originally developed for students with visual impairments.

The IEP committee determines the need for AT devices and services. Most school districts have policies/procedures regarding AT assessments and have teams of professionals that conduct the evaluation. Often the assessment team will include physical or occupational therapists and speech therapists, to address communication and physical needs. The student's teacher(s) and parents are often included in the AT evaluation. Once it has been determined that an AT device or service is needed, the student's IEP team should document the required device(s) in the IEP.

The use of AT may decrease the amount of other support services a student needs to be successful.

In addition to providing the devices, IDEA requires services to support the AT devices. IDEA '97 defines AT services as "any service that directly assists a child with a disability in the selection, acquisition, or use of an assistive technology device." There are a variety of services included in this category.

- Evaluation: A functional evaluation of the child's needs in his or her customary environment.

- Acquisition: Whether by purchasing or leasing, the local education agency is required to acquire the device for the student at no cost to the parent.

- Selection and maintenance of the AT device. Included in this area could be the design, fitting, customizing, adapting, repairing, or replacing as needed to support the needs of the child.

- Coordination with other therapies or interventions, including existing education and rehabilitation plans and programs.

- Training or technical assistance for the student, the family, school personnel, employers, or anyone who provides service to the student with a disability.

Suggestions about selecting and using software were given by Male (1994). First, make sure there is a curriculum correspondence between what students are working on at their desks and what they do at the computers, or whatever AT device is in use. This should follow what he calls stages of learning. Then, make certain the students proceed through the five stages of learning. Computer software should be selected with the following stages in mind:

Acquisition	Introduction of a new skill
Proficiency	Practice under supervision to achieve accuracy and speed
Maintenance	Continued practice without further instruction
Generalization	Application of the new skills in new settings and situations
Adaptation	Modifications of the task to meet new needs and demands of varying situations

Computer-Assisted Instruction

Computers are used to provide a safe, stimulating learning environment for many youth. The computer does not evaluate or offer subjective opinions about the student's work. It merely provides feedback about the correctness or incorrectness of each answer in a series. The computer is like an effective teacher when it

- Provides immediate attention and feedback

- Individualizes to the particular skill level

- Allows students to work at their own pace

- Makes corrections quickly

- Produces a professional looking product

- Keeps accurate records on correct and error rates

- Ignores inappropriate behavior

- Focuses on the particular response

- Is nonjudgmental (Smith & Luckasson, 1992)

Computers are useful in helping teach traditional academic subjects such as math, reading, spelling, geography, and science. Effective teachers allow for drill and practice on the computer, monitor student progress, and reinforce appropriately. When students have mastered a particular level, these teachers help them progress to another level. Reasoning and problem solving are other skill areas that teachers have discovered can be taught using computers.

One type of newly developed computer software is the program Hypertext. It enables further explanation of textbook material. The explanation is accessed by a simple press of a key while the student is working on the learning material. For example, by pressing a single key, students can access definitions of difficult vocabulary words, reworded complicated text, additional detailed maps, and further information about concepts being introduced in the text. By using this program, teachers can help students by creating individualized lessons. Students with learning disabilities especially benefit.

Computer games can enhance learning skills and provide a highly desired reinforcement opportunity. When played alone, the games serve as leisure activities for the individual. When played with classmates, the games can help develop interpersonal relationships. Use of computer games is particularly applicable to youngsters with behavioral disorders and learning and intellectual disabilities, as well as those without any identified disability.

Word Processing Technology and the Process Approach

The process approach to writing is encouraged, especially when using a word processor (Male, 1994). These stages include planning and prewriting, drafting, revising and editing, and sharing and publication. Progressing through these stages is particularly helpful to developing writers.

The planning stage is characterized by written outlines, brainstorming, clustering or mind mapping, and lists of ideas, themes, or key words. These activities are ideally suited to a classroom that has a large television monitor or a computer projection device so that the teacher can list, group, revise, and expand ideas as students share them. Printed copies of what was generated by the group can be distributed at the end of the class session.

In the drafting stage, individuals can do draft work at a computer by themselves, or they can collaborate as a group on the work. Some students may choose to use pencil and paper to do initial draft work, or they may want to dictate stories to the teacher or another student who writes it down for them, or to voice to text computer software.

Students share their work during the revising and editing stage. Students read their stories aloud to a partner, a small group, or the whole class. Classmates are instructed to ask questions and give feedback that will help the writer make revisions to the work. After the content of the story has been completed, attention is given to mechanics and writing conventions. Specific software designed to aid each of these tasks is available.

The sharing and publication stage enables students to experience being authors responding to an audience. Students are encouraged to share their work by reading it aloud and distributing it in printed form. They can do this with or without graphics or illustrations.

Sample Test Questions and Rationale

(Easy)

1. **John learns best through the auditory channel, so his teacher wants to reinforce his listening skills. Through which of the following types of equipment would instruction be most effectively presented?**

   A. Overhead projector

   B. CD player

   C. Microcomputer

   D. Opaque projector

Answer: B. CD player

As he is an auditory learner, the ability to listen to information would help sharpen and further develop John's listening skills.

Sample Test Questions and Rationale (cont.)

(Average)

2. What Assistive Technology (AT) is best for Bob, who can compose well, but has difficulty with both encoding and the physical act of writing?

   A. A peer to write what he dictates

   B. Voice to text computer software

   C. A CD player he can listen to while others write

   D. A slant board for writing

Answer: B. Voice to text computer software

Voice to text computer software is ideal for a student who can compose well (written expression), but who cannot write down his thoughts either because he cannot encode (spell) adequately or because he has a physical disability that makes the physical act of writing difficult. The computer allows him to focus on his expression without worrying about physical mechanics. Dictating to a teacher or a peer will also work, but these are not forms of AT. Listening to a CD while others write is not access to the curriculum.

COMPETENCY 10
ASSESSMENT

> **SKILL 10.1** Use of assessment for screening, diagnosis, placement, and the making of instructional decisions *(e.g., how to select and conduct nondiscriminatory and appropriate assessments; how to interpret standardized and specialized assessment results; how to use evaluation results effectively in development of an individualized family service plan [IFSP]/individualized educational program [IEP]; how to prepare written reports and communicate findings)*

ASSESSMENT: the gathering of information in order to make decisions; in education, assessments typically focus on student performance, progress, and behavior

ASSESSMENT is the gathering of information in order to make decisions. In education, assessments typically focus on student performance, progress, and behavior.

Purposes of Assessment

In the education of students with exceptionalities, assessment is used to make decisions about the following:

- Screening and initial identification of children who may need services

- Diagnosis of specific learning disabilities

- Selection and evaluation of teaching strategies and programs

- Determination of the child's present level of performance in academics

- Classification and program placement

- Development of goals, objectives, and evaluation for the IEP

- Eligibility for a program

- Continuation of a program

- Effectiveness of instructional programs and strategies

- Effectiveness of behavioral interventions

- Accommodations needed for mandated or classroom testing

Types of Assessment

Assessment types can be categorized in a number of ways, most commonly in terms of what is being assessed, how the assessment is constructed, or how it is to be used. It is important to understand these differences so as to be able to correctly interpret assessment results.

Formal vs. informal

This variable focuses on how the assessment is constructed or scored. FORMAL ASSESSMENTS are assessments such as standardized tests or textbook quizzes—objective tests that include primarily questions for which there is only one correct, easily identifiable answer. These can be commercial or teacher-made assessments, given to either groups or individuals. INFORMAL ASSESSMENTS have fewer objective measures and may include anecdotes or observations that may or may not be quantified, interviews, informal questioning during a task, etc. An example might be watching a student sort objects to see what attribute is most important to the student, or questioning a student to see what he or she found confusing about a task.

FORMAL ASSESSMENTS: assessments such as standardized tests or textbook quizzes—objective tests that include primarily questions for which there is only one correct, easily identifiable answer

INFORMAL ASSESSMENTS: have fewer objective measures, and may include anecdotes or observations that may or may not be quantified, interviews, informal questioning during a task, etc.

Standardized tests

Standardized tests are formal tests that are administered to either groups or individuals in a specifically prescribed manner, with strict rules to keep procedures, scoring, and interpretation of results uniform in all cases. Such tests allow comparisons to be made across populations, across ages or grades, or over time for a particular student. Intelligence tests and most diagnostic tests are standardized tests.

Norm-referenced vs. criterion-referenced

This distinction is based on the standard to which the student's performance is being compared. Norm-referenced tests establish a ranking and compare the student's performance to an established norm, usually for age or grade peers. What the student knows is of less importance than how similar the student's performance is to a specific group. Norm-referenced tests are, by definition, standardized. Examples include intelligence tests and many achievement tests. Norm-referenced tests are often used in determining eligibility for special needs services. Criterion-referenced tests measure a student's knowledge of specific content, usually related to classroom instruction. The student's performance is compared to a set of criteria or a preestablished standard of information the student is expected to know. On these tests, what the student knows is more important than how he or she compares to other students. Examples include math quizzes at the end of a chapter, or some state-mandated tests of specific content. Criterion-referenced tests are used to determine whether a student has mastered required skills.

Group vs. individual assessments

This variable simply refers to the manner of presentation, whether given to a group of students or on a one to one basis. Group assessments can be formal or informal, standardized or not, criterion- or norm-referenced. Individual assessments can be found in all these types as well.

Authentic assessments

Authentic assessments are designed to be as close to real life as possible so they are relevant and meaningful to the student's life. They can be formal or informal, depending upon how they are constructed. An example of an authentic test item would be calculating a 20 percent sales discount on a popular clothing item after the student has studied math percentages.

Rating scales and checklists

Rating scales and checklists are generally self-appraisal instruments completed by the student or observation-based instruments completed by teacher or parents. The focus is frequently on behavior or affective areas such as interest, motivation, attention or depression. These tests can be formal or informal and some can be standardized and norm-referenced. Examples of norm-referenced tests of this type would be ADHD rating scales or the Behavior Assessment System for Children.

Screening, diagnosis, and placement

Intelligence tests have historically been considered relatively good predictors of school performance. These tests are standardized and norm referenced. Examples are the Wechsler Intelligence Scale for Children—Fourth Edition (WISC-IV), Stanford-Binet IV, and Kaufman Assessment Battery for Children—Second Edition (KACB-II). Some intelligence tests are designed for use with groups and are used for screening and identification purposes. The individual tests are used for classification and program placement. Since intelligence is a quality that is difficult to define precisely, results of intelligence tests should not be used to discriminate or define the person's potential. In recent years intelligence testing has evolved to include measures of multiple intelligences (Gardner, 1999) and these tests can further refine placement decisions for students with special needs. In many cases a significant discrepancy between scores on different intelligences helps to identify specific learning disabilities. Such measures also help show how a disability impacts performance in different areas of the curriculum.

There are many standardized achievement and educational skills tests, including state-mandated testing, that are also used by school systems to help determine eligibility and placement.

Making Instructional Decisions Based on Assessment Results

Assessment is key to providing differentiated and appropriate instruction to all students, and this is the area in which teachers will most often use assessment. Teachers should use a variety of assessment techniques to determine the existing knowledge, skills, and needs of each student. Depending on the age of the student and the subject matter under consideration, diagnosis of readiness may be accomplished through pretest, checklists, teacher observation, or student self-report. Diagnosis serves two related purposes—to identify those students who are not ready for the new instruction and to identify for each student what prerequisite knowledge is lacking.

Student assessment is an integral part of the teaching-learning process. Identifying student, teacher, or program weaknesses is only significant if the information so obtained is used to remedy those concerns. Lesson materials and lesson delivery must be evaluated to determine relevant prerequisite skills and abilities. The teacher must be capable of determining whether a student's difficulties lie with the new information, with a lack of significant prior knowledge, or with a core learning disability that must be addressed with specialized lesson plans or accommodations. The ultimate goal of any diagnostic or assessment endeavor is improved learning. Thus, instruction is adapted to the needs of the learner based on assessment information.

Using Assessment Information to Modify Plans and Adapt Instruction

Assessment skills should be an integral part of teacher training. Teachers are able to use pre- and post-assessments of content areas to monitor student learning, analyze assessment data in terms of individualized support for students and instructional practice for teachers, and design lesson plans that have measurable outcomes and definitive learning standards. Assessment information should be used to provide performance-based criteria and academic expectations for all students in evaluating whether students have learned the expected skills and content of the subject area.

Assessment information should be used to provide performance-based criteria and academic expectations for all students in evaluating whether students have learned the expected skills and content of the subject area.

For example, in an Algebra I class, teachers can use assessment to see whether students have the prior knowledge to engage in the proposed lesson. If the teacher provides students with a preassessment on algebraic expression and ascertains whether the lesson plan should be modified to include a prealgebraic expression lesson unit to refresh student understanding of the content area, then the teacher can create, if needed, quantifiable data to support the need of additional resources to support student learning. Once the teacher has taught the unit on algebraic expression, a post-assessment test can be used to test student learning, and a mastery examination can be used to test how well students understand and can apply the knowledge to the next unit of math content learning.

A teacher working with students with learning disabilities will use assessment information in additional ways. For example, if assessments show a student has extreme difficulty organizing information in the visual field, a teacher may modify a worksheet in math to present only one problem positioned in a large, squared-off field, with lots of white space around it, or even set up problems to be presented one problem at a time on 4×6 inch cards, etc.

By making inferences on teaching methods and gathering clues for student performance, teachers can use assessment data to inform and have an impact on instructional practices.

By making inferences on teaching methods and gathering clues for student performance, teachers can use assessment data to inform and have an impact on instructional practices. By analyzing the various types of assessments, teachers can gather more definitive information on projected student academic performance. Instructional strategies for teachers would provide learning targets for student behavior, cognitive thinking skills, and processing skills that can be employed to diversify student learning opportunities.

Sample Test Questions and Rationale

(Rigorous)

1. **Formal assessments include standardized tests, norm-referenced Instruments, and _____?**

   A. developmental rating scales

   B. interviews

   C. anecdotes/ observations

   D. textbook chapter tests

Answer: D. Textbook chapter tests

Formal assessments are assessments such as standardized tests or textbook quizzes; objective tests that include primarily questions for which there is only one correct, easily identifiable answer. These can be commercial or teacher made assessments. Informal assessments have less objective measures, and may include anecdotes or observations that may or may not be quantified, interviews, informal questioning during a task, etc.

(Easy)

2. **Which of the following is an advantage of giving informal individual assessments, rather than standardized group tests?**

   A. Questions can be modified to reveal a specific student's strategies or misconceptions

   B. The test administrator can clarify or rephrase questions for the student

   C. They can be inserted into the class quickly on an as needed basis

   D. All of the above

Answer: D. All of the above

Standardized group tests are administered to a group in a specifically prescribed manner, with strict rules to keep procedures, scoring, and interpretation of results uniform in all cases. Such tests allow comparisons to be made across populations, ages or grades. Informal assessments have less objective measures, and may include anecdotes or observations that may or may not be quantified, interviews, informal questioning during a task, etc. An example of an informal individually administered assessment might be watching a student sort objects to see what attribute is most important to the student, or questioning a student to see what he or she found confusing about a task.

(Rigorous)

3. **Criterion referenced tests can provide information about:**

   A. Whether a student has mastered prerequisite skills

   B. Whether a student is ready to proceed to the next level of instruction

   C. Which instructional materials might be helpful in covering program objectives

   D. All of the above

Answer: A. Whether a student has mastered prerequisite skills

In criterion referenced testing, the emphasis is on assessing specific and relevant skills or knowledge bases that have been mastered. Items on criterion-referenced tests are often linked directly to specific instructional objectives.

SKILL 10.2 **Procedures and test materials, both formal and informal, typically used for prereferral, referral, eligibility, placement, and ongoing program monitoring**

Standardized tests will have very specific instructions regarding procedures for administration, and it is the teacher's responsibility to see that these standardized procedures are followed. Failure to follow them will invalidate the resulting scores and make it impossible to correctly interpret the results. Some standardized tests also have lists of accommodations that can be used for students with special needs, and these must be carefully recorded and rules about their use strictly followed.

Even with informal assessments, teachers should be attentive to the procedures for administration and at least record differences in administration to different students so results can be correctly interpreted.

It is important for the teacher to correctly interpret the results of any formal assessments used. Most standardized tests will explain how to interpret results so the teacher does not make errors and assume that a test result means something it does not mean.

Particular care must be taken in interpreting some tests. Intelligence test scores, for example, should be interpreted in terms of performance and not the person's potential. The teacher must read the test manuals and become familiar with the following items:

- Areas measured: Verbal, quantitative, memory, cognitive skills, or the multiple intelligences on some assessments

- Population: Target age groups, lack of cultural bias, adaptations or norms for children with physical handicaps such as blindness

- Standardization information: Mean and standard deviation, scaled scores and what they mean

- Means of comparing performance among subtests, such as the Verbal and Performance IQ scores of the WISC-IV

- Uses of the results: The test manual will contain information about how the results can be used (e.g., using the K-ABC-II to identify gifted children), or how they are not to be used (e.g., assuming that a third grade student who gets a score like a fifth grader on a third grade test is ready to do fifth grade work—an assumption that would not be correct)

- Information on use with special populations, such as Spanish-speaking students, or students with visual impairments, physical impairments, or learning disabilities

- Information concerning reliability and validity

Behavioral and Emotional Assessment

Standardized measures of behavior involve direct observation with a behavior rating scale. Measurement of emotional state involves inference and subjectivity on the part of the examiner.

Behavior rating scales

Examples of these scales are the Revised Behavior Problem Checklist, Behavior Rating Profile, and Burks Behavior Rating Scales. Items may be grouped according to categorical characteristics. For the Revised Behavior Problem Checklist, the four major scales are Conduct Disorder, Socialized Aggression, Attention Problem-Immaturity, and Anxiety-Withdrawn, with minor scales of Psychotic Behavior and Motor Excess. Behavior -rating scales require that the examiner rate examples of behaviors on Likert-type scales, such as 0 = not a problem, 1 = mild problem, and 2 = severe problem.

Each scale has its own set of scoring procedures. Therefore, the teacher must be sure to consult the test manual before attempting to interpret the results. The following are other factors to consider in interpreting behavior-rating scales:

- Reliability and validity information: Norm group information and relevant research on the test instrument

- Sources of information: Some tests include parent and youth reports or measure behavior across a number of settings in and out of school

- Suggested uses of the results: Some tests are intended for screening but not diagnostic purposes

- Scoring and profile information: For example, the Child Behavior Checklist and Revised Behavior Profile lists three social competency scales and behavior problem scales identified by factor analysis for boys and girls in three separate age ranges

Measures of emotional state

These tests are designed to be administered by trained psychologists and psychiatrists. The child's emotional state is inferred by analyzing observable behavior. Types of tests include projective methods, measures of self-concept, and inventories and questionnaires.

Projective methods

The theory behind these methods is that a person will project his or her own meaning, patterns, feelings, and significance onto ambiguous stimuli. Because these tests are subjective, it is difficult to establish reliability and validity; therefore, their usefulness for educational purposes is limited. Some examples of these tests are:

- **Rorschach ink blot test:** The individual states what he "sees" in each of the ten inkblots. Diagnostic interpretation is based on clinical data.
- **Thematic apperception test:** The examiner uses a series of thirty-one pictures and asks the child to tell a story about them. The examiner looks for themes in the stories, especially those relating to the main character.

When interpreting these tests, attention must be paid to the reliability and validity, the training of the examiner, and the subjective quality.

Self-concept measures

Some familiar examples are the Tennessee Self-Concept Scale and Piers-Harris Children's Self-Concept Scale. Most instruments use a system of self-evaluation and self-report. Therefore, the child might choose the answer that he or she believes the examiner wants to see. In addition, because self-concept is a difficult construct to define, there is the problem of adequate validity.

Inventories and questionnaires

Many of these are designed for measuring the emotional and personality characteristics of adolescents and adults. These tests are often self-reported, although some, such as the Personality Inventory for Children (PIC), include a parent report. Results are grouped into such scales as adjustment, achievement, depression, delinquency, and anxiety. These results are generally used with classification and placement decisions. Reliability and validity should be considered when interpreting these tests.

The PIC was designed specifically for evaluating children. The parent completes the true/false items, and three validity scales are included to determine the truthfulness of the responses. Thirteen of the thirty scales are considered the profile scales, with the first three—adjustment, achievement, and intellectual screening—considered the cognitive triad.

> **SKILL 10.3** **How to select, construct, conduct, and modify nondiscriminatory, developmentally and chronologically age-appropriate informal assessments, including teacher-made tests, curriculum-based assessment, and alternatives to norm-referenced testing** *(including observation, anecdotal records, error analysis, miscue analysis, self-evaluation questionnaires and interviews, journals and learning logs, portfolio assessment)*

Several authors have identified principles useful in selecting, designing, and interpreting assessments in the classroom.

Linn and Gronlund (1995) identify five principles of assessment:

1. Clearly specifying what is to be assessed has priority in the assessment process

2. An assessment procedure should be selected because of its relevance to the characteristics or performance to be measured

3. Comprehensive assessment requires a variety of procedure

4. Proper use of assessment procedures requires an awareness of their limitations

5. Assessment is a means to an end, not an end in itself

Stiggins (1997) introduces seven guiding principles for classroom assessment:

1. Assessments require clear thinking and effective communication

2. Classroom assessment is key

3. Students are assessment users

4. Clear and appropriate targets are essential

5. High-quality assessment is a must

6. Understanding personal implication is essential

7. Assessment is a teaching and learning tool

Drummond lists six critical questions to ask about possible assessments when making a choice among them:

1. What specific assessment judgments and decisions have to be made?

2. What information is needed to make the best decisions?

3. What information is already available?

4. What assessment methods and instruments will provide the needed information?

5. How should appropriate instruments be located?

6. What criteria should be used in selecting and evaluating assessment instruments?

Measures of Metacognitive Function

METACOGNITION is the advanced cognitive ability to think about thinking and learning—the degree to which a student is aware of his or her own learning strategies and processes. Teachers can use informal process measures to gain information about a student's metacognitive knowledge associated with a particular task, such as analyzing visual aids. The teacher can give the student a task involving analysis of visual aids, then interview the student with direct and open-ended questions. In these interviews, the teacher attempts to answer the following three questions:

1. What does the student know about the metacognitive processes involved in using visual aids? This addresses the student's knowledge of the function of visual aids and whether the student uses background knowledge to predict or clarify the information in the visual aid.

2. If the student knows that certain strategies are needed to analyze an aid, does the student know how to perform those strategies?

3. What variables influence the student's ability or lack of ability to make efficient use of process strategies?

A teacher-made process assessment can be done with a visual aid and a structured, teacher-prepared interview. Interviews begin with global or general questions that measure what the student knows without being prompted to recall specific techniques. Examples of global or general questions are:

- What types of information can graphics tell you?

- What sort of things make graphics useful?

- What should you do if you cannot figure out a graphic?

Following the global/general questions, the teacher can move on to specific questions about specific strategies and components of the strategies, Examples of specific questions would be:

- What does *identify what is important* mean?

- What does *activating knowledge* mean?

Beginning with general questions lessens the possibility that the student will answer what he believes the teacher wants to hear. During the specific question stage, the teacher can explore specific aspects of the student's use of the process in more detail.

Other Useful Informal Assessments

Anecdotal records

These records are notes recorded by the teacher concerning an area of interest or concern with a particular student. They should focus on observable behaviors and should be descriptive in nature. They should not include assumptions or speculations regarding affective areas such as motivation or interest. These records are usually compiled over a period of several days to several weeks.

Portfolio assessment

The use of student portfolios for some aspect of assessment has become quite common. The purpose, nature, and policies of portfolio assessment vary greatly from one setting to another. In general, though, a student's portfolio contains samples of work collected over an extended period. The nature of the subject, age of the student, and scope of the portfolio all contribute to the specific mechanics of analyzing, synthesizing, and otherwise evaluating the portfolio contents.

In most cases, the student and teacher make joint decisions as to which work samples go into the student's portfolio. A collection of work compiled over an extended time allows teacher, student, and parents to view the student's progress from a unique perspective. Qualitative changes over time can be readily apparent from work samples. Such changes are difficult to establish with strictly quantitative records typical of the scores recorded in the teacher's grade book.

Questioning

One of the most frequently occurring forms of assessment in the classroom is oral questioning by the teacher. As the teacher questions the students, she collects a great deal of information about the degree of student learning and potential sources of confusion for the students. While questioning is often viewed as a component of instructional methodology, it is also a powerful assessment tool.

Sample Test Question and Rationale

(Rigorous)

1. Which of the following purposes of testing calls for an informal test?

   A. Screening a group of children to determine their readiness for the first reader

   B. Analyzing the responses of a student with a disability to various presentations of content material to see which strategy works for him

   C. Evaluating the effectiveness of a fourth-grade math program at the end of its first year of use in a specific school

   D. Determining the general level of intellectual functioning of a class of fifth graders

Answer: B. Analyzing the responses of a student with disability to various presentations of content material to see which strategy works for him

Formal tests such as standardized tests or textbook quizzes are objective tests that include primarily questions for which there is only one correct answer. Some are teacher prepared, but they are often commercially prepared and frequently standardized. To analyze the response of a student to types of presentation, informal methods such as observation or questioning are more useful.

COMPETENCY 11
STRUCTURING AND MANAGING THE LEARNING ENVIRONMENT

> **SKILL 11.1** **Structuring the learning environment** *(e.g., the physical-social environment for learning [expectations, rules, consequences, consistency, attitudes, lighting, acoustic characteristics, seating, access, safety provisions, and strategies for positive interactions]; transitions between lessons and activities; grouping of students; integration of related services [occupational therapy, physical therapy, speech and language therapy])*

Physical Settings

The physical setting of the classroom contributes a great deal toward the propensity for students to learn. An adequate, well-built, well-equipped, and well-organized classroom will invite students to learn. This has been called "invitational learning." The following are among the important factors to consider in the physical setting of the classroom:

- Adequate and appropriately arranged physical space

- Repair status

- Lighting adequacy

- Adequate entry and exit access (including handicap accessibility)

- Ventilation and climate control

- Coloration

A classroom must have adequate physical space so students can conduct themselves comfortably. Some students are distracted by windows, doors, pencil sharpeners, etc. The space must be organized in a manner that makes it easier for students to carry out their daily tasks. Student seating arrangements will be dictated by student needs. *See Skill 9.3 for information on how to modify student seating for students with disabilities.*

The teacher has the responsibility to report any items of classroom disrepair to maintenance staff. Broken windows, falling plaster, exposed sharp surfaces, leaks in ceiling or walls, and other items of disrepair present hazards to students.

Another factor that must be considered is adequate lighting. Report any inadequacies in classroom illumination. Flickering lights can produce headaches in children with latent epilepsy, and some students with Irlen Syndrome, for example, are very sensitive to the glare from florescent lights and will need shades or desk lamps to compensate.

Another consideration is adequate ventilation and climate control. Some students may have disabilities that require them to be kept warmer or cooler than is common. Students with autism spectrum disorders may be extremely sensitive to odors, and students with asthma may react badly to dusty or stuffy rooms.

Classrooms with warmer subdued colors contribute to students' concentration on task items. Neutral hues for coloration of walls, ceiling, and carpet or tile are generally used in classrooms so that distraction because of classroom coloration may be minimized.

Acoustics can be very important when teaching students with learning disabilities. Autistic children can be very sensitive to sounds, and students with auditory processing disorders may have difficulty understanding speech if there is background noise from fans or machinery, etc.

The modern classroom has a great deal of furniture, equipment, supplies, appliances, and learning aids to help the teacher teach and students learn.

The classroom should be provided with furnishings that fit the purpose of the classroom. The kindergarten classroom may have a reading center, a playhouse, a puzzle table, student work desks or tables, a sandbox, and any other relevant learning and interest areas.

Whatever the arrangement of furniture and equipment, the teacher must provide for adequate traffic flow. Rows of desks must have adequate space between them for students to move and for the teacher to circulate. All areas must be open to line-of-sight supervision by the teacher.

In all cases, proper care must be taken to ensure student safety. Furniture and equipment should be situated safely at all times. No equipment, materials, boxes, etc. should be placed where falling over is a danger. Doors must have entry and exit accessibility at all times. *(See Skill 9.4 for other ways the environment can be modified to assist students with disabilities.)*

Scheduling the Day

Schedule development depends upon the type of class (elementary or secondary) and the setting (regular classroom or resource room). However, general rules of thumb apply to both types and settings.

1. Allow time for transitions, planning, and setups.

2. Aim for maximum instructional time by pacing the instruction quickly and allotting time for practice of the new skills.

3. Proceed from short assignments to long ones, breaking up long lessons or complex tasks into short sessions or step-by-step instruction.

4. Follow a less preferred academic or activity with a highly preferred academic or activity.

5. In settings where students are working on individualized plans, do not schedule all the students at once in activities that require a great deal of teacher assistance. For example, have some students work on math or spelling while the teacher works with the students in reading, which usually requires more teacher involvement.

6. Break up a longer segment into several smaller segments with a variety of activities.

7. When working with students with disabilities, it may be necessary to adjust the schedule to fit their best working times; some students take medicine that affects their ability to work, and the schedule must take this into account.

Special Considerations for Elementary Classrooms

1. Determine the amount of time that is needed for activities such as P.E., lunch, or recess.

2. Allow about fifteen to twenty minutes each for opening and closing exercises. Spend this time for such housekeeping activities as collecting lunch money, going over the schedule, cleaning up, reviewing the day's activities, and getting ready to go home.

3. Schedule concentrated academics for periods when the students are more alert and motivated (remember to pay attention to any medication schedules relevant to students with disabilities).

4. Build in time for slower students to finish their work; others may work at learning centers or other enrichment activities of interest. Allowing extra time gives the teacher time to give more attention where it is needed, conduct assessments, or for students to complete or correct work.

Special Considerations for Secondary Classes

Secondary school-days are usually divided into five, six, or seven periods of about fifty minutes, with time for homeroom and lunch. Students cannot stay behind and finish their work, since they have to leave for a different room. Resource room time should be scheduled so that the student does not miss academic instruction in his or her classroom or miss desirable nonacademic activities. In schools where special education teachers also co-teach or work with students in the regular classroom, the regular teacher will have to coordinate lesson plans with those of the special education teacher. Consultation time will also have to be budgeted into the schedule.

Organization and Distribution of Materials

Instructional momentum requires an organized system for material placement and distribution. Inability to find an overhead transparency, a necessary chart page, or the handout worksheet for the day not only stops the momentum, but is very irritating to students. Disorganization of materials frustrates both teacher and students. Effective teachers deal with daily classroom procedures efficiently and quickly so students spend the majority of class time engaged in academic tasks.

Instructional momentum requires an organized system for material placement and distribution.

In the lower grades, an organized system often includes a "classroom helper" for effective distribution and collection of books, equipment, supplies, etc. Care must be taken when using such a system with students with some disabilities, however. Sometimes students can be so distracted by the demands of distributing or organizing materials that learning time is seriously reduced. The teacher must take individual student needs into account.

At higher grade levels, the teacher is concerned with materials such as textbooks, written instructional aids, worksheets, computer programs, etc., which must be produced, maintained, distributed, and collected for future use. One important consideration is the production of sufficient copies of duplicated materials to satisfy classroom needs. Another is the efficient distribution of worksheets and other materials. The teacher may decide to hand out materials as students are in their learning sites (desks, etc.) or to have distribution materials at a clearly specified place (or small number of places) in the classroom. In any case, teachers should have firmly established procedures, completely understood by students, for receiving classroom materials.

An effective teacher will also consider the needs and abilities of his or her students when developing routines or a daily schedule. For routines, a teacher might motivate a low-achieving student with a coveted task (such as taking down the attendance sheet or a recommendation for safety patrol) in order to increase confidence in that child. This increased confidence could lead to an increased interest in school and improved learning. Likewise, a teacher should also consider the needs of his or her students when developing the aspects of the daily schedule. For instance, if faced with a "hard to calm down" group, a teacher might schedule quiet reading time after recess. Being aware of their students' trends and characteristics in developing a classroom routine can significantly impact student learning.

Safety Provisions

Emergency response routines can present significant challenges to students with disabilities. Traditionally, the major emergency responses include two categories for student movement: tornado warning response and building evacuation (fire, bomb threat, etc.). More recently, many schools practice emergency procedures for building invasion, as well. For tornadoes, the prescribed response is to evacuate all students and personnel to the first floor of multi-story buildings and to place students along walls away from windows. All persons, including the teacher, should then crouch on the floor and cover their heads with their hands. These are standard procedures for severe weather, particularly tornadoes.

Most other emergency situations require evacuation of the school building. Teachers should be thoroughly familiar with evacuation routes established for each classroom in which they teach. Teachers should accompany and supervise students throughout the evacuation procedure and account for all students under their supervision. Teachers should then continue to supervise students until the building may be reoccupied (upon proper school or community authority) or until other procedures are followed for students to officially leave the school area and cease to be the supervisory responsibility of the school.

All these scenarios require extra care when working with students with disabilities. Some students have physical disabilities that must be taken into account in such emergencies. Others, such as autistic students, may react strongly to the sounds, sights, and routine disruption of even drills for such emergencies. Extra practice with students with special needs and a clear plan involving additional adult assistance must be in place. For example, the class might have an "emergency response team" that automatically comes to the room when such events—or drills for them—occur.

Homework

Mercer and Mercer recommend that homework be planned at the instructional level of the student and incorporated into the learning process of regular class work. The amount of work and length of time needed will vary according to age and grade level. The following are recommended times for students in regular education classes:

Primary Grades	Three 15-minute assignments per week
Grades 4 to 6	Two to four 15- to 45-minute assignments per week
Grades 7 to 9	As many as five 45- to 75-minute assignments per week
Grades 10 to 12	As many as five 75- to 120-minute assignments per week

Homework assignments may need to be modified for some students with disabilities. Some students with disabilities may be unable to handle the usual amount of homework. Care should be taken to ensure that the homework practice is practice, not new learning. Like many aspects of instruction, homework should be differentiated.

Classroom Transition

TRANSITION refers to changes in class activities that involve movement. Examples are:

- Breaking up from large group instruction into small groups for learning centers and small group instructions

- Moving from the classroom to lunch, to the playground, or to elective classes

- Finishing reading at the end of one period and getting ready for math the next period

- Emergency situations such as fire drills

TRANSITION: changes in class activities that involve movement

MANAGEMENT TRANSITION: when the teacher shifts from one activity to another in a systematic, academically oriented way

Effective teachers use class time efficiently. This efficiency results in higher student–subject engagement and will likely result in more subject matter retention. One way teachers use class time efficiently is through a smooth transition from one activity to another; this activity is also known as management transition. MANAGEMENT TRANSITION is when the teacher shifts from one activity to another in a systematic, academically oriented way. One factor that contributes to efficient management transition is the teacher's management of instructional material. Effective teachers gather their materials during the planning stage of instruction. Doing this, a teacher avoids flipping through items looking for the items necessary for the current lesson. Momentum is lost and student concentration is broken when this occurs.

Teachers who keep students informed of the sequencing of instructional activities maintain systematic transitions because the students are prepared to move on to the next activity.

In addition, teachers who keep students informed of the sequencing of instructional activities maintain systematic transitions because the students are prepared to move on to the next activity. For example, the teacher says, "When we finish with this guided practice together, we will turn to page twenty-three and each student will do the exercises. I will then circulate throughout the classroom helping on an individual basis. Okay, let's begin." Following an example such as this will lead to systematic smooth transitions between activities because the students will be turning to page twenty-three when the class finishes the practice without a break in concentration. These practices are particularly important for students with some disabilities. They may need extra time for transitions, or more advanced warning, or even a physical signal such as a bell or light, to help them manage the change.

Another method that leads to smooth transitions is to move students in groups and clusters rather than one by one. This is called group fragmentation. For example, if some students do seat work while other students gather for a reading group, the teacher moves the students in predetermined groups. Instead of calling the individual names of the reading group, which would be time consuming and laborious, the teacher simply says, "Will the blue reading group please assemble at the reading station. The red and yellow groups will quietly do the vocabulary assignment I am now passing out." As a result of this activity, the classroom is ready to move on in a matter of seconds rather than minutes. Again, this can be particularly helpful for students with some disabilities, as they have the added context of their group's movement to help them figure out what to do next.

The teacher may also employ ACADEMIC TRANSITION SIGNALS, which are "teacher utterance[s] that indicate movement of the lesson from one topic or activity to another by indicating where the lesson is and where it is going." For example, the teacher may say, "That completes our description of clouds; now we will examine weather fronts." Like the sequencing of instructional materials, this method keeps the student informed on what is coming next so they will move to the next activity with little or no break in concentration.

Therefore, effective teachers manage transitions from one activity to another in a systematically oriented way through efficient management of instructional matter, sequencing of instructional activities, moving students in groups, and employing academic transition signals. Through an efficient use of class time, achievement is increased because students spend more class time engaged in on-task behavior.

Successful transitions are achieved by using proactive strategies. Early in the year, the teacher pinpoints the transition periods in the day and anticipates possible behavior problems, such as students habitually returning late from lunch, or an autistic student having difficulty with change. After identifying possible problems with the environment or the schedule, the teacher plans proactive strategies to minimize or eliminate those problems. Proactive planning also gives the teacher the advantage of being prepared, addressing behaviors before they become problems, and incorporating strategies into the classroom management plan right away. Transition plans can be developed for each type of transition and the expected behaviors for each situation taught directly to the students.

Adequate lighting is also important. Flickering lights can produce headaches in children with latent epilepsy, and some students are very sensitive to the glare from florescent lights and will need shades or desk lamps to compensate.

Ventilation and climate control are particularly relevant for students with autism spectrum disorders, who may be extremely sensitive to odors, or students with asthma who react badly to dusty or stuffy rooms.

Warmer subdued colors contribute to students' concentration on task items. Neutral hues for coloration of walls, ceiling, and carpet or tile are generally used in classrooms so that distraction because of classroom coloration may be minimized.

ACADEMIC TRANSITION SIGNALS: teacher utterance[s] that indicate movement of the lesson from one topic or activity to another by indicating where the lesson is and where it is going

Sample Test Questions and Rationale

(Average)

1. Which of the following should be considered when planning the spatial arrangement of your classroom?

   A. Adequate Physical Space

   B. Lighting characteristics

   C. Window location

   D. All of the above

   Answer: D. All of the above

   All of these factors help determine whether the room is "invitational." A classroom must have adequate physical space so students can conduct themselves comfortably. Some students are distracted by windows, doors, pencil sharpeners, etc. The space must be organized in a manner that makes it easier for students to carry out their daily tasks.

   Adequate lighting is also important. Flickering lights can produce headaches in children with latent epilepsy, and some students are very sensitive to the glare from florescent lights and will need shades or desk lamps to compensate.

   Ventilation and climate control are particularly relevant for students with Autism spectrum disorders, who may be extremely sensitive to odors, or students with asthma who react badly to dusty or stuffy rooms.

   Warmer subdued colors contribute to students' concentration on task items. Neutral hues for coloration of walls, ceiling, and carpet or tile are generally used in classrooms so distraction because of classroom coloration may be minimized.

(Average)

2. Appropriate safety features which should be used in learning environments with special needs students include:

   A. Physical barriers

   B. Effective procedures to be used in emergencies

   C. Equal treatment for all students to avoid stigma

   D. Multisensory instructional approach

   Answer: B. Effective procedures to be used in emergencies

   None of the other three choices is a safety feature.

> **SKILL 11.2** **Classroom management techniques** *(e.g., behavioral analysis [identification and definition of antecedents, target behavior, and consequent events]; behavioral interventions; functional analysis; data-gathering procedures [such as anecdotal data, frequency methods, and interval methods]; self-management strategies and reinforcement; cognitive-behavioral interventions; social skills training)*

Treatment models for learning disabilities have evolved in response to theories about their causes. The medical approach of the 1940s and 1950s used instructional practices such as study carrels; movement breaks from seated tasks; structured tasks and schedules corresponding with attention span; reduced noise and distractions; modifying tasks to fit functioning levels; and tape recorded lessons.

During the 1960s, the psychological processing approach advocated identifying student learning styles, using oral administration of tests and books on tape where auditory learning was preferred. It also advocated activities like reproduction of designs, use of simplified, uncluttered worksheets, attention to detail, discrimination of sounds and symbols, interviews, puppetry, role playing, and referential communication.

The instructional practices of the behavioral approach of the 1970s included task analysis; mastery of prerequisite skills; small, sequential learning steps; identification of functioning abilities; use of concrete, hands-on materials; use of oral and written materials simultaneously; use of visual, auditory, and tactile teaching aids; use of compensatory and supportive aids; error analysis; use of color; use of high interest, low vocabulary reading materials; and teacher-made or adapted instructional materials.

In the 1980s and 1990s, strategy approaches were postulated. The instructional strategies included giving clues to identify important information; encouraging "talking through" problems; setting up of homework organizers; teaching how to take notes and organize content read; asking for periodic status reports on long-term assignments; teaching test-taking and study skills; use of mnemonic cues; use of index cards for review; and instruction in use of the calculator, tape recorder, typewriter, and word processor.

At the present time, practices from each of these models are in evidence in special education settings. Most teachers utilize an eclectic approach. The contemporary practice emphasizes cognitive learning strategies in which we teach students how to learn, how to manage their own behaviors in school, and how to generalize information from one setting to another, as the ultimate goal is to produce self-sufficient, independent learners with skills to last a lifetime.

Developing a management plan takes a proactive approach—that is, decide what behaviors will be expected of the class as a whole, anticipate possible problems, and teach the behaviors early in the school year.

Whatever techniques a teacher is using, classroom management plans should be in place when the school year begins. Developing a management plan takes a proactive approach—that is, decide what behaviors will be expected of the class as a whole, anticipate possible problems, and teach the behaviors early in the school year. Be particularly mindful of the needs of students with disabilities when making these plans. Behavior management techniques should focus on positive procedures that can be used at home as well at school. Involving the students in the development of the classroom rules lets the students know the rationale for the rules and allows them to assume responsibility for the rules because they had a part in developing them. When students get involved in helping establish the rules, they will be more likely to assume responsibility for following them. Once the rules are established, enforcement and reinforcement for following the rules should begin right away.

Consequences should be introduced when the rules are introduced, clearly stated, and understood by all of the students. It is preferable to use reward rather than punishment as much as possible. Students with some learning disabilities or behavior problems particularly benefit from extrinsic, concrete rewards, as well as praise for specific acts. When a negative consequence is necessary, the severity of the consequence should match the severity of the offense and must be enforceable. The teacher must apply the consequence consistently and fairly, so the students will know what to expect when they choose to break a rule.

Like consequences, students should understand what rewards to expect for following the rules. The teacher should never promise a reward that cannot be delivered and should follow through with the reward as soon as possible. Consistency and fairness is also necessary for rewards to be effective. Students will become frustrated and give up if they see that rewards and consequences are not delivered fairly and in a timely manner.

About four to six classroom rules should be posted where students can easily see and read them. These rules should be stated positively and describe specific behaviors so they are easy to understand. Certain rules may also be tailored to meet target goals and IEP requirements of individual students. (For example, a new student who has had problems with leaving the classroom may need an individual behavior contract to assist him or her with adjusting to the class rule about remaining in the assigned area.) As the students demonstrate the behaviors, the teacher should provide reinforcement and corrective feedback. Periodic "refresher" practice can be done as needed—for example, after a long holiday or if students begin to "slack off." A copy of the classroom plan should be readily available for substitute use, and the classroom aide should also be familiar with the plan and procedures.

The teacher should clarify and model the expected behavior for the students. In addition to the classroom management plan, a management plan should be developed for special situations, (i.e., fire drills) and transitions (i.e., going to and from the cafeteria). Periodic review of the rules, as well as modeling and practice, may be conducted as needed, such as after an extended school holiday.

Procedures that use social humiliation, withholding of basic needs, pain, or extreme discomfort should never be used in a behavior management plan. Throughout the year, the teacher should periodically review the types of interventions being used, assess the effectiveness of the interventions used in the management plan, and make revisions as needed for the best interests of the children.

Motivation

Before the teacher begins instruction, he or she should choose activities that are at the appropriate level of student difficulty, meaningful, and relevant. Teacher behaviors that motivate students include the following:

- Maintain success expectations through teaching, goal setting, establishing connections between effort and outcome, and self-appraisal and reinforcement.

- Have a supply of intrinsic incentives such as rewards, appropriate competition between students, and the value of the academic activities. It should be noted, however, that many students with disabilities do NOT respond well to competition. For some of them, their lives have involved a long series of failures to do well in competition with peers without disabilities. It is preferable to have students "compete" against themselves; e.g., trying to increase their own score, do better than last time, etc. In addition, many students with disabilities respond better to extrinsic rewards—for example, star charts for elementary students who can trade them in on small treats or prizes. Such charts can be designed to show each individual student's degree of improvement, rather than comparing a student to the rest of the class.

- Focus on students' intrinsic motivation through adapting the tasks to students' interests; provide opportunities for active response, including a variety of tasks; provide rapid feedback; incorporate games into the lesson; allow students the opportunity to make choices, create, and interact with peers.

- Stimulate students' learning by modeling positive expectations and attributions. Project enthusiasm and personalize abstract concepts. Students will be better motivated if they know what they will be learning about. The teacher should also model problem-solving and task-related thinking so students can see how the process is done.

- For adolescents, motivation strategies are usually aimed at getting the student actively involved in the learning process. Since the adolescent has the opportunity to get involved in a wider range of activities outside the classroom (job, car, being with friends), stimulating motivation may be the focus even more than academics.

- Motivation may be achieved through extrinsic reinforcers or intrinsic reinforcers. This is accomplished by allowing the student a degree of choice in what is being taught or how it will be taught. The teacher will, if possible, obtain a commitment either through a verbal or written contract between the student and the teacher. Adolescents also respond to regular feedback, especially when that feedback shows that they are making progress.

- Rewards for adolescents often include free time for listening to music, recreation, or games. They may like extra time for a break or exemption from a homework assignment. They may receive rewards at home for satisfactory performance at school. Other rewards include self-charting progress and tangible reinforcers. In summary, motivational activities may be used for goal setting, self-recording of academic progress, self-evaluation, and self-reinforcement.

Assertive Discipline

Assertive discipline, developed by Canter and Canter, is an approach to classroom control that allows the teacher to constructively deal with misbehavior and maintain a supportive environment for the students. The following are the assumptions behind assertive discipline:

- Behavior is a choice

- Consequences for not following rules are natural and logical, not a series of threats or punishments

- Positive reinforcement occurs for desired behavior

- The focus is on the behavior and the situation, not the student's character

The assertive discipline plan should be developed as soon as the teacher meets the students. The students can become involved in developing and discussing the needs for the rules. Rules should be limited to four to six basic classroom rules that are simple to remember and positively stated (e.g., "Raise hand to speak" instead of "Don't talk without permission").

Recognize and remove roadblocks to assertive discipline

Replace negative expectations with positives and set reasonable limits for students. When dealing with students with certain disabilities, it is particularly important to plan ahead and make classroom modifications that will help the student be successful in following rules. Many students with learning or emotional disabilities have so much experience "failing" to measure up that they have given up trying to please teachers and parents. It may be necessary to "rig" the situation to ensure the student can experience success at first.

Practice an assertive response style

Clearly state teacher expectations and expect the students to comply with them.

Set limits

Take into consideration the students' behavioral needs and the teacher's expectations, and set limits for behavior. Decide what you will do when the rules are broken or complied with.

Follow through promptly with consequences when students break the rules

However, the students should clearly know in advance what to expect when a rule is broken. Conversely, follow through with the promised rewards for compliance and good behavior. This reinforces the concept that individuals choose their behavior and that there are consequences for their behavior.

Devise a system of positive consequences

Positive consequences do not always have to be food or treats. However, rewards should not be promised if it is not possible to deliver them. The result is a more positive classroom.

Nonaversive Techniques

Token economy

Token economy is a system in which individuals receive tokens as a reward for a desired behavior. The tokens are collected and traded for an item or activity. In some cases the token is money, in others it might be stars on a chart. When the person earns enough money (or stars) he or she can buy a certain item or pay to participate in a desirable activity. This technique gives individuals a concrete motivator to perform the targeted behavior.

> *Example: The student is required to stay at his or her seat and work independently while the teacher works with someone else. Each time the student does this successfully, a sticker is put on a chart that, when filled, can be traded for a prize of some sort.*

Planned ignoring

Planned ignoring means the teacher determines that an inappropriate behavior will be ignored. This often works with attention seeking behaviors. In the ideal situation, once the attention is removed the behavior ceases. It is important, however, to ensure that the student has other more appropriate behavioral options for getting the needed attention available, and that the teacher notices them, too.

Example: A student complains that he doesn't want to do a task, folds his arms, and turns away angrily and mutters. The teacher ignores the student and focuses on the students doing their work. The student eventually gets tired of being ignored, stops muttering, and gets to work (and the teacher pays attention to him!).

Proximity control

An adult's close proximity to a student can often reduce or prevent undesirable behaviors.

Example: The rule is no talking. Jack turns to talk to Johnny. The teacher walks by and he stops talking. Sometimes the teacher can use a prearranged signal, such as tapping a book, so the student knows she is watching and will return to work.

Self-assessment

Self-assessment is when the students are responsible for taking part in their own behavior management. The individual may be trained to self-record data. Typically someone may also collect data about the recorder's behavior or observe data recording sessions. Then the results are discussed and the person is rewarded for desirable behaviors. This strategy should be used only with mature individuals.

Example: A student constantly rushes through assignments and receives poor grades. The student is given a questionnaire to answer before turning in a paper. The questionnaire contained the following questions:

Did I put the correct punctuation on all sentences?

Have I capitalized the correct letters?

Have I spaced between words?

Did I thoroughly discuss the topic?

Did I read the paper at least three times to look for errors?

If the student answers yes to all the questions, and it looks like he or she actually did this, he or she would receive a good grade as an incentive to continue self-assessment.

Sample Test Questions and Rationale

(Average)

1. **Positive reinforcers are generally effective if they are desired by the student and:**

   A. Worthwhile in size

   B. Given immediately after the desired behavior

   C. Given only upon the occurrence of the target behavior

   D. All of the above

   Answer: D. All of the above

   Timing and quality of the reinforcer are key to encourage the individual to continue the targeted behavior.

(Easy)

2. **An effective classroom behavior management plan includes all but which of the following?**

   A. Transition procedures for changing activities

   B. Clear consequences for rule infractions

   C. Concise teacher expectations for student behavior

   D. Copies of lesson plans

   Answer: D. Copies of lesson plans

   Effective classroom management includes transition procedures, clear consequences for rule infractions, and concise teacher expectations for student behavior. Lesson plans outline the classroom activities, schedule, and agenda.

(Rigorous)

3. **Morgan frequently talks during instructional time. Her teacher, Mrs. Jenkins, wants to use the assertive discipline approach to behavior management to decrease, and eventually eliminate, Morgan's disruptions. All of the following interventions are appropriate EXCEPT:**

   A. Offering Morgan positive reinforcement when she is quiet during instructional time

   B. Tracking Morgan's talk outs and discussing them with her parents

   C. Promptly following through with expected consequences when Morgan talks out

   D. Focusing on the behavior and the situation rather than on Morgan's character

   Answer: B. Tracking Morgan's talk outs and discussing them with her parents

   Assertive discipline, developed by Canter and Canter, is an approach to classroom control that allows the teacher to constructively deal with misbehavior and maintain a supportive environment for the students. The assumptions behind assertive discipline are:

   • Behavior is a choice

   • Consequences for not following rules are natural and logical, not a series of threats or punishments

   • Positive reinforcement occurs for desired behavior.

   • The focus is on the behavior and the situation, not the student's character

   Mrs. Jenkins should provide opportunities for Morgan to reduce her talk outs and use natural and logical consequences before involving Morgan's parents.

SKILL 11.3   **Behavior management strategies**

Often special educators are faced with behavioral issues that interfere with the student's ability to learn. In many special education programs, a behavior management plan is essential to maintaining a classroom environment that is safe for all students and staff and conducive to learning.

Behavioral Management Defined

Behavior management is establishing behavioral expectations and consequences in a classroom or other setting. Reinforcement of a desired behavior is done when students are rewarded with a token (sticker, treat, privilege) upon completing the behavioral expectations for a given time or activity.

When a behavior management plan is established, ethical considerations must be inherent in it. The behavior management plan should be established with research-based methods and should include positive interactions with students, education of appropriate behavior, and fair, consistent consequences.

Expectations

The teacher must be knowledgeable of appropriate behavioral expectations of non-disabled students of the same age. The teacher must also understand the impact of the individual special education student's disability and medication on behavior. The student's IEP should provide guidance about these issues.

Positive Interaction with Students

Behavior management should incorporate positive, respectful communication with the student as a person. Students should also be taught positive communication skills through modeling, role play, bibliotherapy stories, and self-control.

Special emphasis should also be placed on problem solving and conflict resolution.

Antecedents

The special educator should be aware of antecedents to undesirable behaviors. These may include a time of day, a particular activity, a location, or a combination of people. While some upsetting situations may be avoided, it is often important to work with the student so that the situation is more tolerable. *(See Skill 3.3 for information on functional behavior assessments in this regard.)*

Crisis Intervention

Behavior management is a technique to avoid behavioral crisis incidents. In extreme cases, the special education teacher will need to implement intervention techniques that go beyond verbal expectations. Physical intervention must only be used by individuals trained and certified. In schools where students with severe behavioral needs are taught, it is crucial that staff members be trained.

Sample Test Questions and Rationale

(Easy)

1. Crisis intervention methods are above all concerned with:

   A. Safety and well-being of the staff and students

   B. Stopping the inappropriate behavior

   C. Preventing the behavior from occurring again

   D. The student learning that outbursts are inappropriate

Answer: A. Safety and well-being of the staff and students

Assuring the safety and well-being of the staff and students should be the top priority of any crisis intervention plan. A well designed crisis intervention plan will naturally encompass B, C, and D but the safety and well-being of the staff and students is the top priority.

(Average)

2. Addressing a student's maladaptive behavior right away with a "time out" should be reserved for situations where:

   A. The student has engaged in the behavior continuously throughout the day

   B. Harm might come to the student or others

   C. Lesser interventions have not been effective

   D. The student displayed the behavior the day before

Answer: B. Harm might come to the student or others

The best intervention is to move the student away from the harmful environment.

(Average)

3. Katie frequently is disruptive prior to each day's math lesson. From a behavior management perspective, the math lesson appears to be the ________________ to Katie's undesirable disruptive behavior.

   A. subsequent development

   B. succeeding force

   C. consequence

   D. antecedent

Answer: D. Antecedent

Antecedents are the causes of behaviors and they therefore precede the behavior. The special educator should be aware of antecedents to undesirable behaviors. These may include a time of day, a particular activity, a location, or a combination of people. While some upsetting situations may be avoided, it is often important to work with the student so that the situation is more tolerable.

COMPETENCY 12
PROFESSIONAL ROLES

> **SKILL 12.1** **Specific roles and responsibilities of teachers** (*e.g., teacher as collaborator with other teachers, teacher educators, parents, community groups, and outside agencies; teacher as a multidisciplinary team member; maintaining effective and efficient documentation; selecting appropriate environments and services for students; critical evaluation and use of professional literature and organizations; reflecting on one's own teaching; teacher's role in a variety of teaching settings [self-contained classroom, resource room, itinerant, co-teacher in inclusion setting, etc.]; and maintaining student confidentiality)*

The Teacher's Role

Teaching consists of a multitude of roles. Teachers must plan and deliver instruction in a creative and innovative way so that students find learning both fun and intriguing. The teacher must also research various learning strategies, decide which to implement in the classroom, and balance that information according to the various learning styles and special needs of the students.

When students with special needs are involved, it is the teacher's responsibility to study and follow the IEP and to acquire up to date information on the student's disability. Teachers must facilitate all aspects of the lesson, including preparation and organization of materials, modifications for students with special needs, delivery of instruction, and management of student behavior and attention.

Simultaneously, the teacher must also observe for student learning, interactions, and on-task behavior while making mental or written notes regarding what is working in the lesson and how the students are receiving and using the information. This will provide the teacher with immediate feedback as to whether to continue with the lesson, slow the instruction, or present the lesson in another way. Teachers must also work collaboratively with other adults in the room and use them to maximize student learning. The teacher's job requires the teacher to establish a delicate balance among all these factors.

How the teacher handles this balance depends on the teaching style of the teacher, the content of the lesson, and the individual needs of the students. When using cooperative learning techniques, the teacher must have organized materials ready, perhaps even with instructions for the students. The teacher should conduct a great deal of observations during this type of lesson. Direct instruction methods require that the teacher have an enthusiastic, yet organized, approach to the lesson. When teaching directly to students, the teacher must take care to keep the lesson student-centered and intriguing while presenting accurate information.

Teacher as Community Collaborator

Effective learning for students begins with a collaborative approach by all stakeholders that supports the educational needs of students. Community institutions can have a powerful impact on the current and future goals of students, especially beyond the high schools years when students are competing for college access, student internships, and entry level jobs in the community. Research has shown that schools that involve community institutions have greater retention rates of students graduating and seeking higher education experiences.

When community institutions provide students and teachers with meaningful connections and input, the commitment is apparent in terms of volunteering, loyalty, and professional promotion. Such connections also provide authenticity for classroom learning activities and help put real life goals and objectives into class life.

Placing students in leadership positions such as the ASB (Associated Student Body), the PTSA (Parent Teacher Student Association), school boards, neighborhood sub-committees addressing political or social issues, or government boards that impact and influence school communities creates an avenue for students to explore ethical, participatory, collaborative, transformational leadership that can be applied to all areas of a student's educational and personal life.

Community liaisons help students with accountability and responsibility so they learn about life and how teams work together to accomplish goals and objectives. Teaching social and environmental responsibility and creating public forums that represent student voice increase student interest and motivation. This, in turn, leads to developing and reflecting on individual opinions and understanding the dynamics of the world around them.

Students with disabilities can also participate in such school and community collaborations if their special needs are taken into consideration. For example, they can write letters to congressional representatives, visit various job settings, etc. Even learning to be an advocate for their own needs and inclusion can be useful experience.

When a student sees that the various support systems are in place and working as a team to provide resources and avenues for academic promotion and accountability, it gives them confidence to take the risks needed to grow. Volunteering in local organizations and community institutions provides access to real-world role models and makes the transition to adult responsibilities easier. Teachers of students with disabilities must make a special effort to find ways in which their students can participate in such activities.

SKILL 12.2 **Influence of teacher attitudes, values, and behaviors on the learning of exceptional students**

The responsibility of student progress and success lies to a great extent with the teacher. No Child Left Behind (NCLB) outlines the teacher's role and the expectation of success for every student regardless of exceptional need: All students should learn to read by grade three. The attitude of the teacher should be to incorporate every method of reading instruction necessary to meet this goal. In particular, the incorporation of phoneme awareness exercises and phonics in the curriculum is key to many exceptional students.

In addition to reading skills, NCLB states that all students should show adequate yearly progress as measured by testing. In the case of the exceptional student, the special education and regular education teacher should be aware of the influence of their attitudes, values, and behaviors on the student's learning and reaching the expectations of NCLB.

Attitudes

Special education and regular education teachers should demonstrate the attitude that the exceptional student is a student of both teachers, not a special education student who only goes into a general education classroom at certain times.

Special education and regular education teachers should demonstrate the attitude that the exceptional student is a student of both teachers, not a special education student who only goes into a general education classroom at certain times. Cooperation between these teachers facilitates lesson planning and scheduling. According to IDEA 2004 (Individuals with Disabilities Education Act), exceptional students should be included in regular education lessons and activities to the fullest beneficial extent possible. For some students this will mean full inclusion in a general education classroom. For others it may mean a general education classroom with resource room pull-out, or a subset program in which they spend only part of the day with grade level classmates. In all cases, it is the responsibility of the special education teacher to keep other teachers and staff informed of the needs and accommodations required for the students with disabilities.

Values

The teacher of the exceptional student should demonstrate a sense of value regarding the student's education. This value should be evident in the types of lessons planned and in feedback on student progress. Learning standards should be evident in lesson planning. The goal for exceptional students (IDEA 2004) is to lead to continued education, successful employment, and independence as adults.

Exceptional students as well as their peers without disabilities learn social values from the teacher's example. If an effort is made to include students in simple classroom celebrations such as birthday treats (as opposed to the treat being on the desk when the student returns from a special education setting), students learn respect for themselves and all members of the society. A student's disability should not be allowed to become grounds for exclusion in any activity not actually precluded by the disability.

Behaviors

Exceptional students should not only be included physically in regular classroom lessons and activities, they should be given the opportunity to participate at their level. This can be achieved through differentiated materials and related questions (written or in class discussion). *(See Skill 9.3 for more on differentiated instruction.)*

The speech behavior of the teacher is also influential. Discussion between regular and special education teachers in front of students should not include reference to exceptional students as *your students* or a division of supervision and discipline according to exceptional need. Rather, teachers should work together as a team to plan and implement every aspect of the exceptional student's education.

Sample Test Questions and Rationale

(Average)

1. **The best way to ensure the success of educational interventions is to:**

   A. Give regular education teachers the primary responsibility of teaching special needs students in regular classrooms

   B. Give special education teachers the primary responsibility of teaching special needs students in special education classrooms

   C. Promote cooperative teaching efforts between general and special educators

   D. Have support personnel assume the primary responsibility for the education of special needs students

Answer: C. Promote cooperative teaching efforts between general and special educators

Both types of teachers can learn from each other. Special education and regular education teachers should demonstrate the attitude that the exceptional student is a student of both teachers, not a special education student who only goes into a general education classroom at certain times.

(Average)

2. **A serious hindrance to successful mainstreaming is:**

   A. Lack of adapted materials

   B. Lack of funding

   C. Lack of communication among teachers

   D. Lack of support from administration

Answer: C. Lack of communication among teachers

All four choices are hindrances, but lack of communication and consultation between the service providers is the most serious.

SKILL 12.3 Communicating with parents, guardians, and appropriate community collaborators *(e.g., directing parents and guardians to parent-educators or to other groups and resources; writing reports directly to parents; meeting with parents to discuss student concerns, progress, and IEPs; encouraging parent participation; reciprocal communication and training with other service providers)*

Teachers of exceptional students are expected to manage many roles and responsibilities, not only as concern their students, but also with respect to students' caregivers and other involved educational, medical, therapeutic, and administrative professionals. Because the needs of exceptional students are by definition multidisciplinary, a teacher of exceptional children often serves as the hub of a many-pronged wheel, communicating, consulting, and collaborating with the various stakeholders in a child's educational life. Managing these relationships effectively can be a challenge, but it is central to successful work in exceptional education.

Students

Useful standards developed by the Council for Exceptional Children (CEC) in 2003 outline best practices in communicating and relating to children and their families. For example, CEC guidelines suggest that effective teachers:

- Offer students a safe and supportive learning environment, including clearly expressed and reasonable expectations for behavior

- Create learning environments that encourage self-advocacy and developmentally appropriate independence

- Offer learning environments that promote active participation in independent or group activities

Such an environment is an excellent foundation for building rapport and trust with students, and communicating a teacher's respect for and expectation that they take a measure of responsibility for their educational development. Ideally, mutual trust and respect will afford teachers opportunities to learn of and engage students' ideas, preferences, and abilities.

Effective Communication between Teachers and Families

Research proves that the more families are involved in a child's educational experience, the more that child will succeed academically. Families know students better than almost anyone and are a valuable resource for teachers of exceptional students. Often, an insight or observation from a family member or his or her reinforcement of school standards or activities means the difference between success and frustration in a teacher's work with children. Suggestions for relationship building and collaboration with parents and families include the following:

- Use laypersons' terms when communicating with families and make the communication available in the language of the home.

- Search out and engage family members' knowledge and skills in providing educational and therapeutic services to the student.

- Explore and discuss the concerns of families and help them find tactics for addressing those concerns.

- Plan collaborative meetings with children and their families and help them become active contributors to their educational team.

- Ensure that communications with and about families are confidential and conducted with respect for their privacy.

- Offer parents accurate and professionally presented information about the pedagogical and therapeutic work being done with their child. It is sometimes necessary to provide professional guidance about the child's disability or the techniques that will help. For example, the parent of a third grade child who reads at the first grade level checks out library books at the third grade level and insists that the child labor through trying to read them in the hope this will improve the child's reading skills. The teacher needs to explain that while it would be helpful for the parent to read that third grade level book to the child, books chosen for the child to read should be easy enough for the child to read about 95 percent of the text independently, even if this is below grade level. The teacher might help the parent find material that is age appropriate but written at the child's level.

- Keep parents abreast of their rights, of the kinds of practices that might violate their rights, and of available recourse if needed.

- Acknowledge and respect cultural differences.

One common difficulty occurs when teachers assume that involvement in education simply means that the parents show up to help at school events or participate in parental activities on campus. With this belief, many teachers devise clever strategies to increase parental involvement at school. However, just because a parent shows up to school and assists with an activity does not mean that the child will learn more. Many parents work all day long and cannot assist in the school. Teachers, therefore, have to think of different ways to encourage parental and family involvement in the educational process.

Parent Conferences

The parent-teacher conference is generally for one of three purposes. First, the teacher may wish to share information with the parents concerning the performance and behavior of the child. Second, the teacher may be interested in obtaining information from the parents about the child. Such information may help answer questions or concerns that the teacher has. A third purpose may be to request parent support or involvement in specific activities or requirements. In many situations, more than one of the purposes may be involved.

Planning the conference

When a conference is scheduled, whether at the request of the teacher or the parent, the teacher should allow sufficient time to prepare thoroughly. Collect all relevant information, samples of student work, records of behavior, and other items needed to help the parent understand the circumstances. It is also a good idea to compile a list of questions or concerns you wish to address. Arrange the time and location of the conference to provide privacy and to avoid interruptions.

Conducting the conference

Begin the conference by putting the parents at ease. Take the time to establish a comfortable mood, but do not waste time with unnecessary small talk. Begin your discussion with positive comments about the student. Identify strengths and desirable attributes, but do not exaggerate.

As you address issues or areas of concern, be sure to focus on observable behaviors and concrete results or information. Do not make judgmental statements about parent or child. Share specific work samples, anecdotal records of behavior, etc., that demonstrate clearly the concerns you have. Be a good listener and hear the parent's comments and explanations. Such background information can be invaluable in understanding the needs and motivations of the child.

Finally, end the conference with an agreed plan of action between parents and teacher (and, when appropriate, the child). Bring the conference to a close politely but firmly and thank the parents for their involvement.

After the conference

A day or two after the conference, it is a good idea to send a follow-up note to the parents. In this note, briefly and concisely reiterate the plan or step agreed to in the conference. Be polite and professional; avoid the temptation to be too informal or chatty. If the issue is a long term one such as the behavior or ongoing work performance of the student, make periodic follow-up contacts to keep the parents informed of the progress.

Paraprofessionals and General Education Teachers

Paraprofessionals and general education teachers are also important collaborators with teachers of exceptional students. Although they may have daily exposure to exceptional students, they may not have the theoretical or practical experience to assure their effective interaction with such students. They do bring valuable perspective and opportunities for breadth and variety in an exceptional child's educational experience. General education teachers also offer curriculum and subject matter expertise and a high level of professional support, while paraprofessionals may provide insights born of their particular familiarity with individual students. CEC suggests that teachers can best collaborate with general education teachers and paraprofessionals by

- Offering information about the characteristics and needs of children with exceptional learning needs

- Discussing and brainstorming ways to integrate children with exceptionalities into various settings within the school community

- Modeling best practices and instructional techniques and accommodations and coaching others in their use

- Keeping communication about children with exceptional learning needs and their families confidential

- Consulting with these colleagues in the assessment of individuals with exceptional learning needs

- Engaging them in group problem-solving and in developing, executing, and assessing collaborative activities

- Offering support to paraprofessionals by observing their work with students and offering feedback and suggestions

Related Service Providers and Administrators

Related service providers and administrators offer specialized skills and abilities that are critical to the exceptional education teacher's ability to advocate for his or her student and meet a school's legal obligations to the student and his or her family. Related service providers—such as speech therapists, occupational therapists, and language therapists, psychologists, and physicians—offer expertise and resources unparalleled in meeting a child's developmental needs. Administrators are often experts in the resources available at the school and local education agency levels, as well as the culture and politics of a school system, and can be powerful partners in meeting the needs of exceptional education teachers and students.

A teacher's most effective approach to collaborating with these professionals includes the following:

- Confirming mutual understanding of the accepted goals and objectives of the student with exceptional learning needs as documented in his or her IEP

- Soliciting input about ways to support related service goals in classroom settings

- Understanding the needs and motivations of each professional and acting in support whenever possible

- Facilitating respectful and beneficial relationships between families and professionals

- Regularly and accurately communicating observations and data about the child's progress or challenges

Quite often, teachers have great success with involving families by just informing families of what is going on in the classroom. Newsletters are particularly effective at this. Parents love to know what is going on in the classroom. In newsletters, teachers can provide suggestions on how parents can help with the educational goals of the school. For example, teachers can recommend that parents read with their children for twenty minutes per day. To add effectiveness, teachers can also provide suggestions on what to do when their children come across difficult words or when they ask a question about comprehension. This gives parents practical strategies. In addition, when working with students with special needs, it is a good idea to give frequent updates on the student's progress.

Many IEPs require this on specific intervals. It is also helpful if a means (daily notebook, response sheet, etc.) is provided where parents can alert the teacher to issues at home that might impact the student (e.g., Johnny took his medication late or a change in home routine has upset him).

Parents often equate phone calls from teachers with news about misbehaviors of their children. Teachers can change that tone by calling parents with good news or sending positive notes home with students. This is particularly effective with parents of students with disabilities. Many of these parents have heard so many complaints about their children over the years that they are practically numb to teacher complaints. The teacher should pick only the most essential issues when something negative must be discussed. Then specific, practical remedies need to be provided and the child's positive points need to be emphasized.

Teachers can also provide very specific suggestions to individual parents. For example, if a student needs additional assistance in a particular subject, the teacher can provide tips to parents to encourage and increase deeper understanding in the subject outside of class.

When the teacher finds it necessary to communicate (whether by phone, by letter, or in person) with a parent regarding a concern about a student, it is a good idea to allow a "cooling off" period before making contact with the parent. It is important to remain professional and objective. The purpose for contacting the parent is to elicit support and additional information that may have a bearing on the student's behavior or performance. Care must be taken not to demean the child and not to appear antagonistic or confrontational. The teacher must be aware that the parent is likely to be quite uncomfortable with the bad news and will respond best to a cooperative, problem solving approach to the issue. It is also a nice courtesy to notify parents of positive occurrences with their children.

When the teacher finds it necessary to communicate (whether by phone, by letter, or in person) with a parent regarding a concern about a student, it is a good idea to allow a "cooling off" period before making contact with the parent. It is important to remain professional and objective.

Sample Test Questions and Rationale

(Easy)

1. All of the following are essential components of effective parent-teacher conferences EXCEPT:

   A. Collecting samples of student work, records of behavior, and other relevant information

   B. Beginning the conference with positive comments about the student

   C. Using informal small talk to put the parents at ease

   D. Preparing a list of questions or concerns you wish to address

Answer: C. Using informal small talk to put the parents at ease

While you do want to begin the conference by putting the parents at ease and by taking the time to establish a comfortable mood, you should not waste time with unnecessary small talk. Begin your discussion with positive comments about the student, and be polite and professional. By collecting relevant data and a list of questions or concerns you wish to address, you will be better prepared to keep the conference focused and positive.

(Rigorous)

2. What can you do to create a good working environment with a classroom assistant?

   A. Plan lessons with the assistant.

   B. Write a contract that clearly defines his/her responsibilities in the classroom

   C. Remove previously given responsibilities.

   D. All of the above

Answer: A. Plan lessons with the assistant

Planning with your classroom assistant shows that you respect his/her input and allows you to see where he/she feels confident.

(Average)

3. A paraprofessional has been assigned to assist you in the classroom. What action on the part of the teacher would lead to a poor working relationship?

   A. Having the paraprofessional lead a small group

   B. Telling the paraprofessional what you expect him/her to do

   C. Defining classroom behavior management as your responsibility alone

   D. Taking an active role in his/her evaluation

Answer: C. Defining classroom behavior management as your responsibility alone

When you do not allow another adult in the room to enforce the class rules, you create an environment where the other adult is seen as someone not to be respected. No one wants to be in a work environment where they do not feel respected.

Sample Test Questions and Rationale (cont.)

(Average)

4. **Parent contact should first begin when:**

   A. You are informed the child will be your student

   B. The student fails a test

   C. The student exceeds others on a task

   D. An IEP meeting is scheduled and you have had no previous replies to letters

   Answer: A. You are informed the child will be your student

   Student and parent contact should begin as a getting to know you piece, which allows you to begin on a nonjudgmental platform. It is counterproductive to wait until there is a problem. If you can establish a cordial, team spirit relationship with the parents in the beginning, it will be easier to solve problems when they arise. It also helps the parent to see you as a professional that is willing to work with them.

(Rigorous)

5. **Janice requires occupational therapy and speech therapy services. She is your student. What must you do to ensure her needs are met?**

   A. Watch the services being rendered

   B. Schedule collaboratively

   C. Ask for services to be given in a push-in model

   D. Ask them to train you to give the service

   Answer: B. Schedule collaboratively

   Collaborative scheduling of students to receive services is both your responsibility and that of the service provider. Scheduling together allows for both your convenience and that of the service provider. It also will provide you with an opportunity to make sure the student does not miss important information.

References

Ager, C.L. & Cole, C.L. (1991). A Review of Cognitive-Behavioral Interventions for Children and Adolescents with Behavioral Disorders. *Behavioral Disorders*, 16 (4), 260-275.

Aiken, L.R. (1985). *Psychological Testing and Assessment* (5th Ed.). Boston: Allyn and Bacon.

Alberto, P.A. & Trouthman, A.C. (1990). *Applied Behavior Analysis for Teachers: Influencing Student Performance*. Columbus, Ohio: Charles E. Merrill.

Algozzine, B. (1990). *Behavior Problem Management: Educator's Resource Service*. Gaithersburg, MD: Aspen Publishers.

Algozzine, B., Ruhl, K., & Ramsey, R. (1991). *Behaviorally Disordered: Assessment for Identification and Instruction CED Mini-Library*. Renson, VA: The Council for Exceptional Children.

Ambron, S.R. (1981). *Child Development* (3rd Ed.). New York: Holt, Rinehart and Winston.

Anerson, V., & Black, L. (Eds.). (1987, Winter). National News: U.S. Department of Education Releases Special Report (Editorial). *GLRS Journal* [Georgia Learning Resources System].

Anguili, R. (1987, Winter). The 1986 Amendment to the Education of the Handicapped Act. *Confederation* [a Quarterly Publication of the Georgia Federation Council for Exceptional Children].

Ashlock, R.B. (1976). *Error Patterns in Computation: A Semi-Programmed Approach* (2nd Ed.). Columbus, Ohio: Charles E. Merrill.

Association for Retarded Citizens of Georgia (1987). 1986-87 *Government Report*. College Park, GA: Author

Ausubel, D.P. & Sullivan, E.V. (1970). *Theory and Problems of Child Development*. New York: Grune & Stratton.

Banks, J.A., & McGee Banks, C.A. (1993). *Multicultural Education* (2nd Ed.). Boston: Allyn and Bacon.

Barrett, T.C. (Ed.). (1967). *The Evaluation of Children's Reading Achievement. In Perspectives in Reading, No. 8*. Newark, Delaware: International Reading Association.

Bartoli, J.S. (1989). An Ecological Response to Cole's Interactivity Alternative. *Journal of Learning Disabilities*, 22 (5), 292-297.

Basile-Jackson, J. (1981) *The Exceptional Child in the Regular Classroom*. Augusta, GA: East Georgia Center, Georgia Learning Resources System.

Bauer, A.M., & Shea, T.M. (1989). *Teaching Exceptional Students in Your Classroom*. Boston: Allyn and Bacon.

Bentley, E.L. Jr. (1980). *Questioning Skills* (Videocassette & Manual Series). Northbrook, IL: Hubbard Scientific Company. (Project STRETCH [Strategies to Train Regular Educators to Teach Children with Handicaps], Module 1, ISBN 0-8331-1906-0).

Berdine, W.H., & Blackhurst, A.E. (1985). *An Introduction to Special Education.* (2nd Ed.) Boston: Little, Brown and Company.

Blake, K. (1976). *The Mentally Retarded: An Educational Psychology.* Englewood Cliff, NJ: Prentice-Hall.

Bloom, B.S. (1956). *Taxonomy of Educational Objectives, Handbook I: The Cognitive Domain.* New York: David McKay Co. Inc.

Bohline, D.S. (1985). *Intellectual and Affective Characteristics of Attention Deficit Disordered Children.* Journal of Learning Disabilities, 18 (10), 604-608.

Boone, R. (1983). Legislation and Litigation. In R.E. Schmid, & L. Negata (Eds.). *Contemporary Issues in Special Education.* New York: McGraw Hill.

Brantlinger, E.A., & Guskin, S.L. (1988). Implications of Social and Cultural Differences for Special Education. In Meten, E.L. Vergason, G.A., & Whelan, R.J. *Effective Instructional Strategies for Exceptional Children.* Denver, CO: Love Publishing.

Brewton, B. (1990). Preliminary Identification of the Socially Maladjusted. In Georgia Psycho-Educational Network, Monograph #1. *An Educational Perspective on Emotional Disturbance and Social Maladjustment.* Atlanta, GA Psychoeducational Network.

Brolin, D.E., & Kokaska, C.J. (1979). *Career Education for Handicapped Children Approach.* Renton, VA: The Council for Exceptional Children.

Brolin, D.E. (Ed). (1989). *Life Centered Career Education: A Competency Based Approach.* Reston, VA: The Council for Exceptional Children.

Brown, J.W., Lewis, R.B., & Harcleroad, F.F. (1983). *AV Instruction: Technology, Media, and Methods* (6th Ed.). New York: McGraw-Hill.

Bryan, T.H., & Bryan, J.H. (1986). *Understanding Learning Disabilities* (3rd Ed.). Palo Alto, CA: Mayfield.

Bryen, D.N. (1982). *Inquiries Into Child Language.* Boston: Allyn & Bacon.

Bucher, B.D. (1987). *Winning Them Over.* New York: Times Books.

Bush, W.L., & Waugh, K.W. (1982). *Diagnosing Learning Problems* (3rd Ed.). Columbus, OH: Charles E. Merrill.

Caine, R.N., et al. (2005). *12 Brain/Mind Learning Principles in Action : The Fieldbook for Making Connections, Teaching, and the Human Brain.* Thousand Oaks, CA: Corwin Press.

Campbell, P. (1986). *Special Needs Report* [Newsletter]. 1 (1), 1-3.

Canter, L., & Canter, M. (2001). *Assertive Discipline: Positive Behavior Management for Today's Classroom.* Bloomington, IN: Solution Tree.

Carbo, M., & Dunn, K. (1986). *Teaching Students to Read Through Their Individual Learning Styles.* Englewood Cliffs, NJ: Prentice Hall.

Cartwright, G.P., & Cartwright, C.A., & Ward, M.E. (1984). *Educating Special Learners* (2nd Ed.). Belmont, CA: Wadsworth.

Cejka, J.M. (Consultant), & Needham, F. (Senior Editor). (1976). *Approaches to Mainstreaming.* (Filmstrip and Cassette Kit, Units 1 & 2). Boston: Teaching Resources Corporation. (Catalog Nos. 09-210 & 09-220).

Chalfant, J.C. (1985). *Identifying Learning Disabled Students: A Summary of the National Task Force Report.* Learning Disabilities Focus, 1, 9-20.

Chalfant, J.C., et al. (1979). Teacher Assistance Teams: A Model for Within-Building Problem Solving. *Learning Disability Quarterly* 2 (3), 85-96.

Charles, C.M. (1976). *Individualizing Instructions.* St Louis: The C.V. Mosby Company.

Chrispeels, J.H. (1991). District Leadership in Parent Involvement: Policies and Actions in San Diego. *Phi Delta Kappan*, 71, 367-371.

Cincinnati Children's Hospital Medical Center. Website. http://www.cincinnatichildrens.org.

Clarizio, H.F. (1987). Differentiating Characteristics. In Georgia Psychoeducational Network, Monograph #1, *An Educational Perspective on: Emotional Disturbance and Social Maladjustment.* Atlanta, GA: Psychoeducational Network.

Clarizio, H.F. & McCoy, G.F. (1983). *Behavior Disorders in Children* (3rd Ed.). New York: Harper & Row.

Coles, G.S. (1989). *Excerpts from the Learning Mystique: A Critical Look at Disabilities.* Journal of Learning Disabilities, 22 (5), 267-278.

Collins, E. (1980). *Grouping and Special Students.* (Videocassette & Manual Series). Northbrook, IL: Hubbard Scientific Company. (Project STRETCH [Strategies to Train Regular Educators to Teach Children with Handicaps], Module 17, ISBN 0-8331-1922-2).

Compton, C., (1984). *A Guide to 75 Tests for Special Education.* Belmont, CA., Pitman Learning.

Council for Exceptional Children. (1976). *Introducing P.L. 94-142.* [Filmstrip-Cassette Kit Manual]. Reston, VA: Author.

Council for Exceptional Children. (1987). *The Council for Exceptional Children's Fall 1987 Catalog of Products and Services.* Renton, VA: Author.

Council for Exceptional Children Delegate Assembly. (1983). *Council for Exceptional Children Code of Ethics* (Adopted April 1983). Reston, VA: Author.

Craig, E., & Craig, L. (1990). *Reading in the Content Areas.* (Videocassette & Manual Series). Northbrook, IL: Hubbard Scientific Company. (Project STRETCH [Strategies to Train Regular Educators to Teach Children with Handicaps], Module 13, ISBN 0-8331-1918-4).

Cummins, J. (1994). The Acquisition of English as a Second Language. In K. Spangenberg-Urbschat & Robert Pritchard, *Kids Come in All Languages.* Newark, DE: International Reading Association.

Cummins, J. (1999). BICS and CALP: Clarifying the Distinction. ERIC Document 438551.

Czajka, J.L. (1984). *Digest of Data on Person with Disabilities* (Mathematics Policy Research, Inc.). Washington, D.C.: U.S. Government Printing Office.

Dell, H.D. (1972). *Individualizing Instruction: Materials and Classroom Procedures.* Chicago: Science Research Associates.

Demonbreun, C., & Morris, J. (1980). *Classroom Management* [Videocassette & Manual Series]. Northbrook, IL: Hubbard Scientific Company. Project STRETCH (Strategies to Train Regular Educators to Teach Children with Handicaps]. Module 5, ISBN 0-8331-1910-9).

Deno, E. (1970). Special Education as Developmental Capital. *Exceptional Children* 37 (3), 229-37.

Department of Education. *Education for the Handicapped Law Reports.* Supplement 45 (1981), P. 102: 52. Washington, D.C.: U.S. Government Printing Office.

Department of Health, Education, and Welfare, Office of Education. (1977, August 23). *Education of Handicapped Children.* Federal Register, 42, (163).

Diana vs. State Board of Education, Civil No. 70-37 R.F.P. (N.D.Cal. January, 1970).

Digangi, S.A., Perryman, P., & Rutherford, R.B., Jr. (1990). Juvenile Offenders in the 90's: A Descriptive Analysis. *Perceptions*, 25 (4), 5-8.

Division of Educational Services, Special Education Programs (1986). *Fifteenth Annual Report to Congress on Implementation of the Education of the Handicapped Act.* Washington, D.C.: U.S. Government Printing Office.

Doyle, B.A. (1978). *Math Readiness Skills.* Paper Presented at National Association of School Psychologists, New York.

Drummond, R.J. (2000). *Appraisal Procedures for Counselors and Helping Professionals.* (4th ed.) Englewood Cliffs, NJ: Merrill/Prentice Hall.

Dunn, R.S., & Dunn, K.J. (1978). *Teaching Students through Their Individual Learning Styles: A Practical Approach.* Reston, VA: Reston.

Epstein, M.H., Patton, J.R., Polloway, E.A., & Foley, R. (1989). Mild Retardation: Student Characteristics and Services. *Education and Training of the Mentally Retarded, 24,* 7-16.

ERIC Clearinghouse on Disabilities and Gifted Education. (1993). *Including Students with Disabilities in General Education Classrooms.* ERIC Digest E521. Eric Document 358677.

Ekwall, E.E., & Shanker, J.L. 1983). *Diagnosis and Remediation of the Disabled Reader* (2nd Ed.) Boston: Allyn and Bacon.

Firth, E.E. & Reynolds, I. (1983). Slide Tape Shows: A Creative Activity for the Gifted Students. *Teaching Exceptional Children.* 15 (3), 151-153.

Frymier, J., & Gansneder, B. (1989). The Phi Delta Kappa Study of Students at Risk. *Phi Delta Kappan.* 71 (2) 142-146.

Fuchs, D., & Deno, S.L. (1992). Effects of Curriculum within Curriculum-Based Measurement. *Exceptional Children* 58 (232-242).

Fuchs, D., & Fuchs, L.S. (1989). Effects of Examiner Familiarity on Black, Caucasian, and Hispanic Children. A Meta-Analysis. *Exceptional Children.* 55, 303-308.

Fuchs, L.S., & Shinn, M.R. (1989). Writing CBM IEP Objectives. In M.R. Shinn, *Curriculum-Based Measurement: Assessing Special Students.* New York: Guilford Press.

Gage, N.L. (1990). Dealing with the Dropout Problems? *Phi Delta Kappan.* 72 (4), 280-285.

Gallagher, P.A. (1988). *Teaching Students with Behavior Disorders: Techniques and Activities for Classroom Instruction* (2nd Ed.). Denver, CO: Love Publishing.

Gardner, H. (1999). *Intelligence Reframed: Multiple Intelligences for the 21st Century.* New York: Basic Books.

Gearheart, B.R. (1980). *Special Education for the 80s.* St. Louis, MO: The C.V. Cosby Company.

Gearhart, B.R. & Weishahn, M.W. (1986). *The Handicapped Student in the Regular Classroom* (2nd Ed.). St Louis, MO: The C.V. Mosby Company.

Gearhart, B.R. (1985). *Learning Disabilities: Educational Strategies* (4th Ed.). St. Louis: Times Mirror/ Mosby College of Publishing.

Georgia Department of Education, Program for Exceptional Children. (1986). *Mild Mentally Handicapped* (Vol. II), Atlanta, GA: Office of Instructional Services, Division of Special Programs, and Program for Exceptional Children. Resource Manuals for Program for Exceptional Children.

Georgia Department of Human Resources, Division of Rehabilitation Services. (1987, February).

Request for Proposal [Memorandum]. Atlanta, GA: Author.

Georgia Psychoeducational Network (1990). *An Educational Perspective on: Emotional Disturbance and Social Maladjustment.* Monograph #1. Atlanta, GA Psychoeducational Network.

Geren, K. (1979). *Complete Special Education Handbook.* West Nyack, NY: Parker.

Gillet, P.K. (1988). Career Development. Robinson, G.A., Patton, J.R., Polloway, E.A., & Sargent, L.R. (Eds.). *Best Practices in Mild Mental Disabilities.* Reston, VA: The Division on Mental Retardation of the Council for Exceptional Children.

Gleason, J.B. (1993). *The Development of Language* (3rd Ed.). New York: Macmillan Publishing.

Good, T.L., & Brophy, J.E. (1978). *Looking into Classrooms* (2nd Ed.). New York: Harper & Row.

Haladyna, T.M. (1999). *Developing and Validating Multiple-Choice Items.* Mahwah, NJ: Lawrence Erlbaum Associates.

Hall, M.A. (1979). Language-Centered Reading: Premises and Recommendations. *Language Arts,* 56 664-670.

Halllahan, D.P. & Kauffman, J.M. (1988). *Exceptional Children: Introduction to Special Education.* (4th Ed.). Englewood Cliffs, NJ: Prentice-Hall.

Hallahan, D.P. & Kauffman, J.M. (1994). *Exceptional Children: Introduction to Special Education* (6th Ed.). Boston: Allyn and Bacon.

Halpern, Andrew S. (1991). Transition: Old Wine in New Bottles. *Exceptional Children* 58 (3), 202-11.

Hammill, D.D., & Bartel, N.R. (1982). *Teaching Children with Learning and Behavior Problems* (3rd Ed.). Boston: Allyn and Bacon.

Hammill, D.D., & Bartel, N.R. (1986). *Teaching Students with Learning and Behavior Problems* (4th Ed.). Boston and Bacon.

Hamill, D.D., & Brown, L. & Bryant, B. (1989). *A Consumer's Guide to Tests in Print.* Austin, TX: Pro-Ed.

Haney, J.B. & Ullmer, E.J. (1970). *Educational Media and the Teacher.* Dubuque, IA: Wm. C. Brown Company.

Hardman, M.L., Drew, C.J., Egan, M.W., & Wolf, B. (1984). *Human Exceptionality: Society, School, and Family.* Boston: Allyn and Bacon.

Hardman, M.L., Drew, C.J., Egan, M.W., & Worlf, B. (1990). *Human Exceptionality* (3rd Ed.). Boston: Allyn and Bacon.

Hargrove, L.J., & Poteet, J.A. (1984). *Assessment in Special Education.* Englewood Cliffs, NJ: Prentice-Hall.

Haring, N.G., & Bateman, B. (1977). *Teaching the Learning Disabled Child.* Englewood Cliffs, NJ: Prentice-Hall.

Harris, K.R., & Pressley, M. (1991). The Nature of Cognitive Strategy Instruction: Interactive Strategy Instruction. *Exceptional Children,* 57, 392-401.

Hart, T., & Cadora, M.J. (1980). *The Exceptional Child: Label the Behavior* [Videocassette & Manual Series], Northbrook, IL: Hubbard Scientific Company. (Project STRETCH [Strategies to Train Regular Educators to Teach Children with Handicaps], Module 12, ISBN 0-8331-1917-6).

Hart, V. (1981). *Mainstreaming Children with Special Needs.* New York: Longman.

Henley, M., Ramsey,R.S., & Algozzine, B. (1993). *Characteristics of and Strategies for Teaching Students with Mild Disabilities.* Boston: Allyn and Bacon.

Hewett, F.M., & Forness, S.R. (1984). *Education of Exceptional Learners.* (3rd Ed.). Boston: Allyn and Bacon.

Howe, C.E. (1981). *Administration of Special Education.* Denver: Love.

Human Services Research Institute (1985). *Summary of Data on Handicapped Children and Youth.* (Digest). Washington, D.C.: U.S. Government Printing Office.

Johnson, D.W. (1972). *Reaching Out: Interpersonal Effectiveness and Self-Actualization.* Englewood Cliffs, NJ: Prentice-Hall.

Johnson, D.W. (1978). *Human Relations and Your Career: A Guide to Interpersonal Skills.* Englewood Cliffs, NJ: Prentice-Hall.

Johnson, D.W., & Johnson, R.T. (1990). Social Skills for Successful Group Work. *Educational Leadership.* 47 (4) 29-33.

Johnson, S.W., & Morasky, R.L. *Learning Disabilities* (2nd Ed.) Boston: Allyn and Bacon.

Jones, F.H. (1987). *Positive Classroom Discipline.* New York: McGraw-Hill Book Company.

Jones, V.F., & Jones, L.S. (1986). *Comprehensive Classroom Management: Creating Positive Learning Environments.* (2nd Ed.). Boston: Allyn and Bacon.

Jones, V.F. & Jones, L.S. (1981). *Responsible Classroom Discipline: Creating Positive Learning Environments and Solving Problems.* Boston: Allyn and Bacon.

Joyce, B.R., & Weil, M. (1996). *Models of Technology.* Boston: Allyn & Bacon.

Kauffman, J.M. (1981). *Characteristics of Children's Behavior Disorders.* (2nd Ed.). Columbus, OH: Charles E. Merrill.

Kauffman, J.M. (1989). *Characteristics of Behavior Disorders of Children and Youth.* (4th Ed.). Columbus, OH: Merrill Publishing.

Kellough, R.D., & Roberts, P. (1991). *A Resource Guide for Elementary School Teaching: Planning for Competence.* New York: Macmillan.

Kem, M., & Nelson, M. (1983). *Strategies for Managing Behavior Problems in the Classroom.* Columbus, OH: Charles E. Merrill.

Kerr, M.M., & Nelson, M. (1983). *Strategies for Managing Behavior Problems in the Classroom.* Columbus, OH: Charles E. Merrill.

Kirk, S.A., & Gallagher, J.J. (1986). *Educating Exceptional Children* (5th Ed.). Boston: Houghton Mifflin.

Kirk, S.A., Gallagher, J.J., & Anastasiow, N.J. *Educating Exceptional Children* (10th Ed.). Boston: Houghton Mifflin.

Kohfeldt, J. (1976). Blueprints for Construction. *Focus on Exceptional Children.* 8 (5), 1-14.

Kokaska, C.J., & Brolin, D.E. (1985). *Career Education for Handicapped Individuals* (2nd Ed.). Columbus, OH: Charles E. Merrill.

Lambie, R.A. (1980). A Systematic Approach for Changing Materials, Instruction, and Assignments to Meet Individual Needs. *Focus on Exceptional Children*, 13 (1), 1-12.

Larson, S.C., & Poplin, M.S. (1980). *Methods for Educating the Handicapped: An Individualized Education Program Approach.* Boston: Allyn and Bacon.

Lerner, J. (1976). *Children with Learning Disabilities.* (2nd Ed.). Boston: Houghton Mifflin.

Lerner, J. (1989). *Learning Disabilities: Theories, Diagnosis and Teaching Strategies* (3rd Ed.). Boston: Houghton Mifflin.

Levenkron, S. (1991). *Obsessive-Compulsive Disorders.* New York: Warner Books.

Lewis, R.B., & Doorlag, D.H. (1991). *Teaching Special Students in the Mainstream.* (3rd Ed.). New York: Merrill.

Lindsley, O.R. (1990). Precision Teaching: By Teachers for Children. *Teaching Exceptional Children*, 22 (3), 10-15.

Linn, R.L., Gronlund, N.E., & Gronlund, N.E. (1995). *Measurement and Assessment in Teaching.* Upper Saddle River, NJ: Merrill.

Lindberg, L., & Swedlow, R. (1985). *Young Children Exploring and Learning.* Boston: Allyn and Bacon.

Long, N.J., Morse, W.C., & Newman, R.G. (1980). *Conflict in the Classroom: The Education of Emotionally Disturbed Children.* Belmont, CA: Wadsworth.

Losen, S.M., & Losen, J.G. (1985). *The Special Education Team.* Boston: Allyn and Bacon.

Lovitt, T.C. (1989). *Introduction to Learning Disabilities.* Boston: Allyn and Bacon.

Lund, N.J. Duchan, J.F. (1988). *Assessing Children's Language in Naturalist Contexts.* Englewood Cliffs, NJ: Prentice Hall

Male, M. (1994). *Technology for Inclusion: Meeting the Special Needs of All Children.* (2nd Ed.). Boston: Allyn and Bacon.

Mandelbaum, L.H. (1989). Reading. In G.A. Robinson, J.R., Patton, E.A., Polloway, & L.R. Sargent (Eds.). *Best Practices in Mild Mental Retardation.* Reston, VA: The Division of Mental Retardation, Council for Exceptional Children.

Mannix, D. (1993). *Social Skills for Special Children.* West Nyack, NY: The Center for Applied Research in Education.

Marshall, et al. vs. Georgia. U.S. District Court for the Southern District of Georgia. C.V. 482-233. June 28, 1984.

Marshall, E.K., Kurtz, P.D., & Associates. *Interpersonal Helping Skills.* San Francisco, CA: Jossey-Bass Publications.

Marston, D.B. (1989). A Curriculum-Based Measurement Approach to Assessing Academic Performance: What It Is and Why Do It. In M. Shinn (Ed.). *Curriculum-Based Measurement: Assessing Special Children.* New York: Guilford Press.

McDowell, R.L., Adamson, G.W., & Wood, F.H. (1982). *Teaching Emotionally Disturbed Children.* Boston: Little, Brown and Company.

McGinnis, E., Goldstein, A.P. (1990). *Skill Streaming in Early Childhood: Teaching Prosocial Skills to the Preschool and Kindergarten Child.* Champaign, IL: Research Press.

McLoughlin, J.A., & Lewis, R.B. (1986). *Assessing Special Students* (3rd Ed.). Columbus, OH: Charles E. Merrill.

Mercer, C.D. (1987). *Students with Learning Disabilities.* (3rd. Ed.). Merrill Publishing.

Mercer, C.D., & Mercer, A.R. (1985). *Teaching Children with Learning Problems* (2nd Ed.). Columbus, OH: Charles E. Merrill.

Meyen, E.L., Vergason, G.A., & Whelan, R.J. (Eds.). (1988). *Effective Instructional Strategies for Exceptional Children.* Denver, CO: Love Publishing.

Miller, L.K. (1980). *Principles of Everyday Behavior Analysis* (2nd Ed.). Monterey, CA: Brooks/Cole Publishing Company.

Mills vs. The Board of Education of the District of Columbia, 348F. Supp. 866 (D.C. 1972).

Mopsick, S.L. & Agard, J.A. (Eds.) (1980). *Education Handbook for Parents of Handicapped Children.* Cambridge, MA: Abbott Associates.

Morris, C.G. (1985). *Psychology: An Introduction* (5th Ed.). Englewood Cliffs, NJ: Prentice-Hall.

Morris, J. (1980). *Behavior Modification.* [Videocassette and Manual Series]. Northbrook, IL: Hubbard Scientific Company. (Project STRETCH [Strategies to Train Regular Educators to Teach Children with Handicaps,] Module 16, Metropolitan Cooperative Educational Service Agency.).

Morris, J. & Demonbreun, C. (1980). *Learning Styles* [Videocassettes & Manual Series]. Northbrook, IL: Hubbard Scientific Company. (Project STRETCH [Strategies to Train Regular Educators to Teach Children with Handicaps], Module 15, ISBN 0-8331-1920-6).

Morris, R.J. (1985). *Behavior Modification with Exceptional Children: Principles and Practices.* Glenview, IL: Scott, Foresman and Company.

Morsink, C.V. (1984). *Teaching Special Needs Students in Regular Classrooms.* Boston: Little, Brown and Company.

Morsink, C.V., Thomas, C.C., & Correa, V.L. (1991). *Interactive Teaming, Consultation and Collaboration in Special Programs.* New York: Macmillan Publishing.

Mullsewhite, C.R. (1986). *Adaptive Play for Special Needs Children: Strategies to Enhance Communication and Learning.* San Diego: College Hill Press.

Newcomer, P.L. (1993). *Understanding and Teaching Emotionally Disturbed Children and Adolescents.* Austin, TX: Pro-Ed.

New York State United Teachers. (2007). Consultant Teacher Services. Information Bulletin no. 200709. http://www.nysut.org/cps/rde/xchg/nysut/hs.xsl/k12_4961.htm

North Central Georgia Learning Resources System/Child Serve. (1985). *Strategies Handbook for Classroom Teachers.* Ellijay, GA.

Patton, J.R., Cronin, M.E., Polloway, E.A., Hutchinson, D., & Robinson, G.A. (1988). Curricular Considerations: A Life Skills Orientation. In Robinson, G.A., Patton, J.R., Polloway, E.A., & Sargent, L.R. (Eds.). *Best Practices in Mental Disabilities.* Des Moines, IA: Iowa Department of Education, Bureau of Special Education.

Patton, J.R., Kauggman, J.M., Blackbourn, J.M., & Brown, B.G. (1991). *Exceptional Children in Focus* (5th Ed.). New York: Macmillan.

Paul, J.L. (Ed.). (1981). *Understanding and Working with Parents of Children with Special Needs.* New York: Holt, Rinehart and Winston.

Paul, J.L. & Epanchin, B.C. (1991). *Educating Emotionally Disturbed Children and Youth: Theories and Practices for Teachers.* (2nd Ed.). New York: Macmillan.

Pennsylvania Association for Retarded Children vs. Commonwealth of Pennsylvania, 334 F. Supp. 1257 (E.D., PA., 1971), 343 F. Supp. 279 (L.D. PA., 19972).

Phillips, V., & McCullough, L. (1990). Consultation Based Programming: Instituting the Collaborative Work Ethic. *Exceptional Children.* 56 (4), 291-304.

Podemski, R.S., Price, B.K., Smith, T.E.C., & Marsh, G.E. (1984). *Comprehensive Administration of Special Education.* Rockville, MD: Aspen Systems Corporation.

Polloway, E.A., & Patton, J.R. (1993). *Strategies for Teaching Learners with Special Needs.* (5th Ed.). New York: Merrill.

Polloway, E.A., Patton, J.R., Payne, J.S., & Payne, R.A. (1989). *Strategies for Teaching Learners with Special Needs.* (4th Ed.). Columbus, OH: Merrill Publishing.

Pugach, M.C., & Johnson, L.J. (1989a). The Challenge of Implementing Collaboration between General and Special Education. *Exceptional Children*, 56 (3), 232-235.

Pugach, M.C., & Johnson, L.J. (1989b). Pre-Referral Interventions: Progress, Problems, and Challenges. *Exceptional Children*, 56 (3), 217-226.

Quay, H.C., & Peterson, D.R. (1996). *Revised Problem Behavior Checklist.* Odessa, FL : Psychological Assessment Resources.

Radabaugh, M.T., & Yukish, J.F. (1982). *Curriculum and Methods for the Mildly Handicapped.* Boston: Allyn and Bacon.

Ramsey, R.S. (1981). Perceptions of Disturbed and Disturbing Behavioral Characteristics by School Personnel. (Doctoral Dissertation, University of Florida) Dissertation Abstracts International, 42 (49), DA8203709.

Ramsey, R.S. (1986). Taking the Practicum Beyond the Public School Door. *Journal of Adolescence.* 21 (83), 547-552.

Ramsey, R.S., (1988). *Preparatory Guide for Special Education Teacher Competency Tests.* Boston: Allyn and Bacon, Inc.

Ramsey, R.S., Dixon, M.J., & Smith, G.G.B. (1986). *Eyes on the Special Education: Professional Knowledge Teacher Competency Test.* Albany, GA: Southwest Georgia Learning Resources System Center.

Ramsey R.W., & Ramsey, R.S. (1978). Educating the Emotionally Handicapped Child in the Public School Setting. *Journal of Adolescence.* 13 (52), 537-541.

Redl, F. & Winemand, D. (1965). Hypodermic Effect. In *Controls from Within: Techniques for the Treatment of the Aggressive Child.* New York: Free Press.

Reid, D.K. (1988). *Teaching the Learning Disabled: A Cognitive Developmental Approach.* Boston: Allyn & Bacon.

Reinheart, H.R. (1980). *Children I Conflict: Educational Strategies for the Emotionally Disturbed and Behaviorally Disordered.* (2nd Ed.). St Louis, MO: The C.V. Mosby Company.

Robinson, G.A., Patton, J.R., Polloway, E.A., & Sargent, L.R. (Eds.). (1989a). *Best Practices in Mental Disabilities.* Des Moines, IA Iowa Department of Education, Bureau of Special Education.

Robinson, G.A., Patton, J.R., Polloway, E.A., & Sargent, L.R. (Eds.). (1989b). *Best Practices in Mental Disabilities.* Renton, VA: The Division on Mental Retardation of the Council for Exceptional Children.

Rothstein, L.F. (1995). *Special Education Law* (2nd Ed.). New York: Longman Publishers.

Sabatino, D.A., Sabation, A.C., & Mann, L. (1983). *Management: A Handbook of Tactics, Strategies, and Programs.* Aspen Systems Corporation.

Salvia, J., & Ysseldyke, J.E. (1985). *Assessment in Special Education* (3rd. Ed.). Boston: Houghton Mifflin.

Salvia J., & Ysseldyke, J.E. (1991). *Assessment* (5th Ed.). Boston: Houghton Mifflin.

Salvia, J. & Ysseldyke, J.E. (1995). *Assessment* (6th Ed.). Boston: Houghton Mifflin.

Sattler, J.M. (1982). *Assessment of Children's Intelligence and Special Abilities* (2nd Ed.). Boston: Allyn and Bacon.

Schloss, P.J., Harriman, N., & Pfiefer, K. (1985). Application of a Sequential Prompt Reduction Technique to the Independent Composition Performance of Behaviorally Disordered Youth. *Behavioral Disorders.* 11 (1), 17-23.

Schloss, P.J., & Sedlak, R.A.(1986). *Instructional Methods for Students with Learning and Behavior Problems.* Boston: Allyn and Bacon.

Schmuck, R.A., & Schmuck, P.A. (1971). *Group Processes in the Classroom.* Dubuque, IA: William C. Brown Company.

Schubert, D.G. (1978). Your Teaching - the Tape Recorder. *Reading Improvement,* 15 (1), 78-80.

Schulz, J.B., Carpenter, C.D., & Turnbull, A.P. (1991). *Mainstreaming Exceptional Students: a Guide for Classroom Teachers.* Boston: Allyn and Bacon.

Semmel, M.I., Abernathy, T.V., Butera G., & Lesar, S. (1991). *Teacher Perception of the Regular Education Initiative.* Exceptional Children, 58 (1), 3-23.

Shea, T.M., & Bauer, A.M. (1985). *Parents and Teachers of Exceptional Students: A Handbook for Involvement.* Boston: Allyn and Bacon.

Short, D.J. (1989). Adapting Materials for Content-Based Language Instruction. *ERIC News Bulletin* 13 (1), 4-8.

Simeonsson, R.J. (1986). *Psychological and Development Assessment of Special Children.* Boston: Allyn and Bacon.

Smith, C.R. (1991). *Learning Disabilities: The Interaction of Learner, Task, and Setting.* Boston: Little, Brown, and Company.

Smith, D.D., & Luckasson, R. (1992). *Introduction to Special Education: Teaching in an Age of Challenge.* Boston: Allyn and Bacon.

Smith, J.E., & Patton, J.M. (1989). *A Resource Module on Adverse Causes of Mild Mental Retardation.* (Prepared for the President's Committee on Mental Retardation).

Smith, T.E.C., Finn, D.M., & Dowdy, C.A. (1993). *Teaching Students with Mild Disabilities.* Fort Worth, TX: Harcourt Brace Jovanovich College Publishers.

Smith-Davis, J. (1989a April). *A National Perspective on Special Education.* Keynote Presentation at the GLRS/College/University Forum, Macon, GA.

Stephens, T.M. (1976). *Directive Teaching of Children with Learning and Behavioral Disorders.* Columbus, OH Charles E. Merrill.

Sternburg, R.J. (1990). Thinking Styles: Key to Understanding Performance. *Phi Delta Kappan* 71 (5), 366-371.

Stiggins, R.J. (1997). *Student-Centered Classroom Assessment.* Upper Saddle River, NJ: Merrill.

Sulzer, B., & Mayer, G.R. (1972). *Behavior Modification Procedures for School Personnel.* Hinsdale, IL: Dryden.

Tateyama-Sniezek, K.M. (1990.) Cooperative Learning: Does It Improve the Academic Achievement of Students with Handicaps? *Exceptional Children,* 57 (2), 426-427.

Thiagarajan, S. (1976). Designing Instructional Games for Handicapped Learners. Focus on *Exceptional Children.* 7 (9), 1-11.

Thomas, O. (1980). *Individualized Instruction* [Videocassette & Manual Series]. Northbrook, IL: Hubbard Scientific Company. (Project STRETCH [Strategies to Train Regular Educators to Teach Children with Handicaps]. Module 14, ISBN 0-8331-1919-2).

Thomas, O. (1980). *Spelling* [Videocassette & Manual Series]. (Project STRETCH [Strategies to Train Regular Educators to Teach Children with Handicaps]. Module 10, ISBN 0-83311915-X).

Thorndike, R.M. (1997). *Measurement and Evaluation in Psychology and Education.* Upper Saddle River, NJ: Merrill.

Thornton, C.A., Tucker, B.F., Dossey, J.A., & Bazik, E.F. (1983). *Teaching Mathematics to Children with Special Needs.* Menlo Park, CA: Addison-Wesley.

Tomlinson, C.A. (2001). *How to Differentiate Instruction in Mixed Ability Classrooms.* Alexandria, VA: Association for Supervision and Curriculum Development.

Turkel, S.R., & Podel, D.M. (1984). Computer-Assisted Learning for Mildly Handicapped Students. *Teaching Exceptional Children.* 16 (4), 258-262.

Turnbull, A.P., Strickland, B.B., & Brantley, J.C. (1978). *Developing Individualized Education Programs.* Columbus, OH: Charles E. Merrill.

U.S. Department of Education. (1993). *To Assure the Free Appropriate Public Education of All Children with Disabilities. (Fifteenth Annual Report to Congress on the Implementation of the Individuals with Disabilities Education Act.).* Washington, D.C.

Venn, John J. *Assessing Students with Special Needs.* (3rd ed.) Upper Saddle River, NJ: Merrill.

Vygotsky, L.S. (1986). *Thought and Language.* Cambridge, MA: MIT Press.

Walker, J.E., & Shea, T.M. (1991). *Behavior Management: A Practical Approach for Educators.* New York: Macmillan.

Wallace, G., & Kauffman, J.M. (1978). *Teaching Children with Learning Problems.* Columbus, OH: Charles E. Merrill.

Walther-Thomas, C., et al. (1999). *Collaboration for Inclusive Education: Developing Successful Programs.* Boston: Allyn & Bacon.

Wehman, P., & McLaughlin, P.J. (1981). *Program Development in Special Education.* New York: McGraw-Hill.

Weintraub, F.J. (1987, March). [Interview].

Wesson, C.L. (1991). Curriculum-Based Measurement and Two Models of Follow-Up Consultation. *Exceptional Children.* 57 (3), 246-256.

West, R.P., Young, K.R., & Spooner, F. (1990). Precision Teaching: An Introduction. *Teaching Exceptional Children.* 22 (3), 4-9.

Wheeler, J. (1987). *Transitioning Persons with Moderate and Severe Disabilities from School to Adulthood: What Makes it Work?* Materials Development Center, School of Education, and Human Services. University of Wisconsin-Stout.

Whiting, J., & Aultman, L. (1990). *Workshop for Parents.* (Workshop Materials). Albany, GA: Southwest Georgia Learning Resources System Center.

Wiederholt, J.L., Hammill, D.D., & Brown, V.L. (1983). *The Resource Room Teacher: A Guide to Effective Practices* (2nd Ed.). Boston: Allyn and Bacon.

Wiig, E.H., & Semel, E.M. (1984). *Language Assessment and Intervention for the Learning Disabled.* (2nd Ed.). Columbus, OH: Charles E. Merrill.

Will, M.C. (1984). An Advocate for the Handicapped. *American Education* 20 (1), 4-6.

Wolfgang, C.H., & Glickman, C.D. (1986). *Solving Discipline Problems: Strategies for Classroom Teachers* (2nd Ed.). Boston: Allyn and Bacon.

Wood, B.S. (1981). *Children and Communication: Verbal and Nonverbal Language Development.* Englewood Cliffs, NJ: Prentice-Hall.

Ysselkyke, J.E., Algozzine, B. (1990). *Introduction to Special Education* (2nd Ed.). Boston: Houghton Mifflin.

Ysseldyke, J.E., Algozzine, B., & Thurlow, M.L. (1992). *Critical Issues in Special Education* (2nd Ed.). Boston: Houghton Mifflin Company.

Yssedlyke, J.E., Thurlow, M.L., Wotruba, J.W., Nania, PA.A (1990). Instructional Arrangements: Perceptions from General Education. *Teaching Exceptional Children,* 22 (4), 4-8.

Zabala, J. (2000). *Introduction to Assistive Technology.* Georgia Project for Assistive Technology.

Zargona, N., Vaughn, S., 7 & McIntosh, R. (1991). Social Skills Interventions and Children with Behavior Problems: A Review. *Behavior Disorders,* 16 (4), 260-275.

Zigmond, N., & Baker, J. (1990). Mainstream Experiences for Learning Disabled Students (Project Meld): Preliminary Report. *Exceptional Children,* 57 (2), 176-185.

Zirpoli, T.J., & Melloy, K.J. (1993). *Behavior Management.* New York: Macmillan.

SAMPLE TEST

SAMPLE TEST

(Average) (Skill 1.1)

1. Which behavior would be expected at the mild level of emotional/behavioral disorders?

   A. Attention seeking

   B. Inappropriate affect

   C. Self-injurious

   D. Poor sense of identity

(Rigorous) (Skill 1.1)

2. Short attention span, daydreaming, clumsiness, and preference for younger playmates are associated with:

   A. Conduct disorder

   B. Personality disorders

   C. Immaturity

   D. Socialized aggression

(Rigorous) (Skill 1.2)

3. Skilled readers use all but which one of these knowledge sources to construct meanings beyond the literal text:

   A. Text knowledge

   B. Syntactic knowledge

   C. Morphological knowledge

   D. Semantic knowledge

(Rigorous) (Skill 1.2)

4. Celia, who is in first grade, asked, "Where are my ball?" She also has trouble with passive sentences. Language interventions for Celia would target:

   A. Morphology

   B. Syntax

   C. Pragmatics

   D. Semantics

(Rigorous) (Skill 1.2)

5. Mr. Mendez is assessing his students' written expression. Which of these is not a component of written expression?

   A. Vocabulary

   B. Morphology

   C. Content

   D. Sentence structure

(Average) (Skill 1.4)

6. Muscular Dystrophy is a condition which affects the _________ system of the body.

   A. cardiopulmonary

   B. musculoskeletal

   C. neurological

   D. All of the above

(Rigorous) (Skill 2.1)

7. A child with intellectual disabilities who is fairly clumsy and possesses poor social awareness, but who can be taught to communicate and to perform semi-skilled labor and maintains himself under supervision, as an adult, probably belongs to which level of classification:

    A. Mild

    B. Moderate

    C. Severe

    D. Profound

(Rigorous) (Skill 2.2)

8. **Individuals with mild mental retardation can be characterized as:**

    A. Often indistinguishable from normal developing children at an early age

    B. Having a higher than normal rate of motor activity

    C. Displaying significant discrepancies in ability levels

    D. Uneducable in academic skills

(Average) (Skill 3.2)

9. **Across America there is a toxic substance that widely contributes to the creation of disabilities in our children. What is it?**

    A. Children's aspirin

    B. Fluoride water

    C. Chlorine gas

    D. Lead

(Average) (Skill 3.2)

10. ________ is an environmental reason for mild learning and behavioral disabilities:

    A. Poverty

    B. Genetics

    C. Biochemical factors

    D. Maturational lag

(Average) (Skill 3.2)

11. **Parents are more likely to have a child with a learning disability if:**

    A. They smoke tobacco

    B. The child is less than 5 pounds at birth

    C. If the mother drank alcohol on a regular basis until she planned for a baby

    D. The father was known to consume large quantities of alcohol during the pregnancy

(Easy) (Skill 3.3)

12. **Duration is an appropriate measure to take with all of these behaviors EXCEPT:**

    A. Thumb sucking

    B. Hitting

    C. Temper tantrums

    D. Maintaining eye contact

(Average) (Skill 3.3)

13. **All children cry, hit, fight, and play alone at different times. Children with behavior disorders will perform these behaviors at a higher than normal:**

    A. Rate

    B. Topography

    C. Duration

    D. Magnitude

(Rigorous) (Skill 3.4)

14. **Which of the following is typical of attention problems that a youngster with a learning disability might display?**

    A. Lack of selective attention

    B. Does not consider consequences before acting

    C. Unable to Control Own Actions or impulses

    D. Poor fine motor coordination

(Average) (Skill 3.4)

15. **Echolalia, repetitive stereotyped actions, and a severe disorder of thinking and communication are indicative of:**

    A. Psychosis

    B. Schizophrenia

    C. Autism

    D. Paranoia

(Average) (Skill 3.4)

16. **In which of the following exceptionality categories may a student be considered for inclusion if his IQ score falls more than two standard deviations below the mean?**

    A. Mental retardation

    B. Specific learning disabilities

    C. Emotionally/behaviorally disordered

    D. Gifted

(Rigorous) (Skill 5.1)

17. **What legislation started FAPE?**

    A. Section 504

    B. EHCA

    C. IDEA

    D. Education Amendment 1974

(Average) (Skill 5.1)

18. **What is true about IDEA? In order to be eligible, a student must:**

    A. Have a medical disability

    B. Have a disability that fits into one of the categories listed in the law

    C. Attend a private school

    D. Be a slow learner

(Average) (Skill 5.1)

19. **According to IDEA 2004, students with disabilities are to do what:**

   A. Participate in the general education program to the fullest extent that it is beneficial for them

   B. Participate in a vocational training within the general education setting

   C. Participate in a general education setting for physical education

   D. Participate in a modified program that meets his/her needs

(Average) (Skill 5.2)

20. **What determines whether a person is entitled to protection under Section 504?**

   A. The individual must meet the definition of a person with a disability

   B. The person must be able to meet the requirements of a particular program in spite of his or her disability

   C. The school, business or other facility must be the recipient of federal funding assistance

   D. All of the above

(Rigorous) (Skill 5.4)

21. **How was the training of special education teachers changed by the No Child Left Behind Act of 2002?**

   A. It required all special education teachers to be certified in reading and math

   B. It required all special education teachers to take the same coursework as general education teachers

   C. If a special education teacher is teaching a core subject, he or she must meet the standard of a highly-qualified teacher in that subject

   D. All of the above

(Easy) (Skill 6.1)

22. **One of the most important goals of the special education teacher is to foster and create with the student:**

   A. Handwriting skills

   B. Self-advocacy

   C. An increased level of reading

   D. Logical reasoning

(Easy) (Skill 6.2)

23. **Greg is a three-year-old boy who has recently survived a bout of meningitis. The pediatrician who treated Greg during his illness had to inform Greg's parents about some brain dysfunction which he had medically diagnosed. A reaction which would be anticipated upon learning of Greg's condition is:**

   A. Shock

   B. Disbelief

   C. Denial

   D. All of the above

(Average) (Skill 6.3)

24. **Early nineteenth century is considered a period of great importance in the field of special education because principles presently used in working with exceptional students were formulated by Itard. These principles included:**

   A. Individualized instruction

   B. Sequence of tasks

   C. Functional life-like skills curriculum

   D. All of the above

(Rigorous) (Skill 6.4)

25. **Acceptance of disabilities by parents and siblings is most influenced by:**

    A. Students obtain career training from elementary through high school

    B. Students acquire specific training in job skills prior to exiting school

    C. Students need specific training and supervision in applying skills learned in school to requirements in job situations

    D. Students obtain needed instruction and field-based experiences that help them to be able to work in specific occupations

(Easy) (Skill 7.2)

26. **Students with disabilities develop greater self-images and recognize their own academic and social strengths when they are:**

    A. Included in the mainstream classroom

    B. Provided community based internships

    C. Socializing in the hallway

    D. Provided 1:1 instructional opportunity

(Average) (Skill 7.4)

27. **Vocational training programs are based on all of the following ideas except:**

    A. Students obtain career training from elementary through high school

    B. Students acquire specific training in job skills prior to exiting school

    C. Students need specific training and supervision in apply skills learned in school to requirements in jog situations

    D. Student obtain needed instruction and field-based experiences that help them to be able to work in specific occupations

(Rigorous) (Skill 8.1)

28. **An educational implication of cognitive learning stages is the importance given to:**

    A. Defining behavior

    B. Modifying behavior

    C. Assessing entry-level skills

    D. Knowing the ages of the students

(Rigorous) (Skill 8.1)

29. **Advocates of cognitive learning stages support the idea that behavior is:**

    A. Variable

    B. Predictable

    C. Learned

    D. Practical

(Rigorous) (Skill 8.2)

30. **Which components of the IEP are required by law?**

    A. Present level of academic and functional performance; statement of how the disability affects the student's involvement and progress; evaluation criteria and timeliness for instructional objective achievement; modifications of accommodations

    B. Projected dates for services initiation with anticipated frequency, location and duration; statement of when parent will be notified; statement of annual goals

    C. Extent to which child will not participate in regular education program; transitional needs for students age 16

    D. All of the above

(Rigorous) (Skill 8.2)

31. **What does the section of the IEP entitled "Present Levels" or "Present Levels of Educational Performance" address?**

    A. Academic achievement and functional performance

    B. English as a second language

    C. Functional performance

    D. Academic achievement

(Average) (Skill 8.2)

32. **Which of the following must be provided in a written notice to parents when proposing a child's educational placement?**

    A. A list of parental due process safeguards

    B. A list of family services available through the school

    C. A list of persons responsible for the child's education

    D. A list of academic subjects the child has passed

(Easy) (Skill 8.3)

33. **Which of the following teaching activities is LEAST likely to enhance observational learning in students with special needs?**

    A. A verbal description of the task to be performed, followed by having the children immediately attempt to perform the instructed behavior

    B. A demonstration of the behavior, followed by an immediate opportunity for the children to imitate the behavior

    C. A simultaneous demonstration and explanation of the behavior, followed by ample opportunity for the children to rehearse the instructed behavior

    D. Physically guiding the children through the behavior to be imitated, while verbally explaining the behavior

(Rigorous) (Skill 9.1)

34. **The minimum number of IEP meetings required per year is:**

    A. As many as necessary

    B. One

    C. Two

    D. Three

(Rigorous) (Skill 9.2)

35. **The Integrated approach to learning utilizes all resources available to address student needs. What are the resources?**

    A. The student, his/her parents, and the teacher

    B. The teacher, the parents, and the special education team

    C. The teacher the student, and an administrator to perform needed interventions

    D. The student, his/her parents, the teacher and community resources

(Easy) (Skill 9.3)

36. **Teaching techniques that stimulate active participation and understanding in the mathematics class include all but which of the following?**

    A. Having students copy computation facts for a set number of times

    B. Asking students to find the error in an algorithm

    C. Giving immediate feedback to students

    D. Having students chart their progress

(Easy) (Skill 9.3)

37. **The social skills of students with mental retardation disabilities are likely to be appropriate for children of their mental age, rather than chronological age. This means that the teacher whose class contains children with these disabilities will need to do all of the following except:**

    A. Model desired behavior

    B. Provide clear instructions

    C. Expect age appropriate behaviors

    D. Adjust the physical environment when necessary

(Rigorous) (Skill 9.4)

38. **Which type of grouping arrangement would be MOST effective for teaching basic academic skills such as math facts or reading?**

    A. Large group with teacher

    B. Peer tutoring

    C. Small group instruction

    D. Cooperative learning

(Rigorous) (Skill 9.5)

39. **A transition or vocational curriculum approach focuses on:**

    A. Remediation of basic academic skills

    B. Preparation for functioning in society as adults

    C. Preparation for the world of work

    D. Daily living and social skills

(Easy) (Skill 9.6)

40. **John learns best through the auditory channel, so his teacher wants to reinforce his listening skills. Through which of the following types of equipment would instruction be most effectively presented?**

    A. Overhead projector

    B. CD player

    C. Microcomputer

    D. Opaque projector

(Average) (Skill 9.6)

41. **What Assistive Technology (AT) is best for Bob, who can compose well, but has difficulty with both encoding and the physical act of writing?**

    A. A peer to write what he dictates

    B. Voice to text computer software

    C. A CD player he can listen to while others write

    D. A slant board for writing

(Rigorous) (Skill 10.1)

42. **Formal assessments include standardized tests, norm-referenced Instruments, and____?**

    A. developmental rating scales

    B. interviews

    C. anecdotes/observations

    D. textbook chapter tests

(Easy) (Skill 10.1)

43. **Which of the following is an advantage of giving informal individual assessments, rather than standardized group tests?**

    A. Questions can be modified to reveal a specific student's strategies or misconceptions

    B. The test administrator can clarify or rephrase questions for the student

    C. They can be inserted into the class quickly on an as needed basis

    D. All of the above

(Rigorous) (Skill 10.1)

44. **Criterion referenced tests can provide information about:**

    A. Whether a student has mastered prerequisite skills

    B. Whether a student is ready to proceed to the next level of instruction

    C. Which instructional materials might be helpful in covering program objectives

    D. All of the above

(Rigorous) (Skill 10.3)

45. **Which of the following purposes of testing calls for an informal test?**

    A. Screening a group of children to determine their readiness for the first reader

    B. Analyzing the responses of a student with a disability to various presentations of content material to see which strategy works for him

    C. Evaluating the effectiveness of a fourth-grade math program at the end of its first year of use in a specific school

    D. Determining the general level of intellectual functioning of a class of fifth graders

(Average) (Skill 11.1)

46. **Which of the following should be considered when planning the spatial arrangement of your classroom?**

    A. Adequate Physical Space

    B. Lighting characteristics

    C. Window location

    D. All of the above

(Average) (Skill 11.1)

47. **Appropriate safety features which should be used in learning environments with special needs students include:**

    A. Physical barriers

    B. Effective procedures to be used in emergencies

    C. Equal treatment for all students to avoid stigma

    D. Multisensory instructional approach

(Average) (Skill 11.2)

48. **Positive reinforcers are generally effective if they are desired by the student and:**

    A. Worthwhile in size

    B. Given immediately after the desired behavior

    C. Given only upon the occurrence of the target behavior

    D. All of the above

(Easy) (Skill 11.2)

49. **An effective classroom behavior management plan includes all but which of the following?**

    A. Transition procedures for changing activities

    B. Clear consequences for rule infractions

    C. Concise teacher expectations for student behavior

    D. Copies of lesson plans

(Rigorous) (Skill 11.2)

50. **Morgan frequently talks during instructional time. Her teacher, Mrs. Jenkins, wants to use the assertive discipline approach to behavior management to decrease, and eventually eliminate, Morgan's disruptions. All of the following interventions are appropriate EXCEPT:**

    A. Offering Morgan positive reinforcement when she is quiet during instructional time

    B. Tracking Morgan's talk outs and discussing them with her parents

    C. Promptly following through with expected consequences when Morgan talks out

    D. Focusing on the behavior and the situation rather than on Morgan's character

(Easy) (Skill 11.3)

51. **Crisis intervention methods are above all concerned with:**

    A. Safety and well-being of the staff and students

    B. Stopping the inappropriate behavior

    C. Preventing the behavior from occurring again

    D. The student learning that outbursts are inappropriate

(Average) (Skill 11.3)

52. **Addressing a student's maladaptive behavior right away with a "time out" should be reserved for situations where:**

    A. The student has engaged in the behavior continuously throughout the day

    B. Harm might come to the student or others

    C. Lesser interventions have not been effective

    D. The student displayed the behavior the day before

(Average) (Skill 11.3)

53. **Katie frequently is disruptive prior to each day's math lesson. From a behavior management perspective, the math lesson appears to be the ________________ to Katie's undesirable disruptive behavior.**

    A. subsequent development

    B. succeeding force

    C. consequence

    D. antecedent

(Average) (Skill 12.2)

54. **The best way to ensure the success of educational interventions is to:**

    A. Give regular education teachers the primary responsibility of teaching special needs students in regular classrooms

    B. Give special education teachers the primary responsibility of teaching special needs students in special education classrooms

    C. Promote cooperative teaching efforts between general and special educators

    D. Have support personnel assume the primary responsibility for the education of special needs students

(Average) (Skill 12.2)

55. **A serious hindrance to successful mainstreaming is:**

    A. Lack of adapted materials

    B. Lack of funding

    C. Lack of communication among teachers

    D. Lack of support from administration

(Easy) (Skill 12.3)

56. **All of the following are essential components of effective parent-teacher conferences EXCEPT:**

    A. Collecting samples of student work, records of behavior, and other relevant information

    B. Beginning the conference with positive comments about the student

    C. Using informal small talk to put the parents at ease

    D. Preparing a list of questions or concerns you wish to address

(Rigorous) (Skill 12.3)

57. **What can you do to create a good working environment with a classroom assistant?**

    A. Plan lessons with the assistant.

    B. Write a contract that clearly defines his/her responsibilities in the classroom.

    C. Remove previously given responsibilities.

    D. All of the above

(Average) (Skill 12.3)

58. **A paraprofessional has been assigned to assist you in the classroom. What action on the part of the teacher would lead to a poor working relationship?**

    A. Having the paraprofessional lead a small group

    B. Telling the paraprofessional what you expect him/her to do

    C. Defining classroom behavior management as your responsibility alone

    D. Taking an active role in his/her evaluation

(Average) (Skill 12.3)

59. **Parent contact should first begin when:**

    A. You are informed the child will be your student

    B. The student fails a test

    C. The student exceeds others on a task

    D. An IEP meeting is scheduled and you have had no previous replies to letters

(Rigorous) (Skill 12.3)

60. Janice requires occupational therapy and speech therapy services. She is your student. What must you do to ensure her needs are met?

   A. Watch the services being rendered

   B. Schedule collaboratively

   C. Ask for services to be given in a push-in model

   D. Ask them to train you to give the service

ANSWER KEY								
1. A	8. A	15. C	22. B	29. B	36. A	43. D	50. B	57. A
2. C	9. D	16. A	23. D	30. D	37. C	44. A	51. A	58. C
3. C	10. A	17. A	24. D	31. A	38. C	45. B	52. B	59. A
4. B	11. B	18. B	25. C	32. A	39. B	46. D	53. D	60. B
5. B	12. B	19. A	26. A	33. A	40. B	47. B	54. C	
6. B	13. A	20. D	27. A	34. B	41. B	48. D	55. C	
7. B	14. A	21. C	28. C	35. D	42. D	49. D	56. C	

RIGOR TABLE	
Rigor level	**Questions**
Easy 25%	12, 22, 23, 26, 33, 36, 37, 40, 43, 49, 51, 56
Average Rigor 50%	1, 6, 9, 10,11, 13, 15, 16, 18, 19, 20, 24, 27, 32, 41, 46, 47, 48, 52, 53, 54, 55, 58, 59
Rigorous 50%	2, 3, 4, 5, 7, 8, 14, 17, 21, 25, 28, 29, 30, 31, 34, 35, 38, 39, 42, 44, 45, 50, 57, 60

PASS THE FIRST TIME

with over 300 titles!

PRAXIS   NYSTCE   TExES   MTEL

FTCE   PLACE   CEOE   ICTS

GACE   MTTC   AEPA   WEST

ORELA   VCLA   CSET   NMTA

Call or visit us online!
1.800.301.4647
www.XAMonline.com

CPSIA information can be obtained at www.ICGtesting.com
Printed in the USA
LVOW09s1927121113

361035LV00007B/557/P